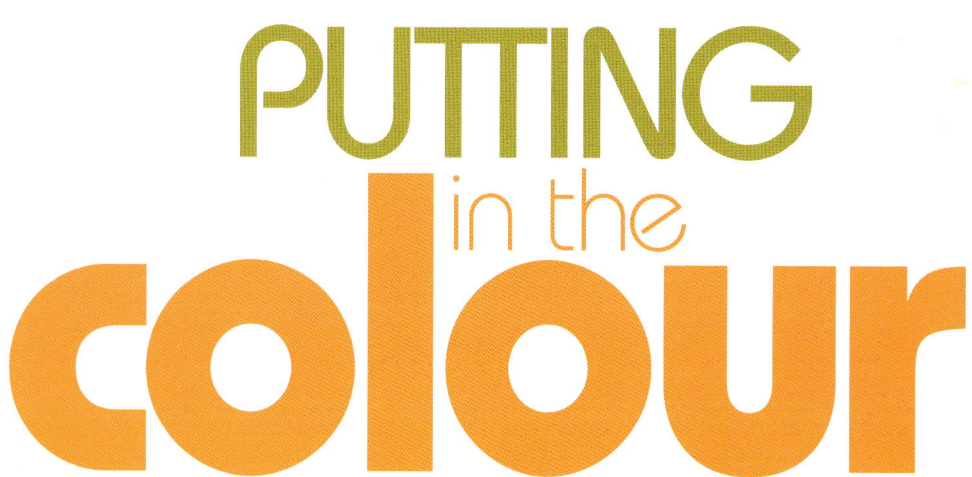

Contemporary Aboriginal textiles

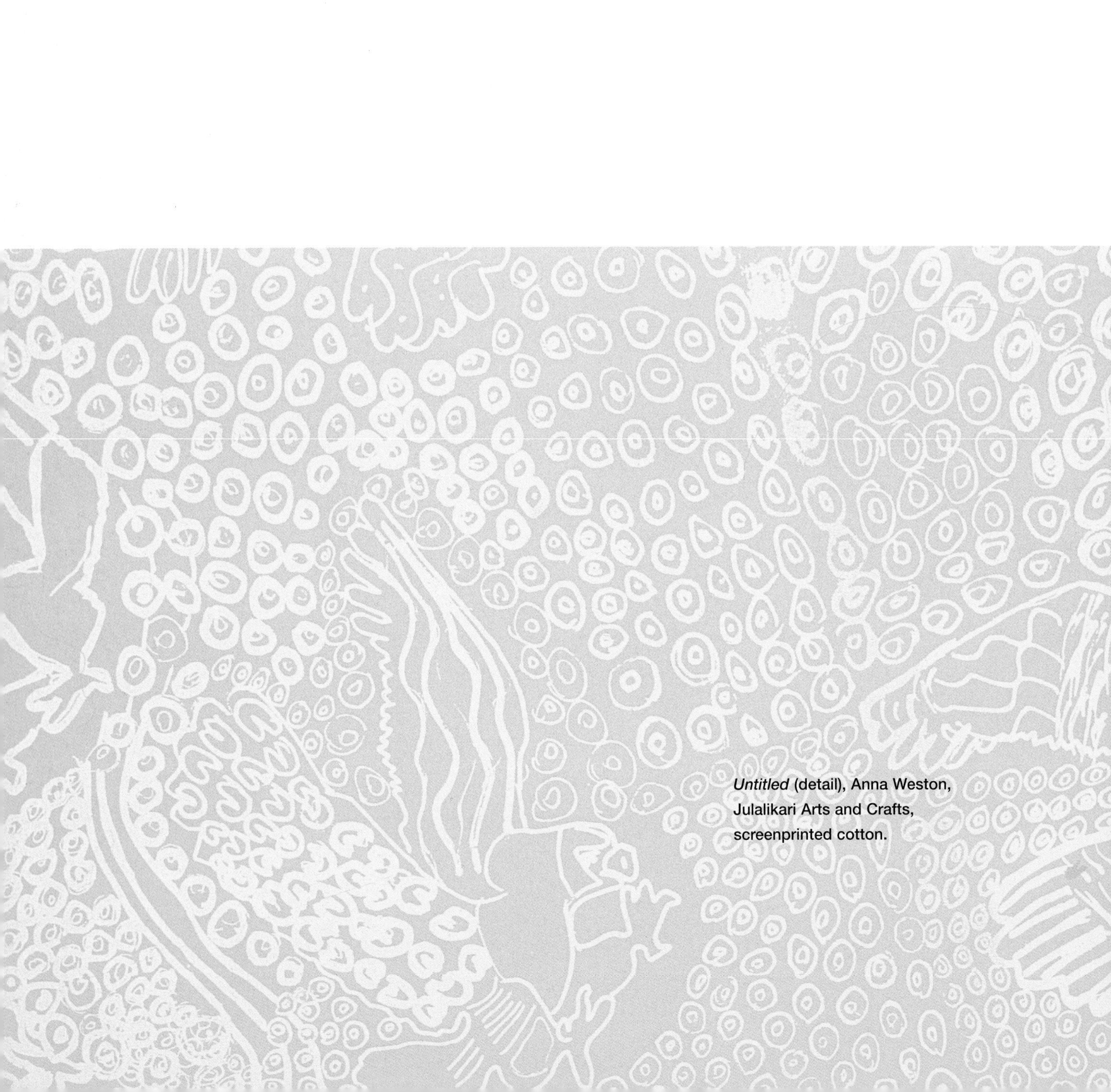

Untitled (detail), Anna Weston,
Julalikari Arts and Crafts,
screenprinted cotton.

PUTTING in the colour

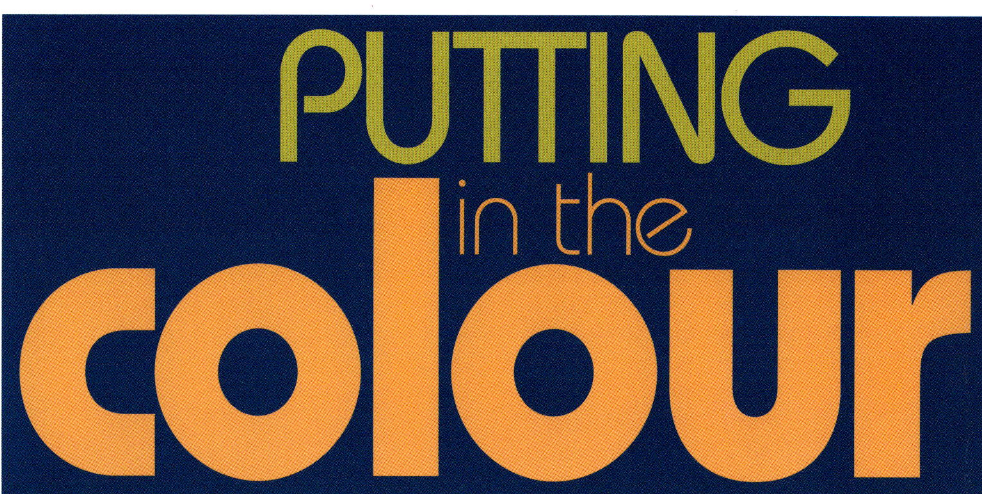

Contemporary Aboriginal textiles

Compiled by Mary-Lou Nugent
for Desart: the Association of Central Australian Aboriginal Art and Craft Centres

jukurrpa books

First published in 2001 by Jukurrpa Books, an imprint of
IAD Press
PO Box 2531
Alice Springs NT 0871
Ph: 08 8951 1334
Fax: 08 8952 2527
Email: iadpress@ozemail.com.au

National Library of Australia Catalogue-in-Publication data:

Putting in the colour: contemporary Aboriginal textiles.

 Bibliography.
 ISBN 1 86465 028 1.

 1. Textile artists – Australia, Central. 2. Textile artists – Australia, Northern.
 3. Aborigines, Australian – Australia, Central – Interviews. 4. Aborigines,
 Australian – Australia, Northern – Interviews. 5. Textile artists – Australia,
 Central – Interviews. 6. Textile artists – Australia, Northern – Interviews.
 7. Textile crafts – Australia, Central. 8. Textile crafts – Australia, Northern.
 9. Aborigines, Australian – Australia – Textile industry and fabrics.
 I. Nugent, Mary-Lou, 1960– . II. Desart Inc.

 746.09942

Compiled by Mary-Lou Nugent
Edited and designed by Christine Bruderlin
Map by Brenda Thornley
Photography by Barry Skipsey, unless otherwise credited

Front cover: (top left) *Barramundi*, Gabriel Maralngurra and Ray Young, Injalak Arts and Crafts Association, screenprinted cotton twill, 8 m length (photo courtesy Injalak Arts and Crafts Association); (top right) Mary Oliver of Keringke Arts handpaints silk; (bottom) silk batik of Utopia by (left to right) Ollie Akemarr, Joy Apetyarr, Jeanni Apetyarr and Lorna Penunga.

Desart

Desart gratefully acknowledges the financial assistance of the Aboriginal and Torres Strait Islander Commission, the Australia Council, the Northern Territory Department of Arts and Museums, and the Gordon Darling Foundation.

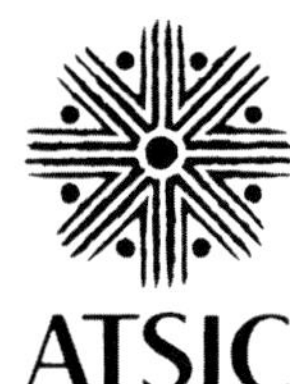
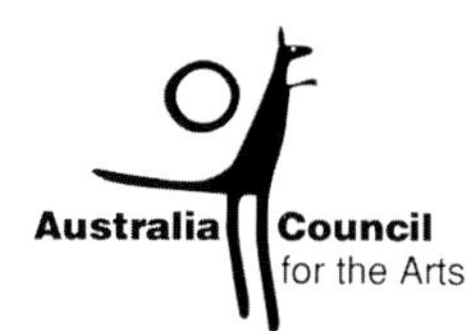
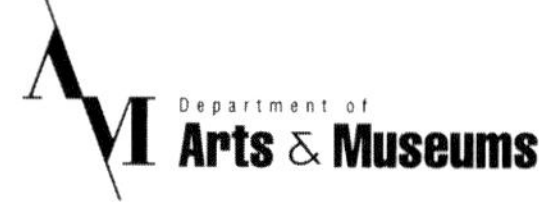
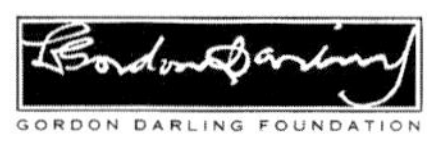

foreword

Desart is the association of Central Australian Aboriginal art centres. The organisation consists of over thirty member groups situated in often remote Aboriginal communities across the southern part of the Northern Territory and the far northern regions of South Australia. Desart's primary objectives are to raise the profile of the art centres it represents and to improve equity and access issues for the artists working through these centres. Importantly, Desart's work also covers the commercial viability of the work being created by Aboriginal art centres, and its function extends to seeking and securing new marketing opportunities for Central Australian Aboriginal art.

There are about five thousand members of Desart; about half of these are textile artists. Until recently, the primary textile work produced was for the fine-art market. The work consisted of one-off handmade batik and handpainted lengths and T-shirts. While the value and position of the fine-art product is unquestionable, financial pressures and shifting market demands have made it necessary, in some places at least, to adopt a more commercial approach. For this reason, Desart has established a commercial and marketing arm. It has secured licensing and manufacturing deals both in Australia and internationally with the intention of drawing upon and promoting the art centres' richly varied and uniquely beautiful textile work.

Kaltjiti Arts and Crafts in South Australia has been one of the first centres to secure a commercial deal. Their batik designs are being reproduced on men's and women's shirts and sarongs. Jukurrpa Artists Corporation artist Bessie Liddle, from Alice Springs, has created a range of designs which are being licensed for use in fabric for purses, shoulder bags, cushion covers and tablecloths. Hermannsburg Potters of Hermannsburg have designed fabric for Hawaiian-style shirts depicting Namatjira watercolour landscape images.

Desart's aim is to ensure that artists in Central Australia can continue a high standard of fine-art practice, while benefiting financially from the licensing and commercial distribution of their designs. Work can be produced off-site, for example, thus avoiding the difficulties that distance and isolation can bring to technical operations. It also means that artists' families can benefit from the regular income generated by royalties.

Desart is controlled by and responsive to the Aboriginal artists it represents. It allows them to have control over their work and receive proper exposure and appropriate representation of their art. Artists have a say in how they are portrayed within the wider community.

Putting in the Colour is a unique publication. It is the first book of its kind, concerned entirely with the textile art of the Aboriginal art centres of Central Australia and the Top End. Included from Central Australia are the textiles of Ernabella Arts of Ernabella, Kaltjiti Arts and Crafts of Fregon, Keringke Arts from Ltyentye Apurte, Urapuntja Artists of Utopia, Julalikari Arts and Crafts in Tennant Creek, and the smaller textile centres of Minymaku Arts at Amata, and Titjikala Women's Centre at Titjikala. The work of several Top End centres is included: Bima Wear and Tiwi Design, both based on Bathurst Island; Dunnilli Arts based at Nungalinya College in Darwin; Jilamara Arts and Crafts Association, and Munupi Arts and Crafts Centre, both on Melville Island; and Injalak Arts and Crafts Association at Gunbalanya in Arnhem Land.

This book is the artists' own, it comes from the artists themselves. It will further raise the profile of Aboriginal textiles, and help to ensure that the medium continues to gain the high international reputation it deserves.

Ron Brien
Executive Officer
Desart

acknowledgements

Desart would like to thank its staff involved in the production of this book: the project coordinator Mary-Lou Nugent, Ron Brien and Katie Yeowart, and the Desart Executive: Inawinytji Williamson, June Smith, Andrea Martin, Clara Inkamala, Bessie Liddle, Audrey Napanangka Martin, Maureen Williams and Margaret Turner.

All the contributors to the book provided considerable support and assistance, and are listed on page 86.

Many other individuals assisted Desart in gathering information. They include Felicity Green, Anna McLeod, Kevin Quigley, Una Rey, Bev Peacock, Alison Alder, Cheryl Hawkins-Clarke, Hilary Houlihan, Simon Turner, Tracey-Lea Smith and Jennifer Coombs.

Thanks especially to Christine Bruderlin for the editing and design of the book, to Mandy Brett, Brenda Thornley and Simon MacDonald at Jukurrpa Books, Norm Wilson at Aboriginal and Torres Strait Islander Commission, and Maggie Kavanagh and Geraldine Tyson.

Input was also gratefully received from Tim Rowse, Michael Richards and Doreen Mellor.

Interpretive assistance has been given by Jenny Green (for the Utopia interviews), Suzy Bryce (for the interviews from the Pitjantjatjara Lands), Margaret Dagg, Therese Ryder, Jude Kenny, Penny Watson and Inawinytji Williamson.

Desart gratefully acknowledges the financial assistance of the Australia Council, the Aboriginal and Torres Strait Islander Commission, the Northern Territory Department of Arts and Museums, and the Gordon Darling Foundation.

contents

getting started

a brief historical overview

In the early 1990s, inspired by the success of the batik artists of Ernabella and Utopia, the women of Nyirrpi in Central Australia decided they wanted to try their hand at the same work. A trainer and some equipment were sent from Alice Springs to the isolated Western Desert community 150 km west of Yuendumu. Work tables were constructed from the walls of the recently pulled-down freezer room and balanced on old 44-gallon drums, desks from the nearby school were used as sewing tables, and the textile work of the community began. The experience of the women of Nyirrpi has been the same as many other textile artists working in remote Aboriginal communities across northern Australia. Some artists began working from the back of a truck, some through the local school, others in small groups in backyards. From humble beginnings like these, a vibrant textiles-based art industry has developed and flourished for over three decades in many remote communities of the Northern Territory and South Australia.

This same period has marked the evolution of textiles—a relatively new art form for Aboriginal artists—into a significant movement within the contemporary art scene. It has developed in many cases alongside extant practices, such as painting onto canvas, bark, wood and paper, though the soft texture and fluid skin of fabric has provided artists with a new and sometimes challenging surface for their mark making. The introduction of the techniques of batik, silk-screening and fabric painting has offered new and exciting possibilities to Aboriginal artists in Central Australia and the Top End to extend their idiom or to present traditional imagery in a fresh way.

In Central Australia, the textile movement began at Ernabella, 400 km south of Alice Springs in the Musgrave Ranges. Ernabella began as a mission station in the late 1930s and many

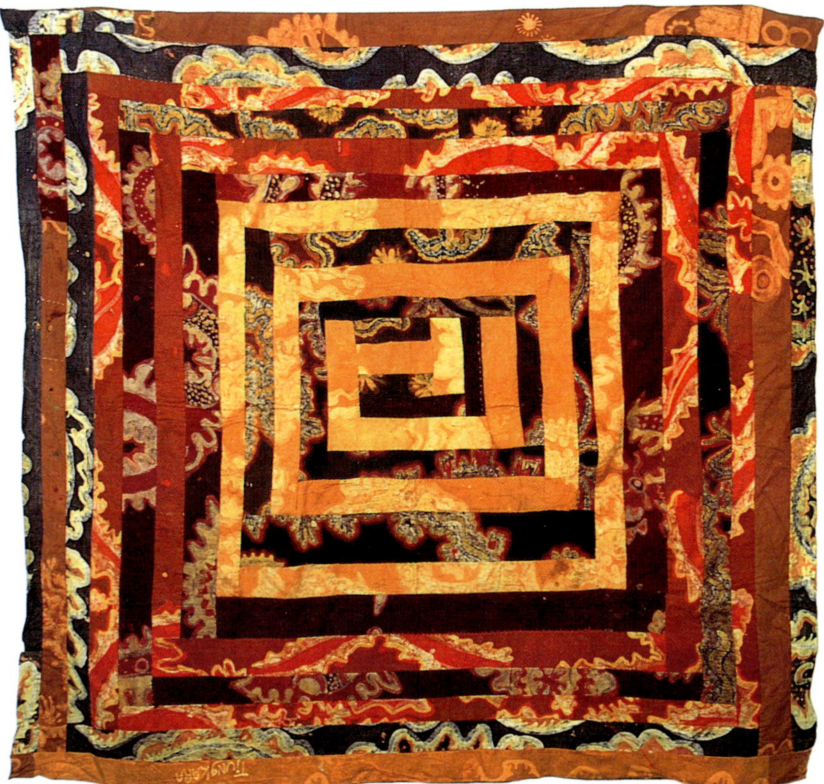

A patchwork of batiks, handsewn by Tinpula Tjutjupai of Puta Puta (near Pipalyatjara), 1982, cotton, 2 m square (collection Suzy Bryce).

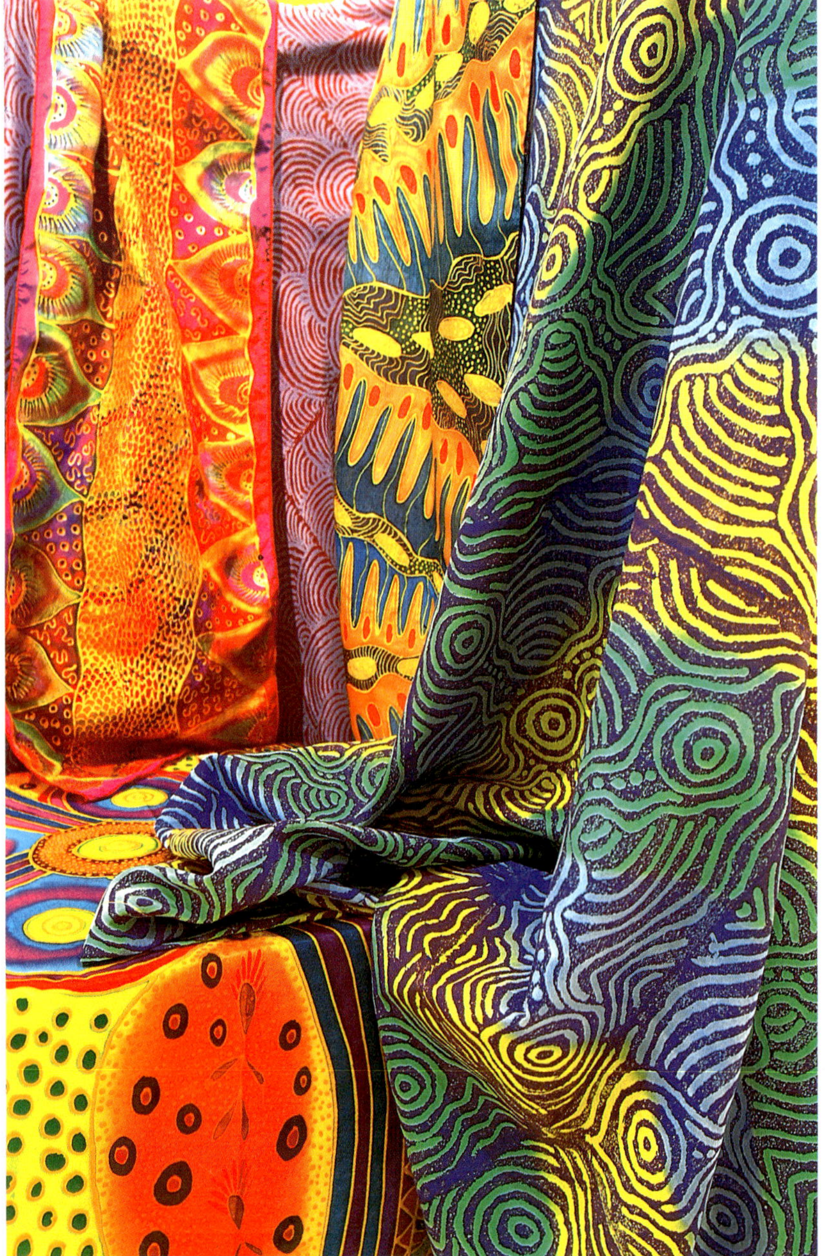

Untitled textiles by Rene Boko and Doris Thomas of the Titjikala Women's Centre, shown as part of the Desert Mob Show at the Araluen Centre, 1998, lino-blocked and handpainted silks.

Pitjantjatjara women who lived there worked at the community's art and craft centre which was set up with help of art adviser Winifred Hilliard. They worked for many years on the production of woven and hand-loomed rugs and by the early 1970s had begun to experiment with batik.

Artists such as Daisy (Nyukana) Baker took readily to the art form, transferring imagery from the strongly linear and elongated shapes of the *walka,* or art, of the Pitjantjatjara people and onto the flowing surface of silk or cotton.

The women of Amata, 150 km to the west of Ernabella, were the next to learn batik. Janet Inyika and Josephine Mick were among the young artists of the time who learnt from Vivienne McKlintock, a teacher at Ernabella, and Eve Rainow, who provided a craft room in her house.

With the development of the out-station movement and the natural flow of traffic between communities in the region, the batik technique spread quickly across the Pitjantjatjara lands over the next 10 years. Suzy Bryce, a trainer from the Institute for Aboriginal Development in Alice Springs, worked with Kunytjitja Brown around Pipalyatjara and Kalka to the west of Ernabella, introducing both sewing and batik to women of the communities. Art centres emerged at Amata and at Fregon, 60 km to the south. At Fregon, women such as Inawinytji Williamson were the first of many artists to embrace batik, working through the then Aparawatatja Arts and Crafts, later to become Kaltjiti Arts and Crafts. The batik form continued to spread across the northern reaches of South Australia and into the Western Australian communities of Warburton and Blackstone.

In the late 1970s Suzy Bryce and Kunytjitja Brown, working for the Institute for Aboriginal Development, travelled to Utopia, 275 km to the north-east of Alice Springs, to conduct a course in batik. Emily Kngwarray, Glory Angal and Lena Apwerl were just three of the women from Utopia who immediately began producing batik lengths. Jenny Green, one of the early arts workers at Utopia, writes in the 1999 publication *Raiki Wara* that the first Aboriginal group exhibition of batik textiles was held in 1980 at Mona Burns' gallery in Alice Springs. The Utopia artists went on to achieve fame through their silk lengths, characterised by free-form imagery and colourful gesture centred on women's *awely,* or ceremony. In 1996 they travelled to Indonesia on an exchange training program with artists from Yogyakarta, in order to revitalise their art. The Hot Wax project, as it became known, developed into a travelling exhibition curated by the Museum and Art Gallery of the Northern Territory and in later years formed the basis for further exchanges between the Indonesian and Australian artists.

The cross-fertilisation of ideas and techniques also continued at a local level. In 1984, with the support of the Northern Territory Department of Education, women artists from Ernabella travelled to Yuendumu in the Western Desert region of Central Australia and introduced batik to the region. After a brief but important period of batik production at Yuendumu the technique declined in popularity as acrylic painting became established. Textile production did resume, however, in 1990 with the establishment of Yurrampi Arts and a screenprinting facility was built through the Northern Territory Department of Education's Adult Education scheme. At its peak the centre produced multiple runs of screenprinted fabric from screens masked with photo emulsion developed on site in Yurrampi Arts' darkroom. Artists from the community made clothes and T-shirts for local events and for sale in the local store. Perry Japanangka Langdon, Aboriginal trainer at Yurrampi Arts, said in 1996 of his work at Yurrampi: 'At first we didn't know

anything. Then we learnt through trainers how to make our own screens and print professionally. We went to Bathurst Island for a look and to get ideas from them and now we have built it up.' Later in the decade, Yurrampi Arts began operating under the wing of Warlukurlangu Artists, the painting centre in Yuendumu, with a shift in emphasis towards fine-art prints on paper.

Short-term courses in textiles, run through the Northern Territory Open College, were conducted in the early 1990s at communities close to Yuendumu, such as Nyirrpi and Mt Allan. Interestingly, these were run through the local women's centres where a range of activities was concentrated, from preparing children's and old people's meals, to running sewing, art and nutrition classes. These centres provided women with a haven away from community and family pressures and allowed them to practise their art in peace. At many women's centres across the region textile production blossomed until it became the focus of women's work, such as happened at Nyirrpi. There the artists printed in repeat with lino blocks on fabric, and sewed clothes from the fabric for their families or for sale in Alice Springs. At Titjikala, to the south-east of Alice Springs, and at about the same time, artists began to use similar

techniques to those practised at Nyirrpi. Lino-block printing on fabric is still preferred by many art and craft centres for the immediacy and simplicity of its effect, negating the need for sophisticated equipment and complex technique.

At Ltyentye Apurte, Santa Teresa, east of Alice Springs, artists were introduced to lino-block printing in 1987 through a 15-week fabric-painting course, funded by the Northern Territory's Adult Education scheme and conducted by Cait Wait in the art room of the community school. The group evolved into Keringke Arts which soon had a purpose-built centre near the sacred site after which the art centre is named. Keringke Art's reputation was built on works of art on silk. Experienced textile artists such as Kathleen Wallace and Camilla Young have their fabrics held in the collections of major art galleries around the country. Subsequent art coordinators, such as Tim Rollason, have assisted in promoting the work of Keringke Arts internationally.

Training workshops encouraged the spread of textile production at Aboriginal art centres across the southern part of the Territory through the 1990s. Iwantja Arts at Indulkana in South Australia, about 200 km south of Fregon, is renowned for the production of limited edition prints on paper. After a series of workshops in 1997 by visiting textile artist Johanna Weiss, artists such as Valerie Cullinan and Marion Baker were able to transfer their extensive experience in lino-block printing on paper to block printing with ink on fabric. They used the strongly linear monotone designs to great effect in tabular repeats on a hand-dyed background of cotton fabric. In the late 1980s, textile artist Pauline Clack ran a series of silk handpainting workshops at Areyonga in Central Australia under the auspices of the Northern Territory Open College. The textile arts remained strong at this centre for a number of years.

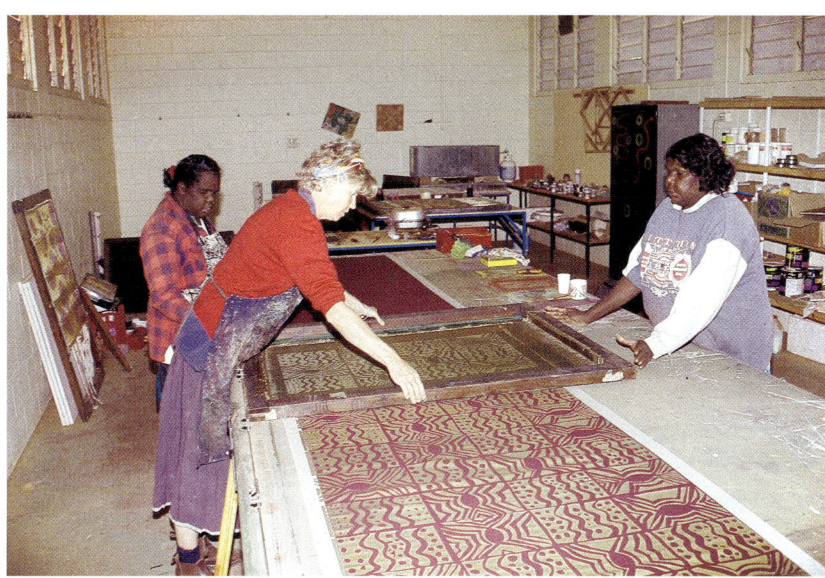

During this period in the Barkly Tablelands, art centres were also becoming increasingly interested in learning about textiles. At Tennant Creek, screenprinter and artist-in-residence Alison Alder worked with artists such as Peggy Napangardi Jones at Julalikari Arts and Crafts creating two- and three-colour repeat lengths on cotton twill. Peggy's fluid linear representation of her country through bushtucker motifs transferred well onto screen for printing and were also handpainted onto stretched silk. Formal training has made a valuable contribution to the evolution of textiles at this centre. In 1996, Penny Watson from Batchelor Institute of Indigenous Tertiary Education conducted workshops in handpainting and printing silks with fibre-resist dyes. By the end of the 1990s the textile arts—screenprinting, batik, handprinting and handpainting—were practised in Aboriginal art and craft centres across the Northern Territory and the northern edge of South Australia.

The Top End

The development of textile art in the Top End has been similar to the Central Australian experience, especially in the 1980s and early 1990s when the popularity of hand-decorated fabrics in the marketplace was on the rise. Paralleling the situation in the Centre, around half of community-based enterprises in the North have made, or still produce, some form of textile art. In the Top End region where the main visual arts practitioners are male, textiles became yet another medium for the transference of ancestral imagery. Even though the number of women visual artists is gradually increasing, their affiliation with customary fibre weaving remains strong. Using textiles as surfaces for mark making is, therefore, not the exclusively female activity that it is in the Centre, although it has certainly opened up new opportunities for women in a number of Top End communities.

Many women's induction into the fabric arts was the result of special training programs, often run out of women's centres. This was the case at Nauiyu Nambiyu, Daly River. In 1986 when adult education classes began at the women's centre, the women wanted to learn skills that would differentiate their work from the men's customary bark painting. With initial training from Eileen Farrelley, they began applying their decorative bushtucker motifs onto fabric with silk-screenprinting and batik. The popularity of these activities led to the foundation of Merrepen Arts in 1987. Since then, the women have maintained a core of textile-based artwork, including screenprinting, batik and handpainted artwork and fabric lengths, as an adjunct to weaving and

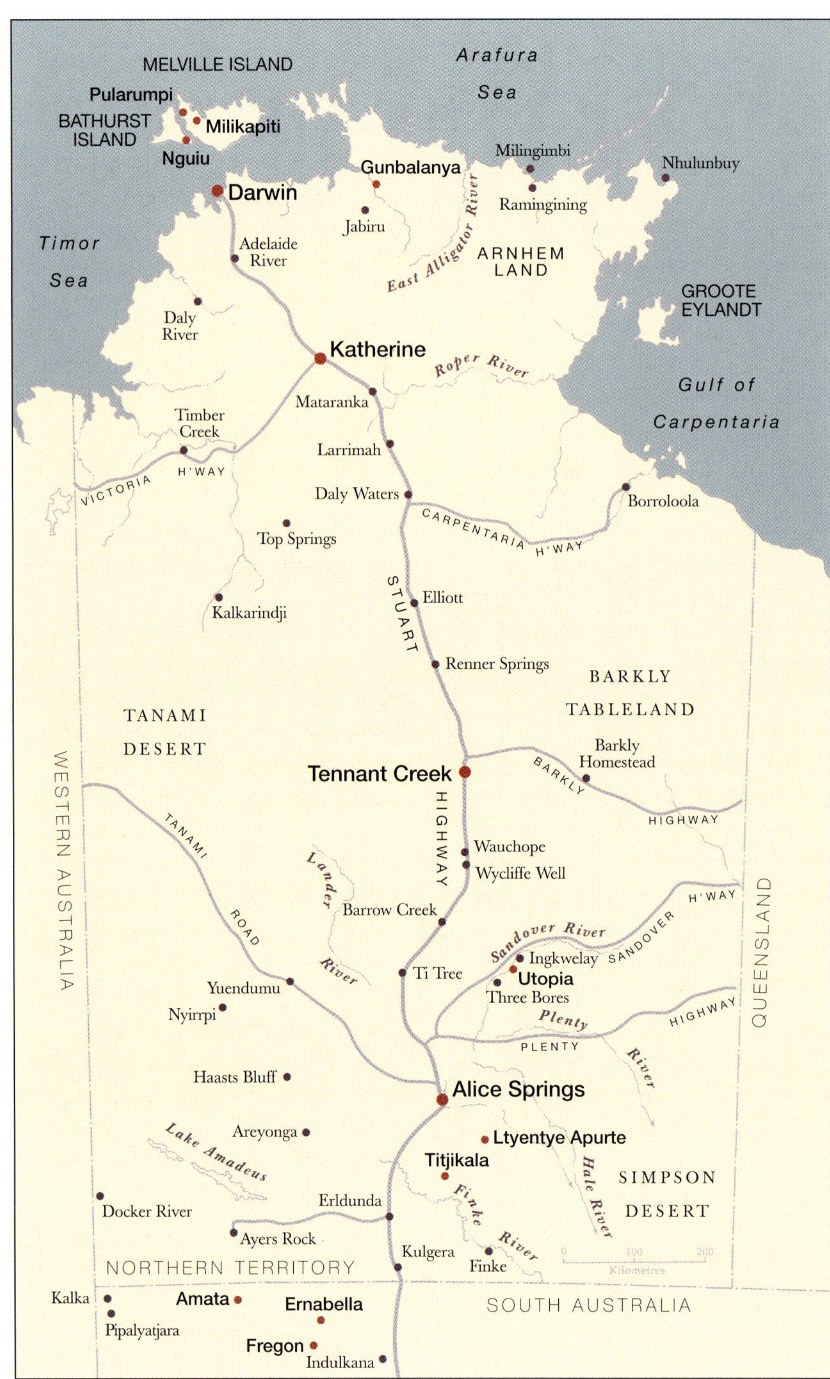

Map showing the Aboriginal communities mentioned in this book.

acrylic painting. The same situation occurred at Jabiru where the Duluk Duluk printery developed out of TAFE-funded classes at the women's centre in 1986. With financial support from the Gagadju Association, the women produced a range of textiles and printed T-shirts for sale, providing a much-needed outlet for artists in Kakadu National Park, until their (temporary) closure in the late 1990s.

A number of Arnhem Land communities were also part of this move into textiles during the 1980s. At Ramingining in central Arnhem Land a purpose-built screenprint workshop was incorporated into the new Bula Bula art centre in 1984. The first printer was Moree artist Laurence Lesley who worked with the male artists to produce a range of printed 'art to wear' T-shirts and fabrics. Other interstate practitioners, such as Fiona Foley and Joe Hurst, also shared their printmaking skills with the artists, resulting in an experimental printmaking and lithography program in 1991—an activity that has continued on an intermittent basis, despite the loss of funding for a dedicated silk-screen trainer in 1995.

Gunbalanya in western Arnhem Land also set up a modest printmaking workshop in 1986 under the auspices of the Northern Territory's Adult Education scheme. Three years later, a large studio was incorporated into the new Injalak Arts and Crafts Association centre where the men of the community continue to produce a range of printed fabric lengths, T-shirts and limited edition prints. Injalak's first trainer was Ray Young who worked for six years prior to this in Australia's first and most successful Indigenous silk-screenprintery: Tiwi Design on Bathurst Island. Since its establishment by Bede Tungatalum and Giovanni Tipungwuti in 1970, Tiwi Design has become the focus for art production on the island, with carvers, painters and printers engaged under the same roof in a continual artistic exchange. Like Ernabella in Central Australia, Tiwi Design has provided the market leadership and inspiration for many Indigenous artists wanting to start their own textile enterprises.

This inspiration began locally, when the women employed at the Bima Wear sewing factory at Nguiu branched into textile decoration in 1982. Interest spread to neighbouring Melville Island where, in 1983, an adult education course was started to train women in basic silk-screen techniques. Raelene Kerinauia, the sister of one of Tiwi Design's influential printers, Vivian, was one of the principal artists involved in what was to become Jilamara Arts and Crafts Association in 1988.

Batik was introduced to Tiwi Design in 1986 by manager Kathy Barnes who had previously worked as arts adviser to the batik artists at Utopia. Skills were consolidated with an intensive batik workshop conducted jointly with Tiwi Design and Jilamara Arts and Crafts Association by Yogyakarta-based batik artists Agus Ismoyo and Nia Flam, practitioners who have worked with many Indigenous communities over the years, including Daly River, Utopia and Ernabella. The Indonesian-based instructors returned the following year to undertake a three-month dyeing and batik workshop at Jilamara Arts and Crafts facilitated by then arts coordinator James Bennett, a professional textile artist with a special interest in batik. It was during this time that a greater subtlety and texture in the fabric was achieved through the introduction of fibre-reactive dyes on silk.

Interest in fabric has created a network of cultural exchanges over the years, linking seasoned textile proponents at Tiwi Design, Ernabella and Utopia with practitioners from other desert and saltwater countries. Many artists have visited these centres prior to launching their own enterprises. For example, Banunydji Yunupingu and other senior Yolngu women from Yirrkala, including Dhuwarrwarr Marika, visited Tiwi Design and Ernabella Arts before establishing their silk-screenprintery, Djulwanbirra Galupa Screenprints, at Drummie Head. A breakaway member of this organisation went on to found the Laynhapuy Silkscreen enterprise, based at Yirrkala's outstation resource centre. Even before this, interest in printmaking had been promoted though classes at Yirrkala's Dhupuma College, and the community's most famous printmaker, Banduk Marika, had already collaborated in textile printing as early as 1983 with Sydney-based designer Jenny Kee.

The interest in textiles continued, with some Yolngu students

---

Untitled cotton screenprints on handpainted backgrounds, created at Indulkana in South Australia.

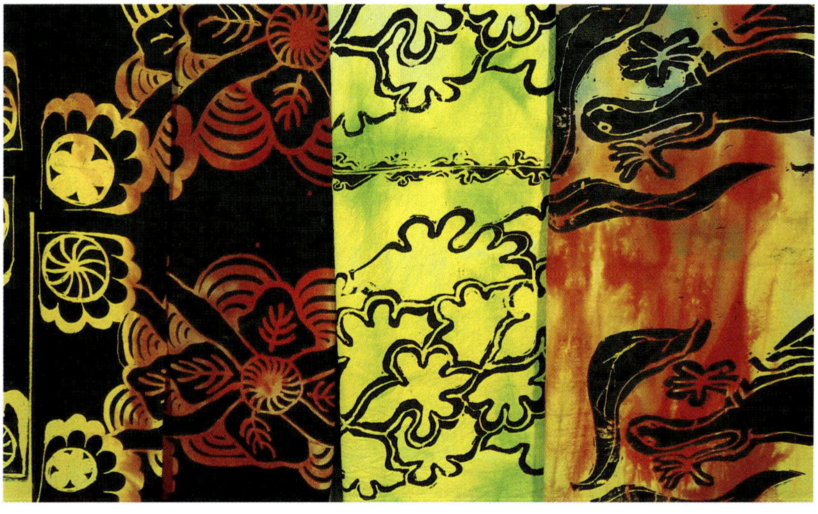

undertaking an exchange visit to study batik at Utopia in 1986. Later, in 1990, these skills were passed on at Yirrkala's adult education centre. Out of this, a large collaborative batik commemorating the program was presented to the funding supporter: the Northern Territory Government's Aboriginal Development Unit. It's perhaps worth noting that for many years before its closure, the Aboriginal Development Unit funded many textile workshops in Territory communities, usually with encouragement from Lenore Dembski, a major promoter of the art form. She went on to establish her own enterprise in Darwin, Paperbark Woman, that has become an important retail outlet for a range of Indigenous fabrics from Tiwi Design, Bima Wear, Daly River, Jilamara Arts and Crafts Association, Injalak Arts and Crafts Association, and Dunnilli Arts. The certificate course in textiles offered at Dunnilli at Darwin's Nungalinya College and the modules offered as part of the certificate course in art and craft at Batchelor Institute of Indigenous Tertiary Education, continue to foster interest in the textile arts amongst many Territory artists.

Where to from here

Despite all the activity described above, textiles still hold a minor position in the art-practice hierarchy and have been, at times, relatively unfashionable in the fine-art world. One reason is that textiles have been viewed by non-Indigenous Australians as being further removed from cultural and ceremonial activity than, for example, acrylic painting on canvas, a medium seen as providing an acceptable modern translation of traditional 'sandpainting'. The production of textiles, whether a batik length or a handpainted silk scarf, requires complex equipment and techniques. The introduction and evolution of textiles in many centres has often coincided with the rise of painting, and the latter's popularity and

unquestionable success within the contemporary international art scene is often at the cost of lesser-known art forms—textiles included.

The growth of acrylic painting by men has, in fact, been well chronicled from the early 1970s, while the development of textiles, which occurred around the same time, has received less media attention. As Judith Ryan writes in *Raiki Wara*: 'The history of Aboriginal men's painting has generally had a louder voice in literature than women's painted textiles. This reflects a preoccupation with men's ritual designs in some of the anthropological texts

that accords with the patriarchal obsessions of white Australia.' While there is truth in this statement, the reality is more complex. In some regions, especially the Top End, motifs all have ancestral references, whether applied to cloth, bark or canvas. At other art centres, such as Ernabella and Utopia, the women artists started out deliberately depicting non-controversial imagery based upon expressive

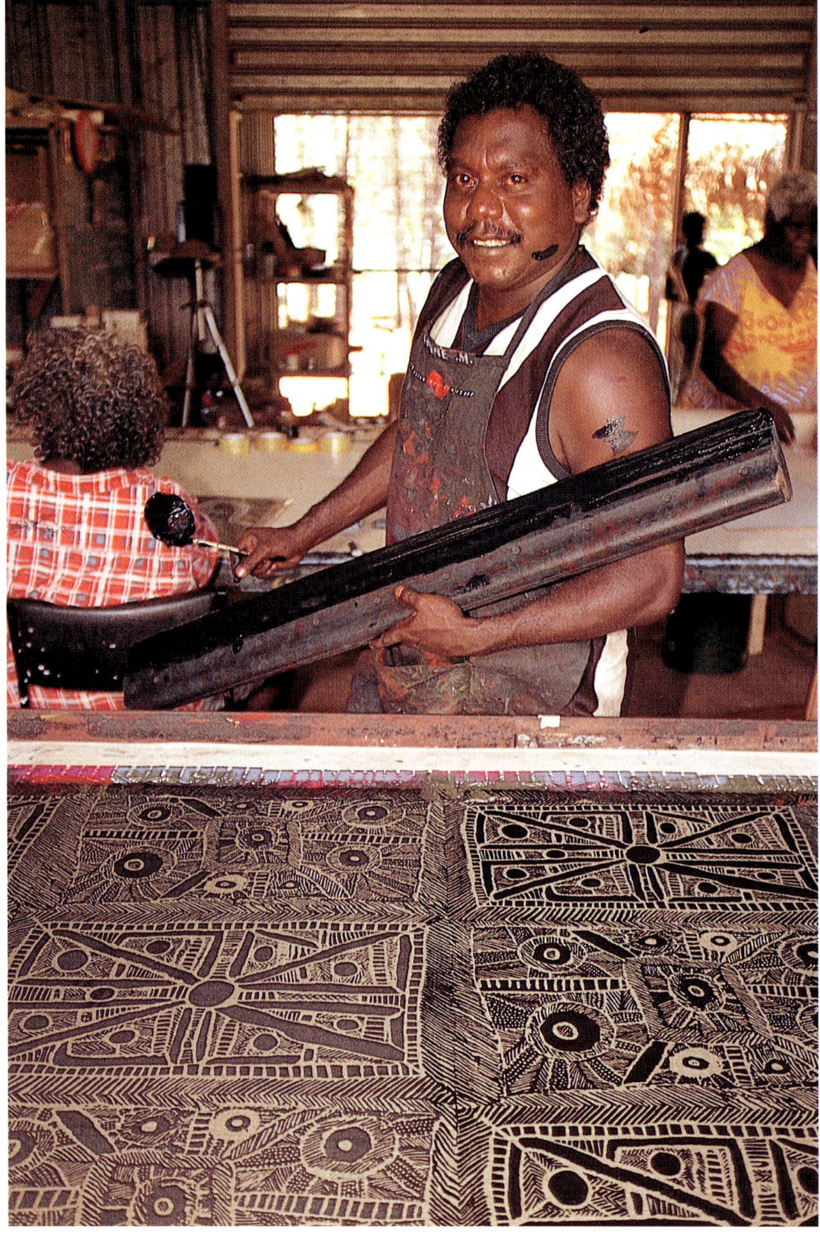

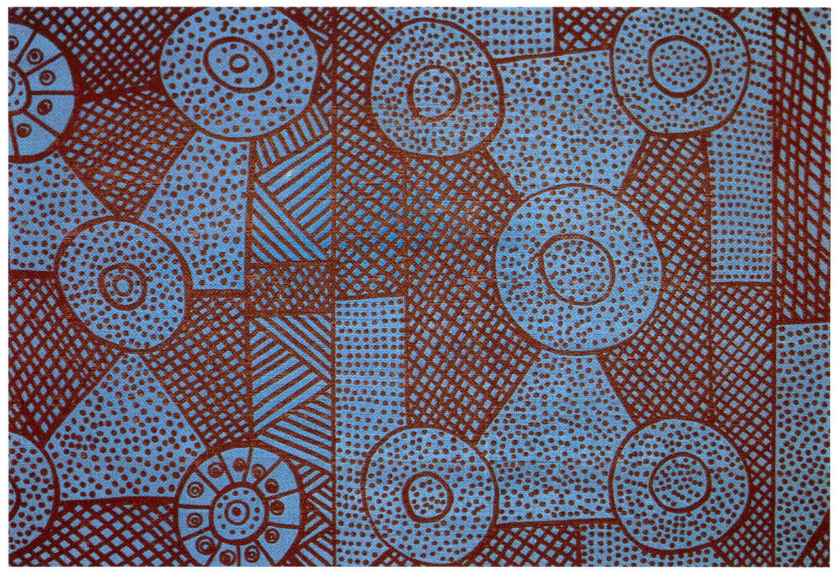

Kurlama (Yam Ceremony), based on a painting by Marie Josette Orsto (1994), developed as a screenprint by Osmond Kantilla, Tiwi Design, 1995, screenprinted cotton length (collection Powerhouse Museum, courtesy Powerhouse Museum).

interpretations of familiar flora and fauna. However, in response to outside interest, the Anmatyerr and Alyawarr of the Utopia area have increasingly incorporated images pertaining to their *awely,* or ceremonial activities, into their fabrics. It seems that the market prejudice against textiles—made by men and women, and to those illustrated with non-traditional content as well as traditional imagery—is based on the arbitrary division between 'art' and 'craft'. 'Craft' products are further ranked in descending order from one-off handpainted wall hangings to repeat motif silk-screenprinted lengths to T-shirts.

There are very practical considerations that have further affected the spread and popularity of textiles. The art form generally requires a sound skill base, and the training required to ensure a quality fabric product is more rigorous and time-consuming than the skills of acrylic painting. Producing two- and three-colour repeat lengths, for example, is

an exacting process that requires technical skill and experience, and good equipment. The standard of a screenprinted length more obviously reflects the standard of the equipment used to produce it than does the use of a bad paintbrush or cheap canvas in acrylic painting. Producing a textile length can also be hard work: batik is physically demanding and fumes from dyes and melted wax can cause sickness in poorly ventilated work areas. Jillian Davey, an artist from Ernabella Arts, has commented, 'I can't do it any more, my lungs got sore from all those dyes, now I paint—it's much better for me.'

Throughout, however, and despite the difficulties, Aboriginal artists have maintained their enthusiasm for the textile art form. While the outcome is always important, the process itself, though often time consuming and involved, is an enjoyable one. Inawinytji Williamson of Kaltjiti Arts and Crafts has said of her batik work: 'It's good to make and to learn. Through the batik we create stories and pictures, of rivers, dog tracks, spinifex, trails and waterholes. We can sit and work together, and help each other as the batik takes shape.' Doris Thomas of Titjikala Women's Centre says of her work, 'We put the tile [lino block] on one print at a time, every corner, and put the others as well… when I saw

my work I was really happy, I made something lovely.' Of the artists of Utopia, Judith Ryan writes in *Raiki Wara,* 'Some of the most committed batik artists [at Utopia] such as Lena [Apwerl], Hilda [Cookie Apwerl] and Glory [Angal] have adopted painting, but have continued to keep their batik alive, which bears testimony to their genuine love of the medium.'

While the product is indisputably deserving, the marketing of Aboriginal textiles has historically presented a challenge to producers. In the 1980s government funds were readily available to support the production of textiles on communities. However, securing external financial support has become increasingly competitive and some art centres have already lost their funding for textile production or simply reverted back to more viable art forms. Other art centres are now questioning their approach to textiles as they look at new, more cost-efficient ways of generating income. They have, for example, weighed the cost of production (including both labour and materials costs) with what the market can realistically stand. Decisions have had to be made as to whether it is better to produce off-site, in the nearest capital city, and risk losing control of a local product, or maintain the effort of developing local industry-standard textile production centres.

Decisions also have had to be made at a community level about what is actually being produced: Aboriginal artists are very experienced in the production of handcrafted one-off products, but where do these textiles fit in the art market? Are they to be marketed as craft or fine art? How are they to be presented at the gallery or exhibition level: are they to be hung as lengths, stretched or framed, or even transformed into homewares such as pillowcase covers and lamps? Added to this situation is a recent shift by many Aboriginal art centres towards producing fine-art prints on paper. Many artists see this practice as a natural progression from screenprinting on fabric, and paper prints are competing more and more with textiles in the marketplace.

The soul searching—and the possibilities—are not necessarily negative. Art centres, such as Minymaku Arts in remote South Australia, are investigating the internet as a means of selling work and establishing new local and international markets. Aboriginal art organisations such as Desart in Alice Springs are working to place licensed Aboriginal textile designs in the mainstream fashion and tourist market. Major exhibitions are also helping to promote the work of Aboriginal textile artists. In 1996 the exhibition Raiki Wara (Long Cloth) assembled by the National Gallery of Victoria, travelled Australia highlighting the work of Aboriginal artists from all over the country.

One of the features of Aboriginal design work lies in its transferability. The graphic quality of the imagery and the strength of its linework make it adaptable to a wide range of media. Howard Morphy, in *Aboriginal Art*, writes, 'Designs are an inheritance from the ancestral past and producing an artwork often involves fitting the design to the shape of the surface or nature of the space as well as taking advantage of the particular medium concerned.'

This 'adaptability' ensures the role that Aboriginal textiles play as a powerful medium for cultural promotion. In the Tiwi Islands, designs often derived from customary *jilamara,* or body painting, or utilising figurative imagery such as ceremonial artefacts, have been developed for use on the screenprinted fabrics of the region. Tiwi cloth is often screenprinted with specific local designs for use during mourning ceremonies. James Bennett writes in his contribution to *Putting in the Colour*, 'The wide variety of armbands and body ornaments—ritual weapons once essential to ceremonial regalia—and richly carved funeral poles are all favoured themes of contemporary silk-screen designs.' At

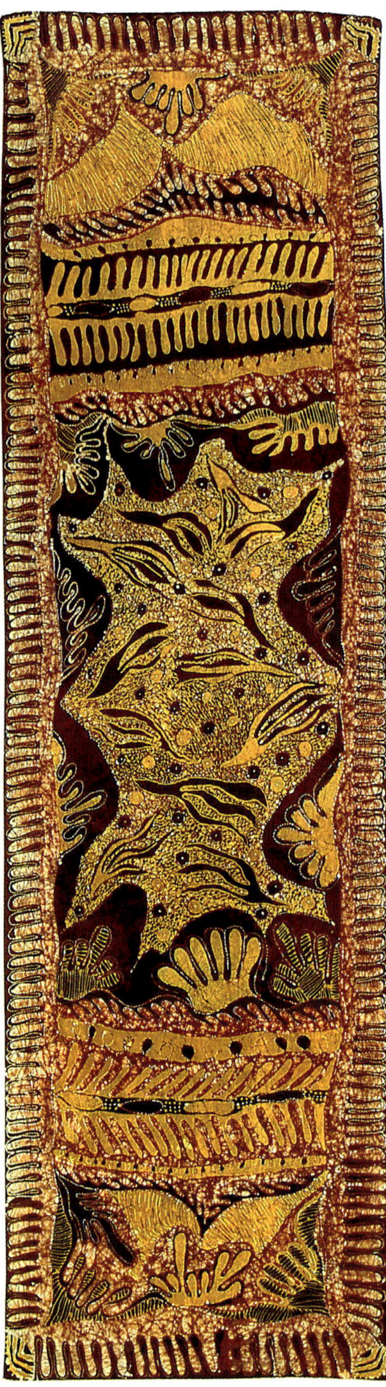

Untitled, Katey Curley, Kaltjiti Arts and Crafts, cotton batik, 300 cm x 90 cm.

Utopia imagery from women's *awely,* or ceremony, is used in the more recent fabric designs of the region. At Keringke Arts near Alice Springs, the Kangaroo Dreaming, the story of the site where the art centre stands, has been put onto T-shirts promoting the work of Keringke Arts.

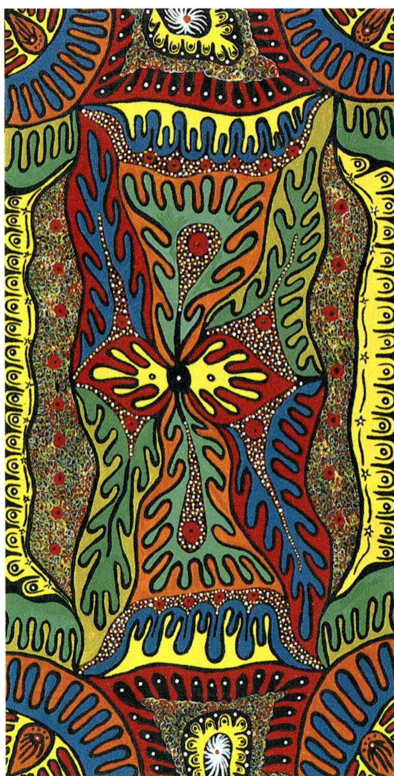

Untitled, Tjangili George, Kaltjiti Arts and Crafts, acrylic on canvas.

The painting of *batik walka* such as this was influenced by batik designs like the one shown on the left. (*Walka* is the name given to the abstract images used in artwork from the Anangu Pitjantjatjara Lands.)

Aboriginal textile art is a meeting of traditional and contemporary forces: artists are working together to produce a marketable product while interacting on their own social and cultural level. It demands of artists a high level of proficiency, at all levels, and adapting these skills to the particular, and in many cases, formidable physical environment can present interesting challenges and inspire surprising and unusual results. At all times, however, the very nature of textile work—the flow of silk, the spread and movement of colour across a fluid surface, the bold or subtle feel of shape and linework—constitute the perfect union between tradition and mastery of technique.

Mary-Lou Nugent and Margie West

the fabric

Top End
Bima Wear Association
Dunnilli Arts
Injalak Arts and Crafts Association
Jilamara Arts and Crafts Association
Munupi Art and Craft Centre
Tiwi Design

Central Australia
Ernabella Arts Inc.
Julalikari Arts and Crafts
Kaltjiti Arts and Crafts
Keringke Arts
Minymaku Arts
Titjikala Women's Centre
Urapuntja Artists

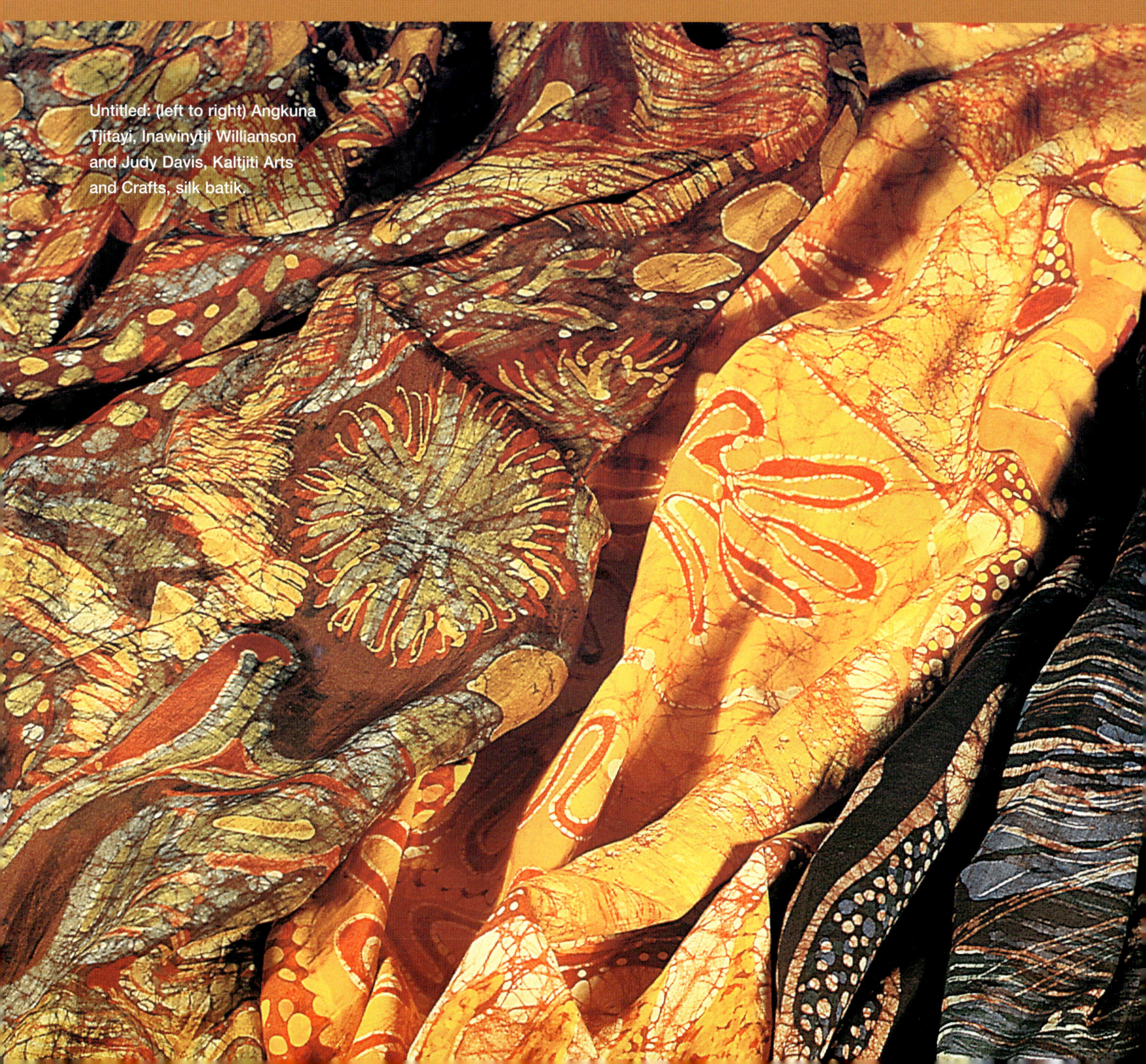

Untitled: (left to right) Angkuna Tjitayi, Inawinytji Williamson and Judy Davis, Kaltjiti Arts and Crafts, silk batik.

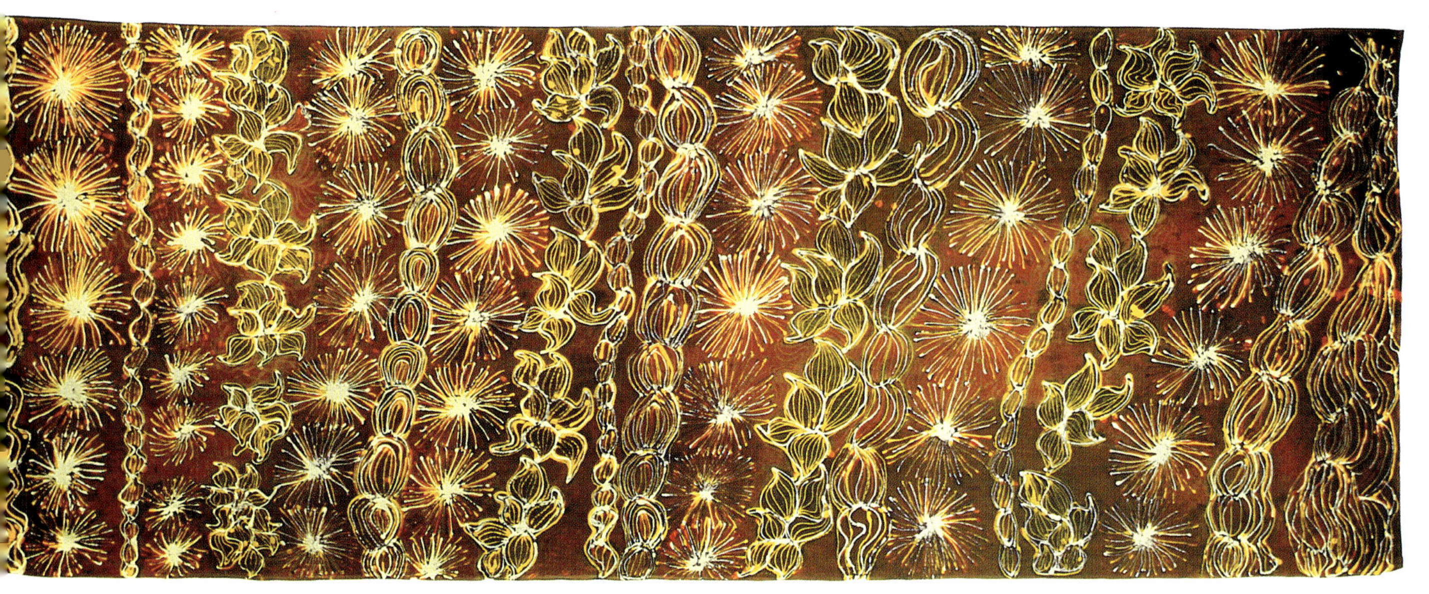

1 *Bush Potato String,* Mavis Akemarr
Utopia
Silk batik, 3 m length

2 *Untitled,* Mona Mitakiki
Minymaku Arts
Cotton batik, 90 cm wide

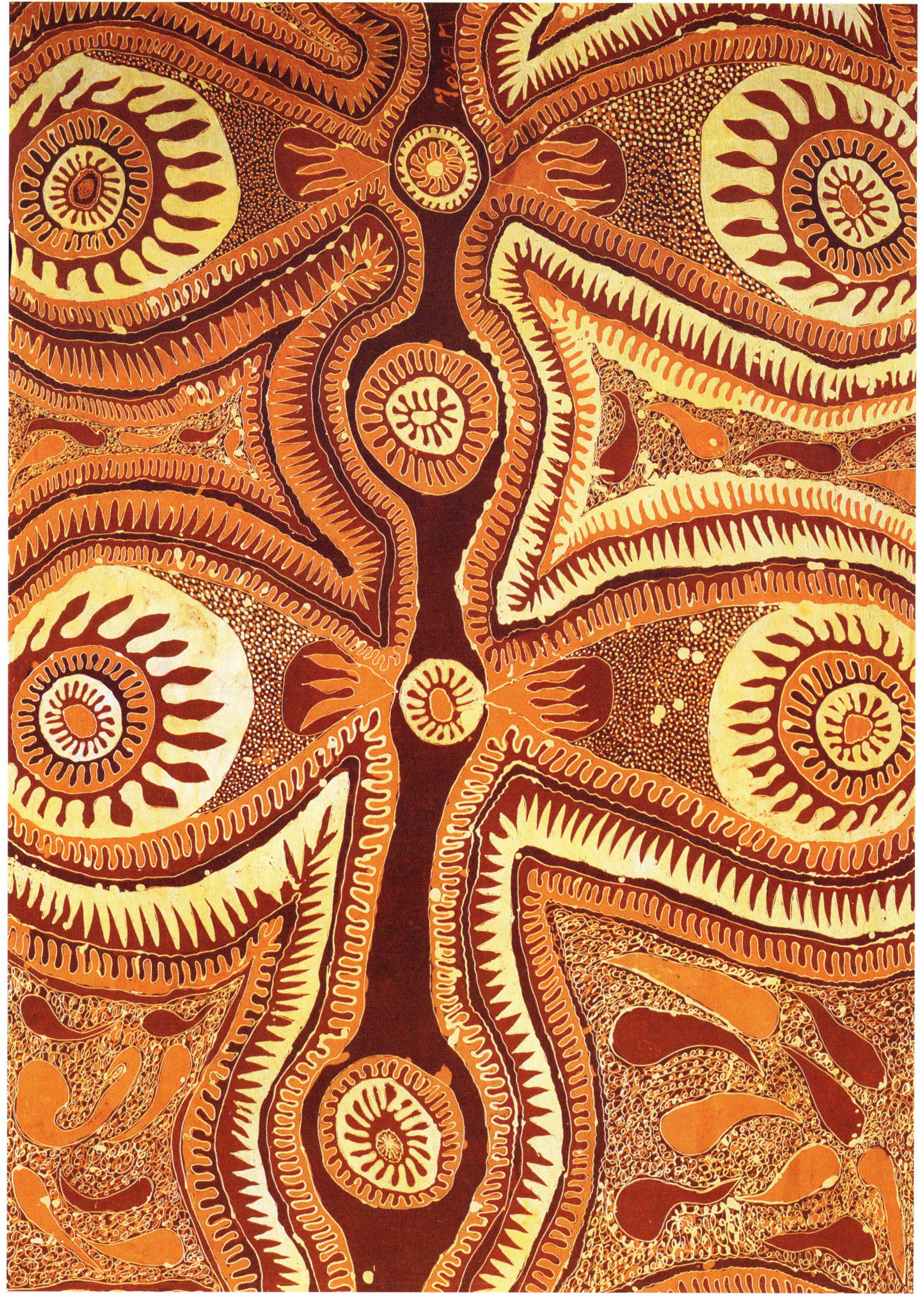

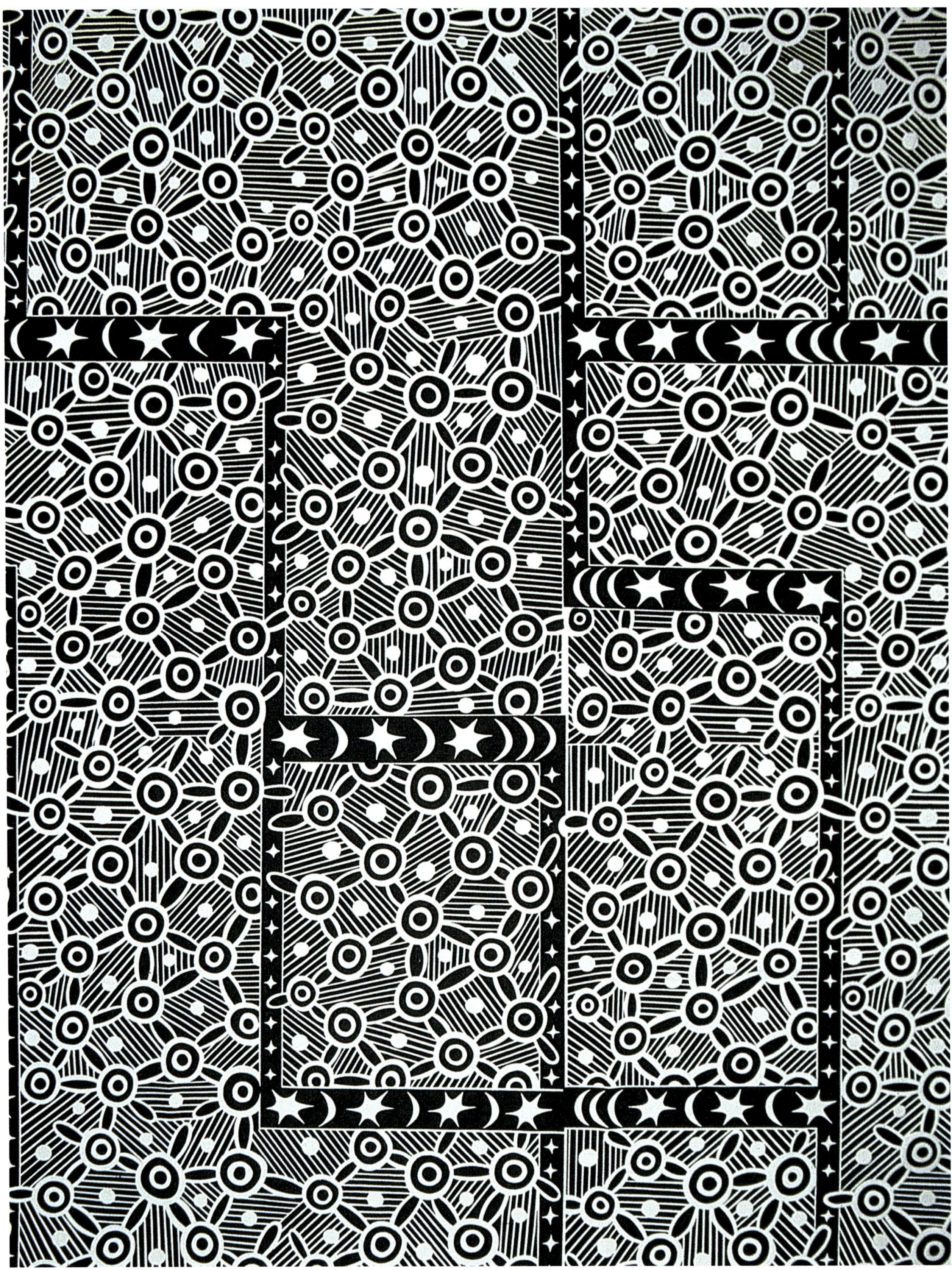

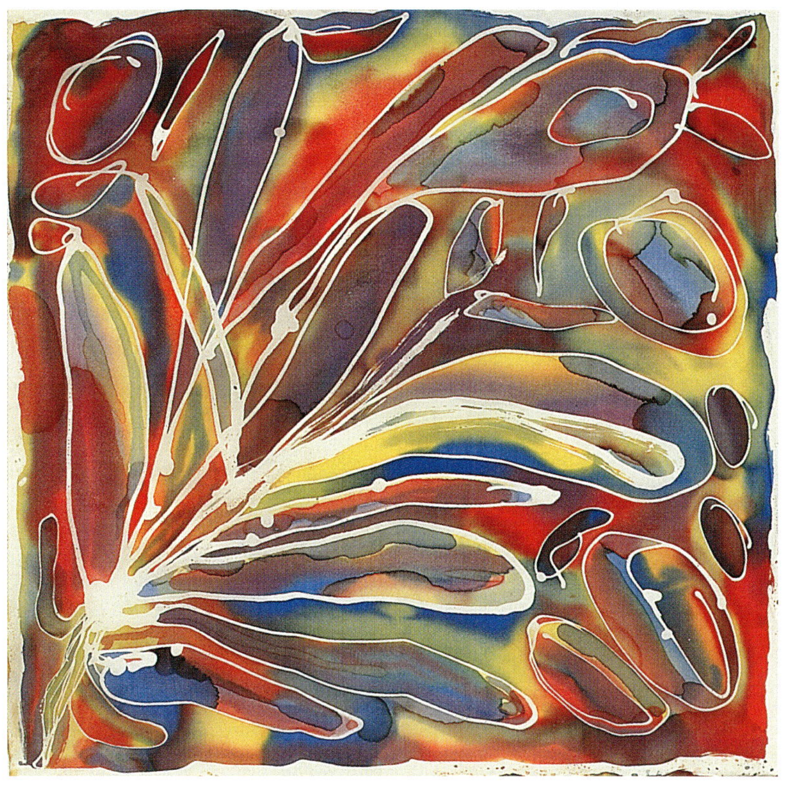

3 *Tapalinga (Star and Moon),*
designed by Danny Munkara,
screenprint developed by Ray Young
Tiwi Design
Screenprinted cotton, 400 cm x 150 cm
Collection: Powerhouse Museum

4 *Untitled,* Peggy Napangardi Jones
Julalikari Arts and Crafts
Handpainted silk, 90 cm x 90 cm

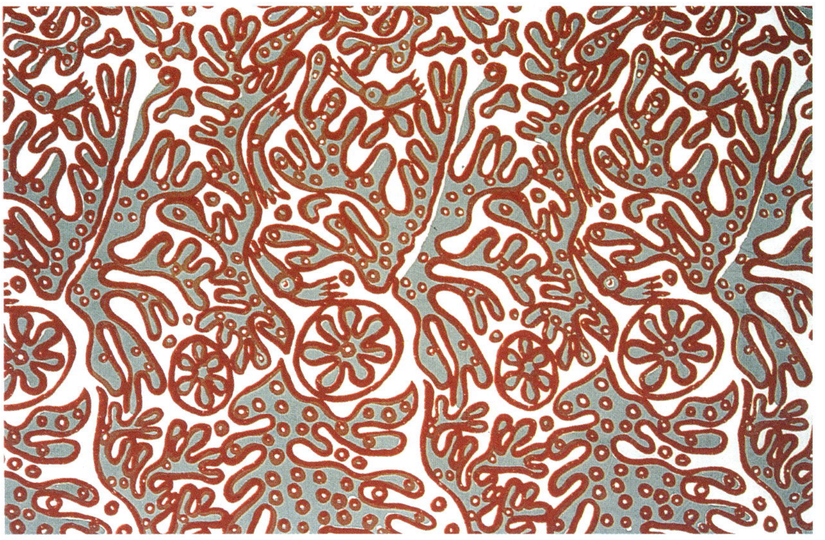

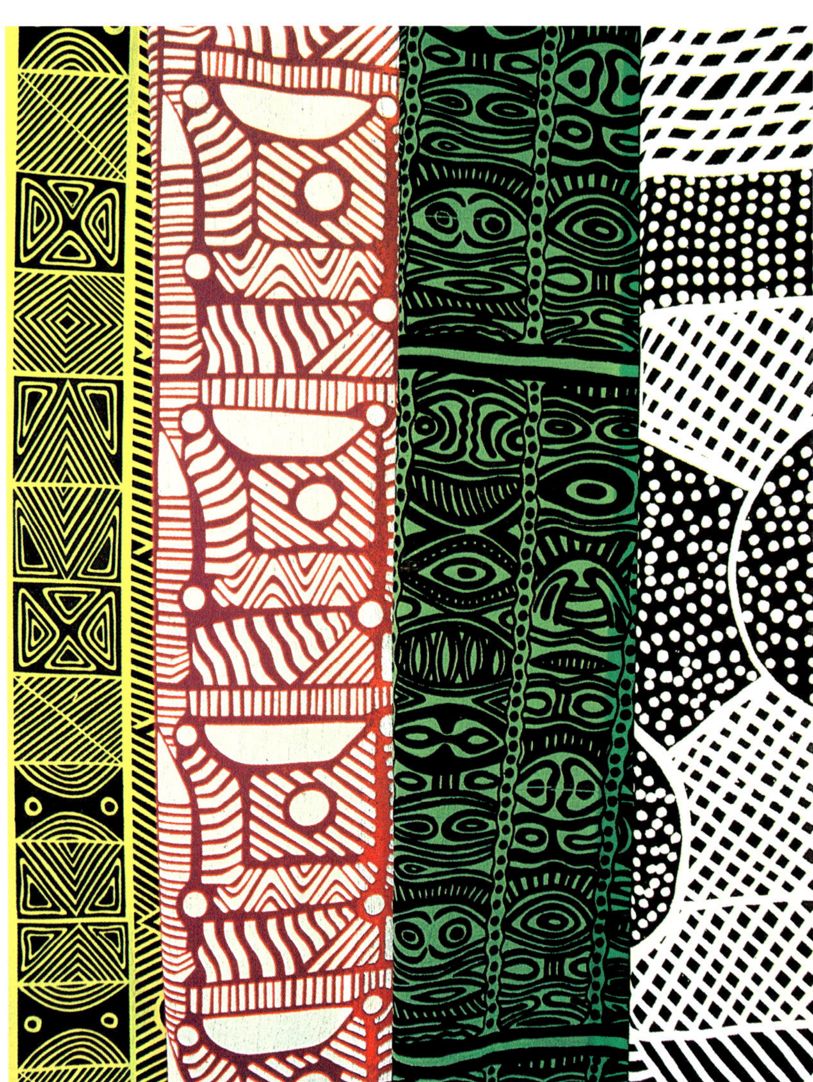

5 *Untitled,* Inawinytji Williamson
Kaltjiti Arts and Crafts
Screenprinted cotton hemp,
120 cm wide

6 (Left to right)
Untitled, Osmond Kantilla
Spider Web, Bede Tungatulum
Body Painting, Jock Pautjimi
Kurlama, Marie Josette Orsto
Tiwi Design
Screenprinted cotton

7 *Lizard Trails,* Polly Nelson Angal
Utopia
Silk batik with brush design,
500 cm x 110 cm
Collection: Powerhouse Musuem

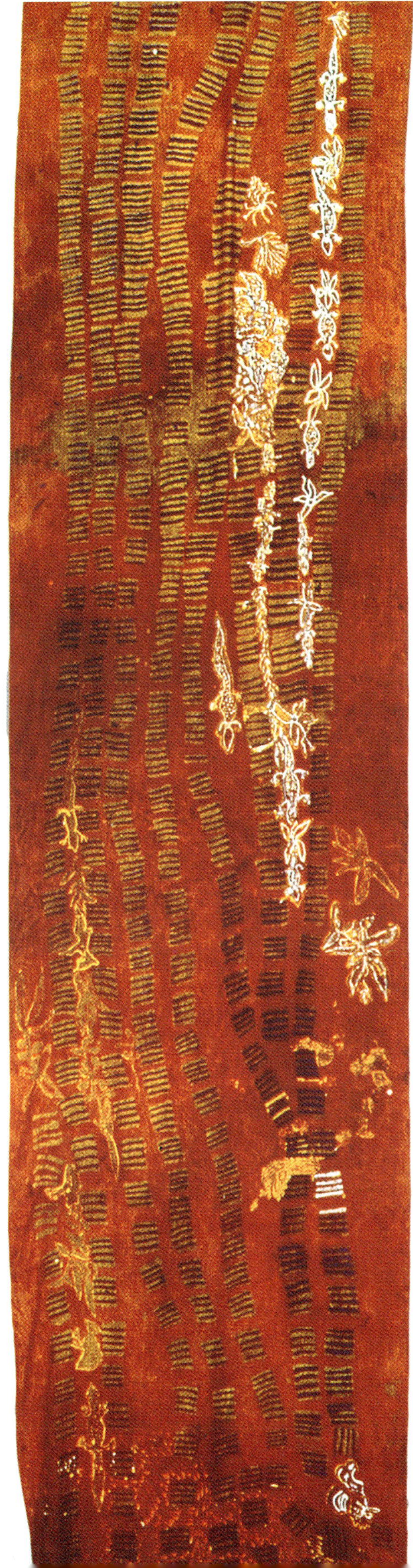

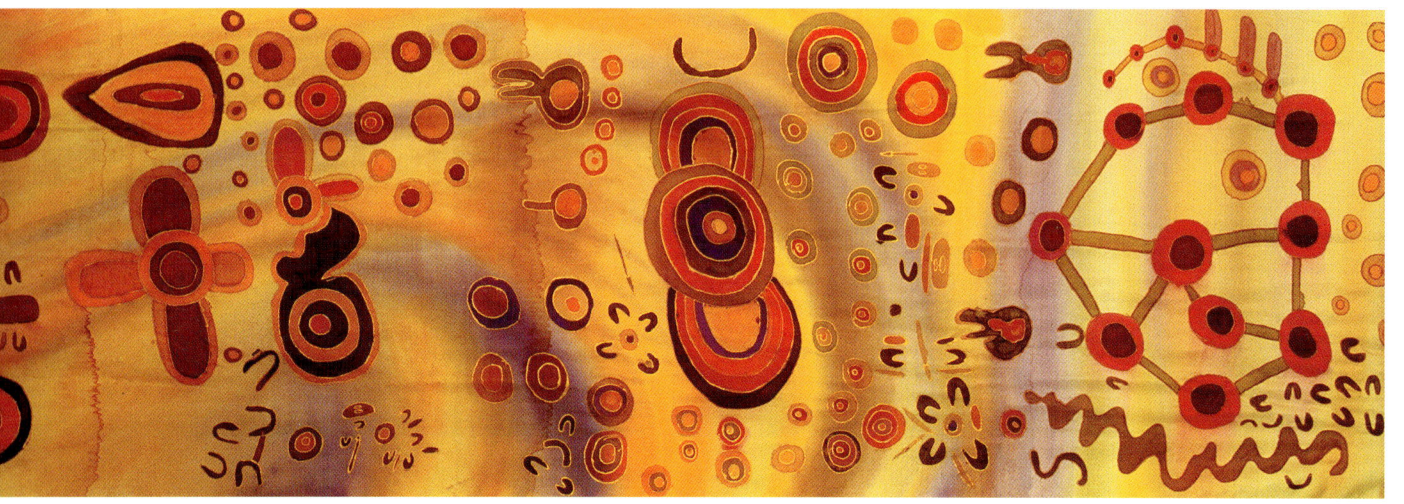

8   *Atyelpe Dreaming,* Agnes Abbott
Keringke Arts
Handpainted silk
500 cm x 100 cm
Collection: Araluen Arts Centre

9   *Barramundi,* Gabriel Maralngurra
and Ray Young
Injalak Arts and Crafts Association
Screenprinted cotton twill, 8 m length
(Photo courtesy Injalak Arts and Crafts
Association)

10   *Untitled,* Yanyi Wells
Kaltjiti Arts and Crafts
Screenprinted cotton hemp,
120 cm wide

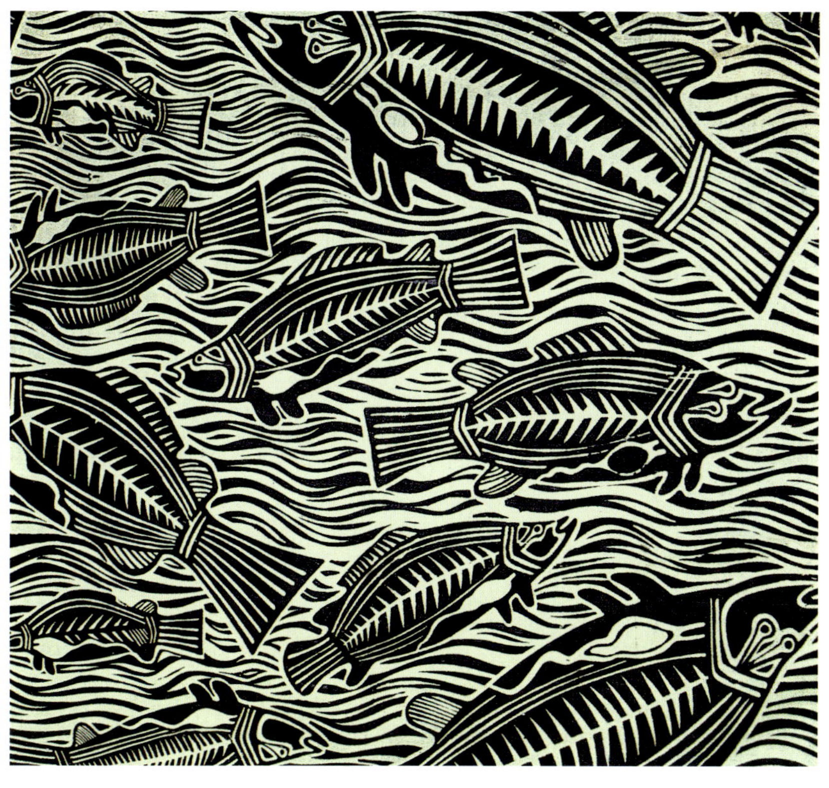

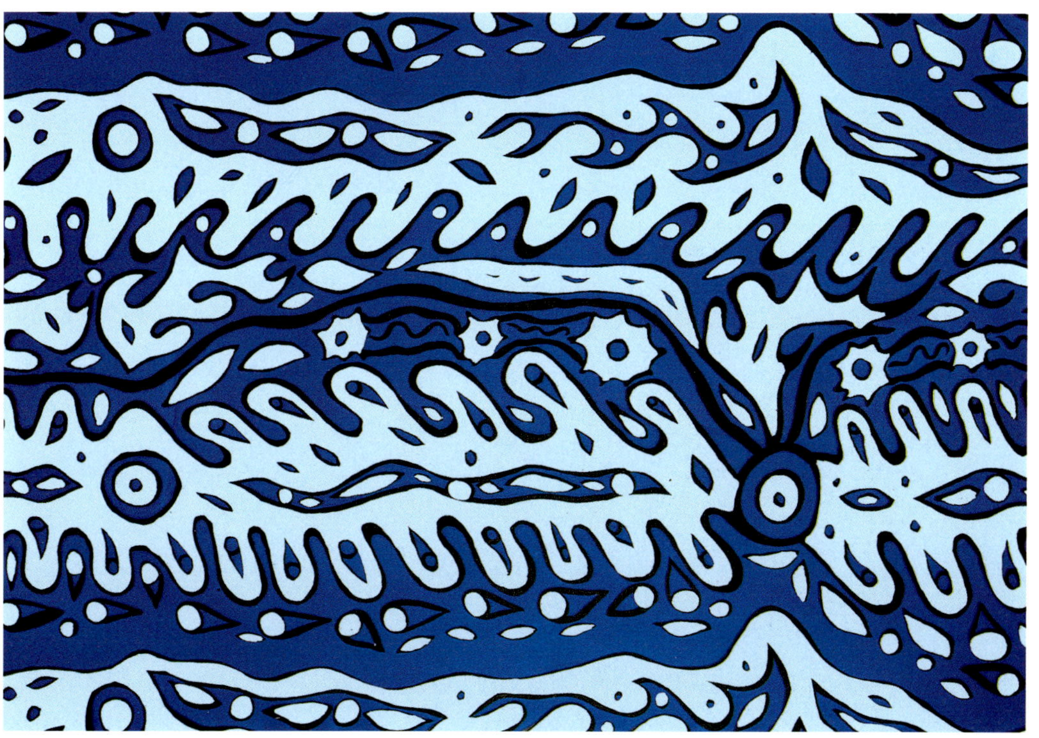

11 *Untitled,* Alison Carroll
Ernabella Arts
Handpainted silk scarf, 90 cm x 90 cm

12 *Untitled,* various artists
Jilamara Arts and Crafts
Screenprinted cotton

13 *Untitled,* Peggy Napangardi Jones
Julalikari Arts and Crafts
Screenprinted cotton twill,
120 cm wide

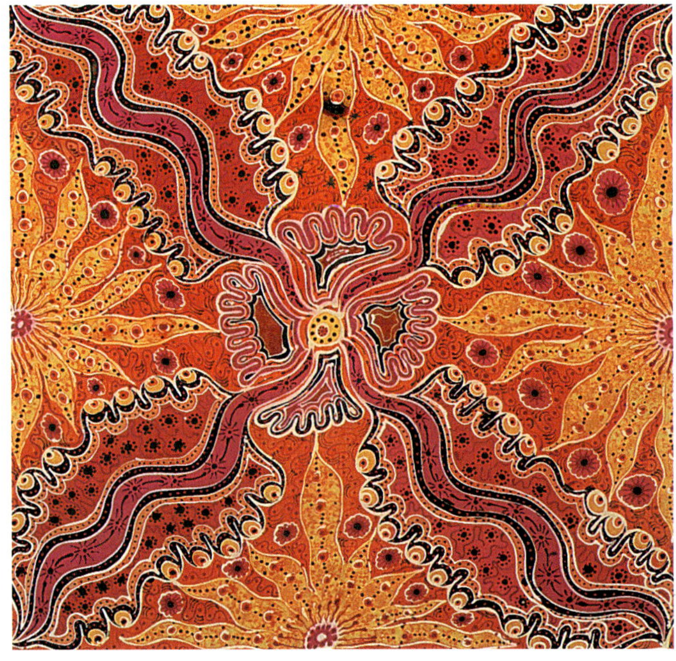

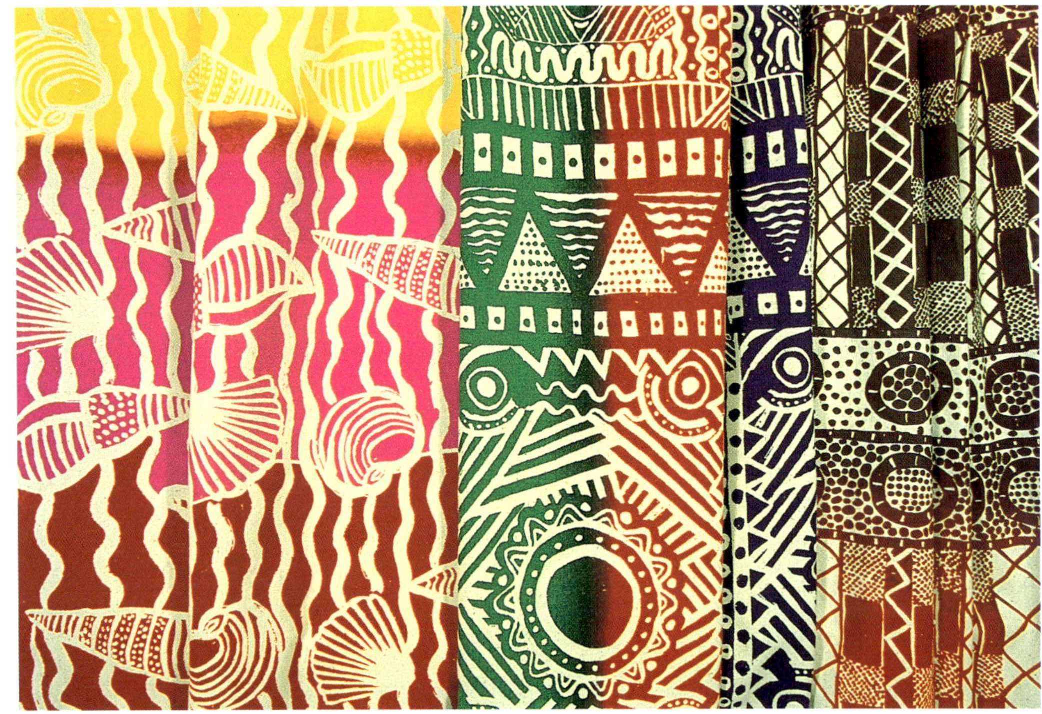

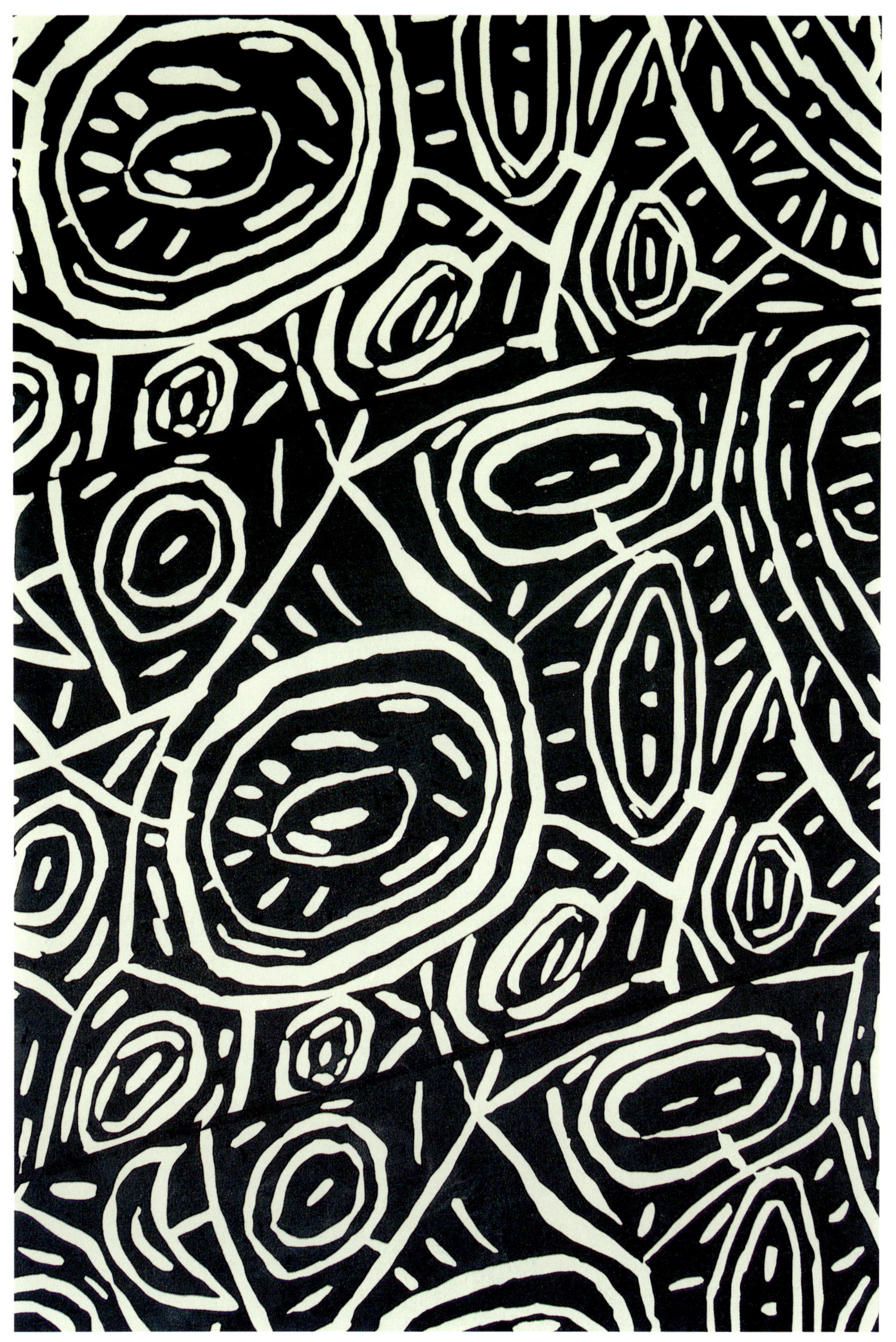

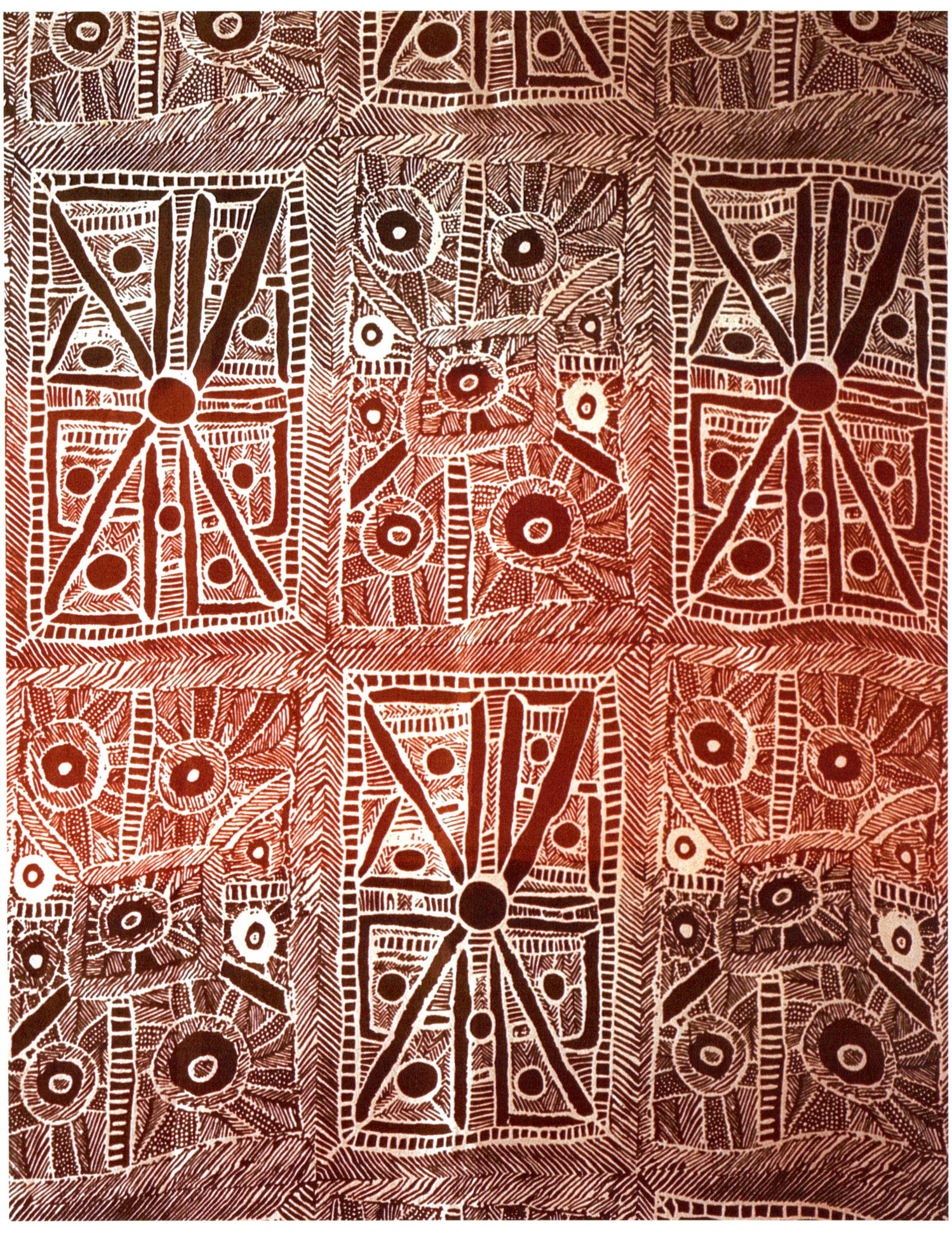

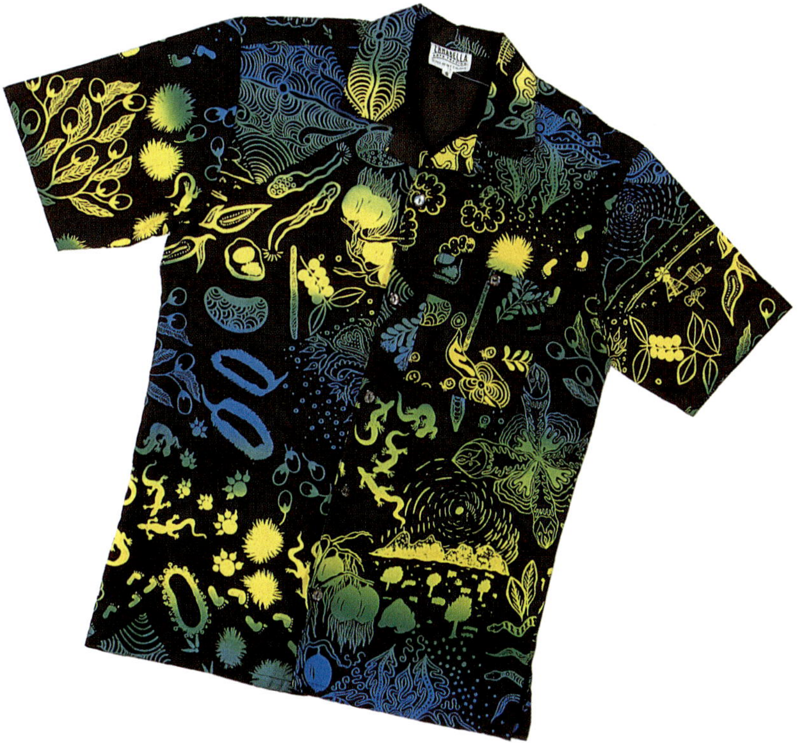

14 *Ngini Parlini Jilamara* (from old designs *Crocodile* and *Spider Woman Dreamings),* **Jilamara Arts and Crafts**
Screenprinted dyes on silk,
400 cm x 92 cm
Collection: Powerhouse Museum

15 *Shirt*
Ernabella Trading Company
Screenprinted cotton

16 *Mimi Figures,* **Lofty Bardayal**
Injalak Arts and Crafts Association
Screenprinted cotton twill, 8 m length
(Photo courtesy Injalak Arts and
Crafts Association)

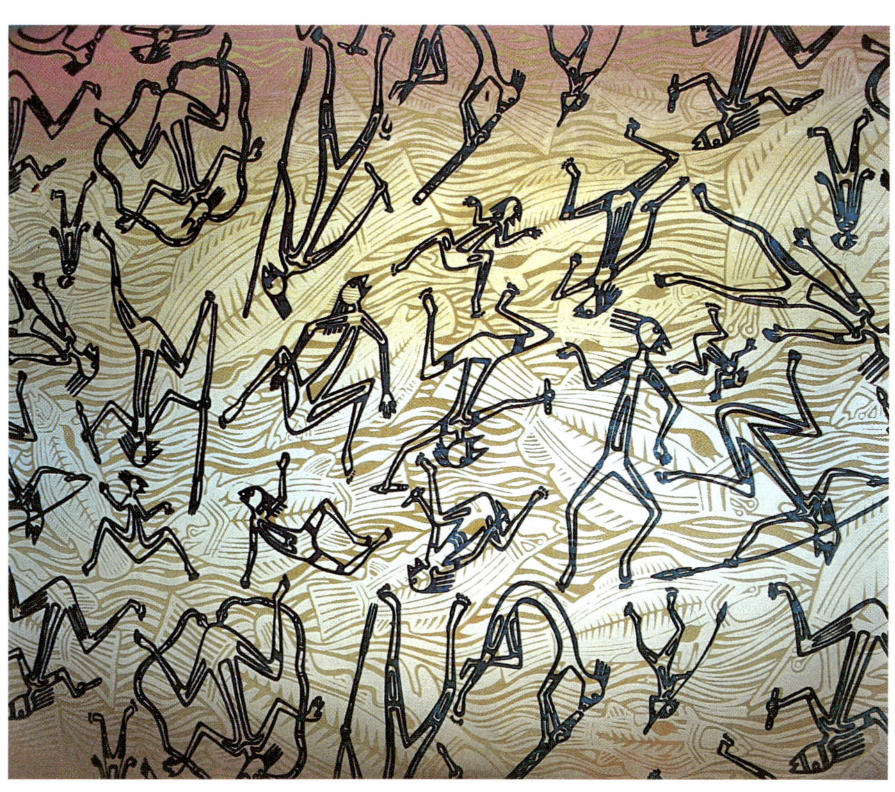

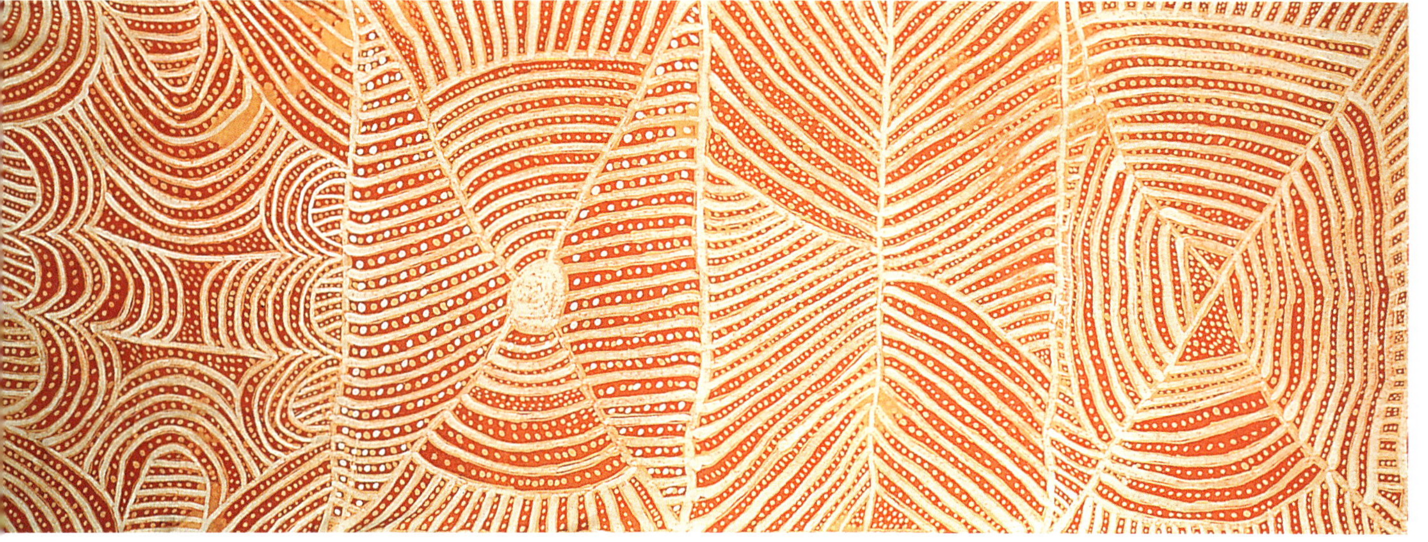

17 *Untitled,* Ada Bird Apetyarr
Utopia
Silk batik, 3 m length

18 (Left to right)
Yam; Bone Design; Sea Life;
artists unknown
Tiwi Design
Screenprinted cotton

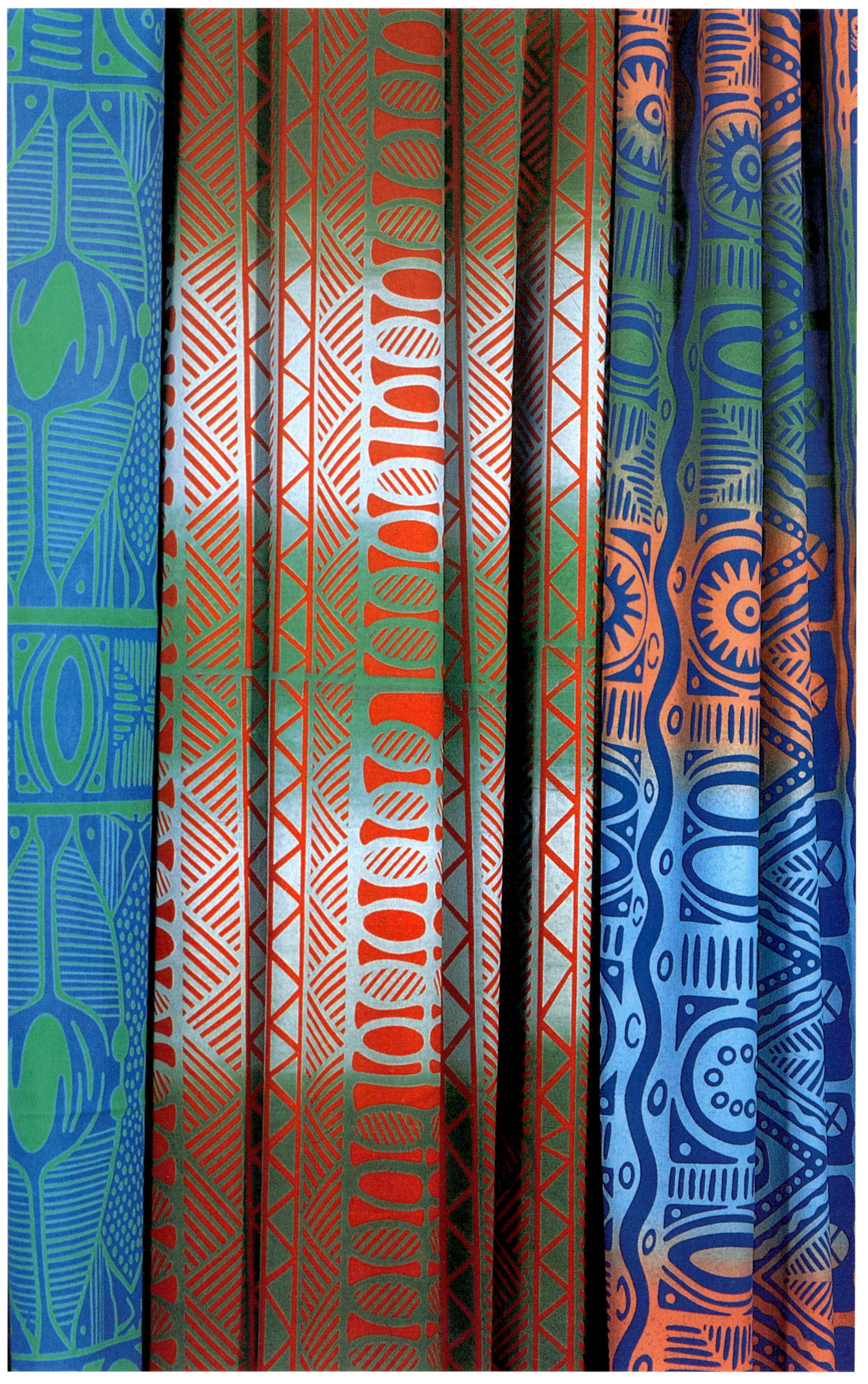

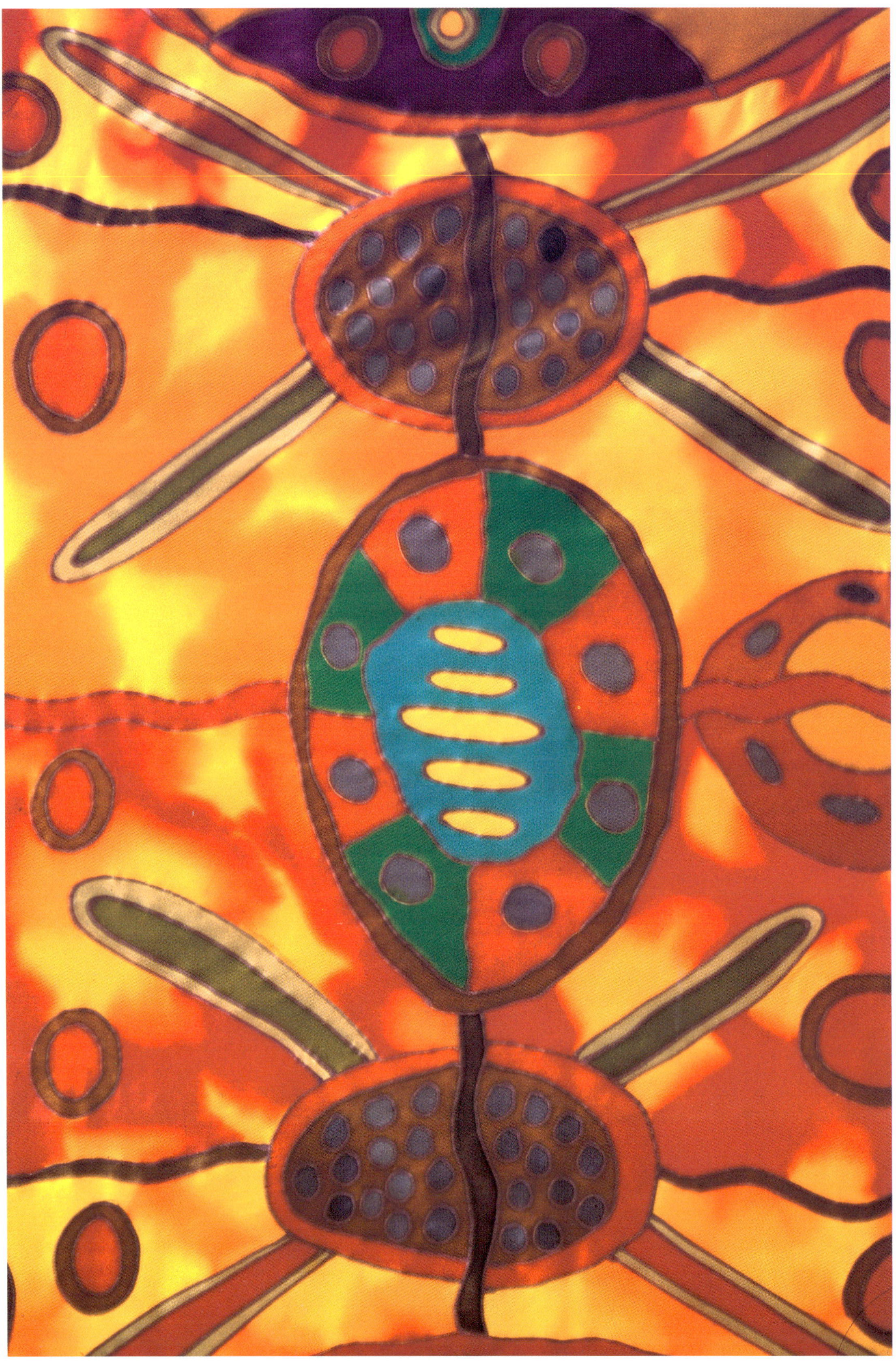

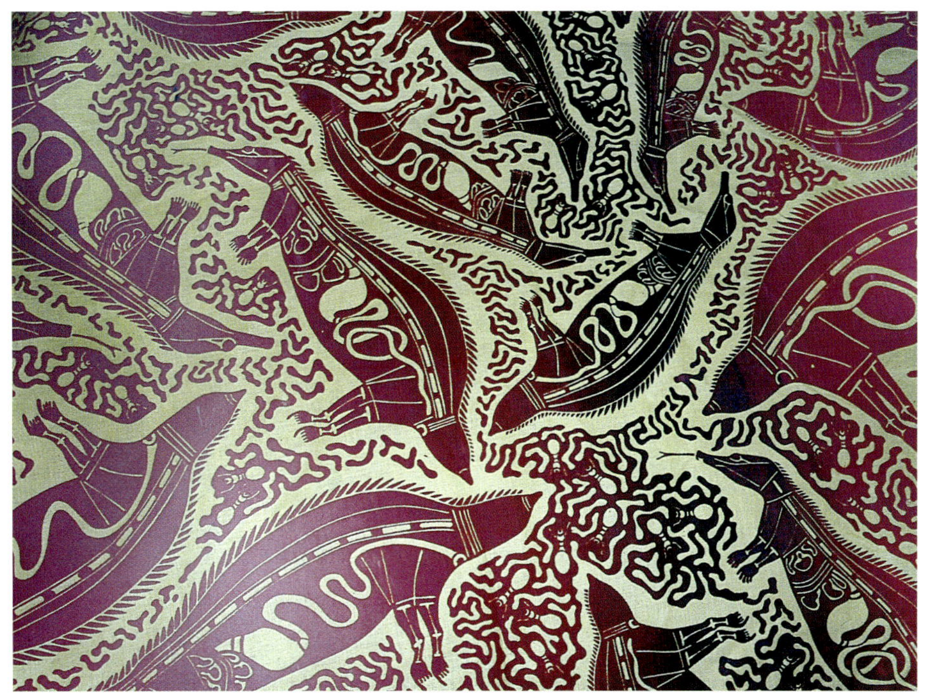

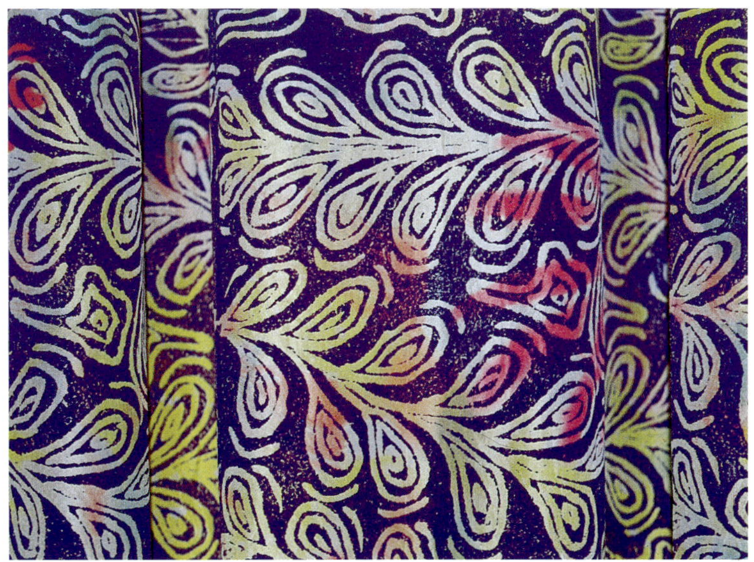

19 *Untitled*, June Smith
Keringke Arts
Handpainted silk
(Photo Mary-Lou Nugent)

20 *Ngarrbek (Echidna)*, Lofty Bardayal
Injalak Arts and Crafts Association
Screenprinted cotton twill, 8m length
(Photo courtesy Injalak Arts and
Crafts Association)

21 *Untitled*, Rene Boko
Titjikala Women's Centre
Lino-block print over handpainted
cotton

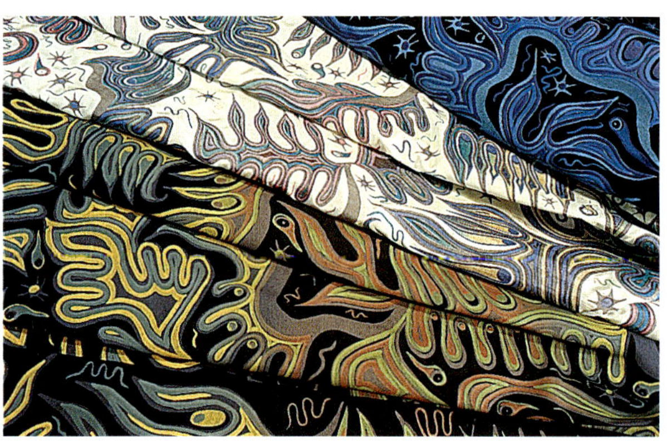

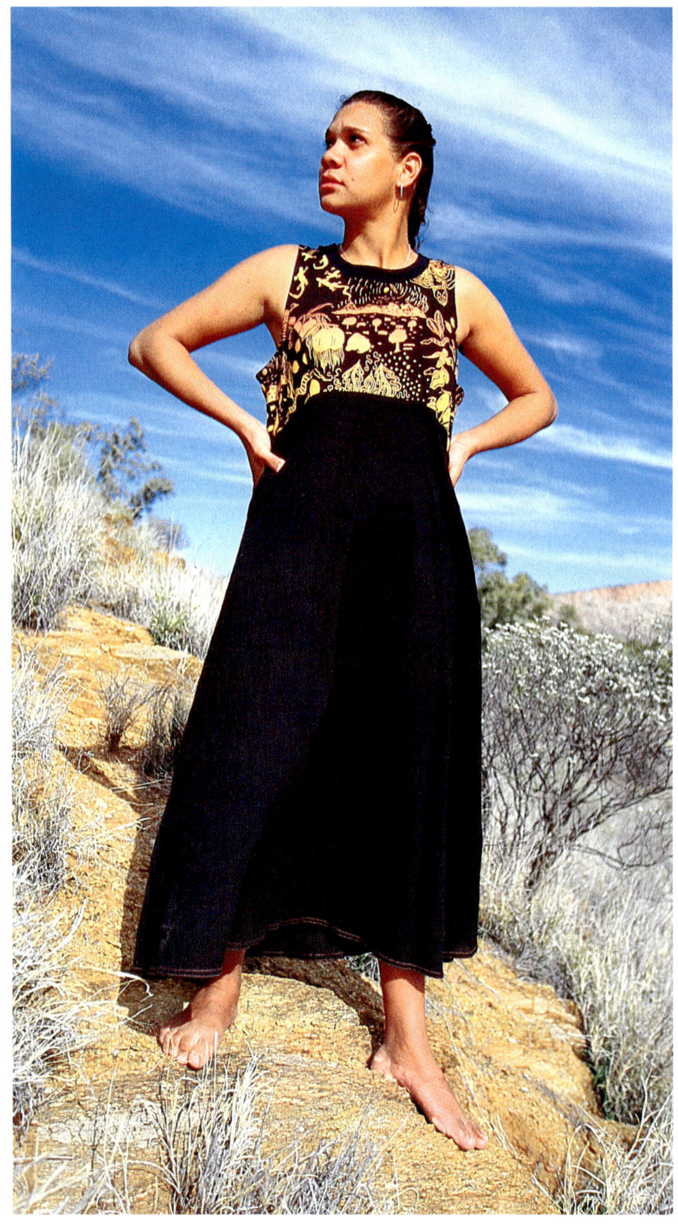

22 *Puti (Bush)* (shown in a number of
colourways)**, Nyuwara Tapaya and
Nyukana Baker**
Ernabella Arts
Screenprinted cotton, 120 cm wide
lengths, printed by Marie Warren

23 *Dress*
Ernabella Trading Company
Screenprinted cotton, modelled by
Desart employee Amelia Forrester

24 *Untitled* (shows bushtucker and river
in flood)**, Rosie Apwerl**
Utopia
Silk satin batik with brush and
canting design, 300 cm x 120 cm
Collection: Powerhouse Museum

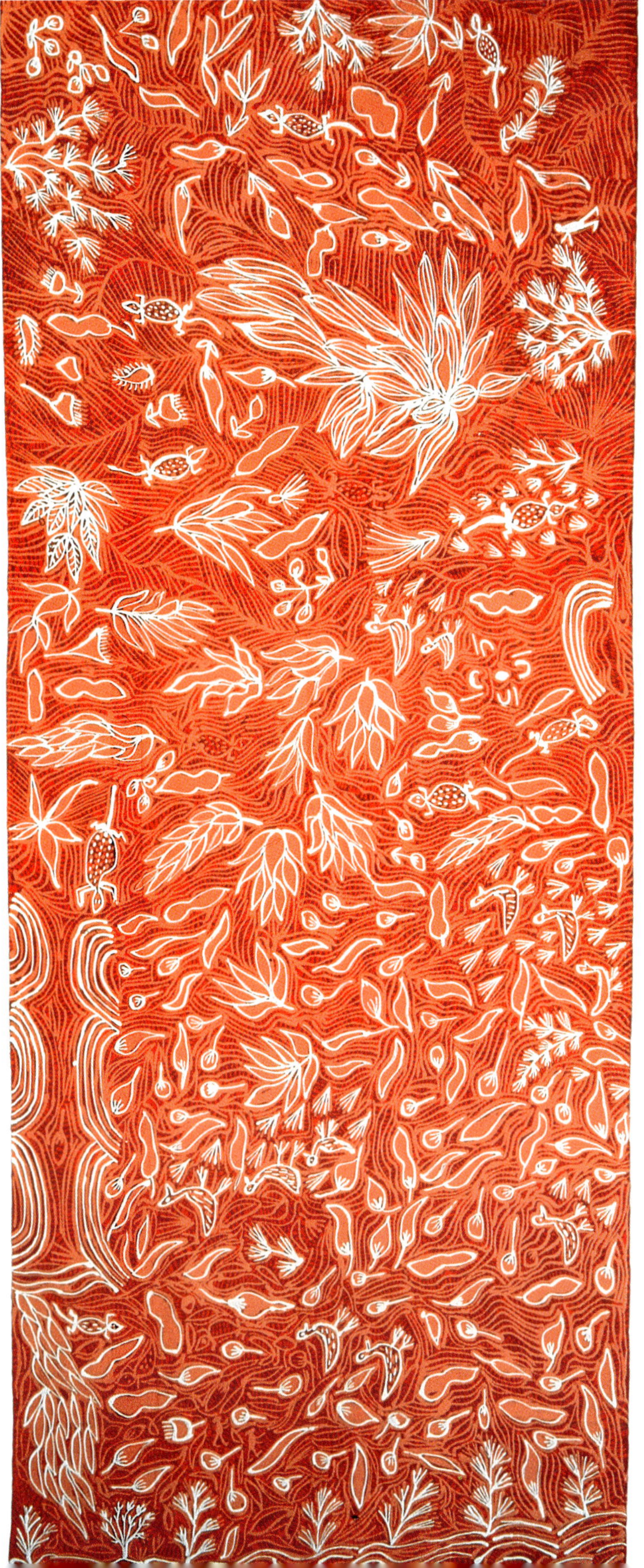

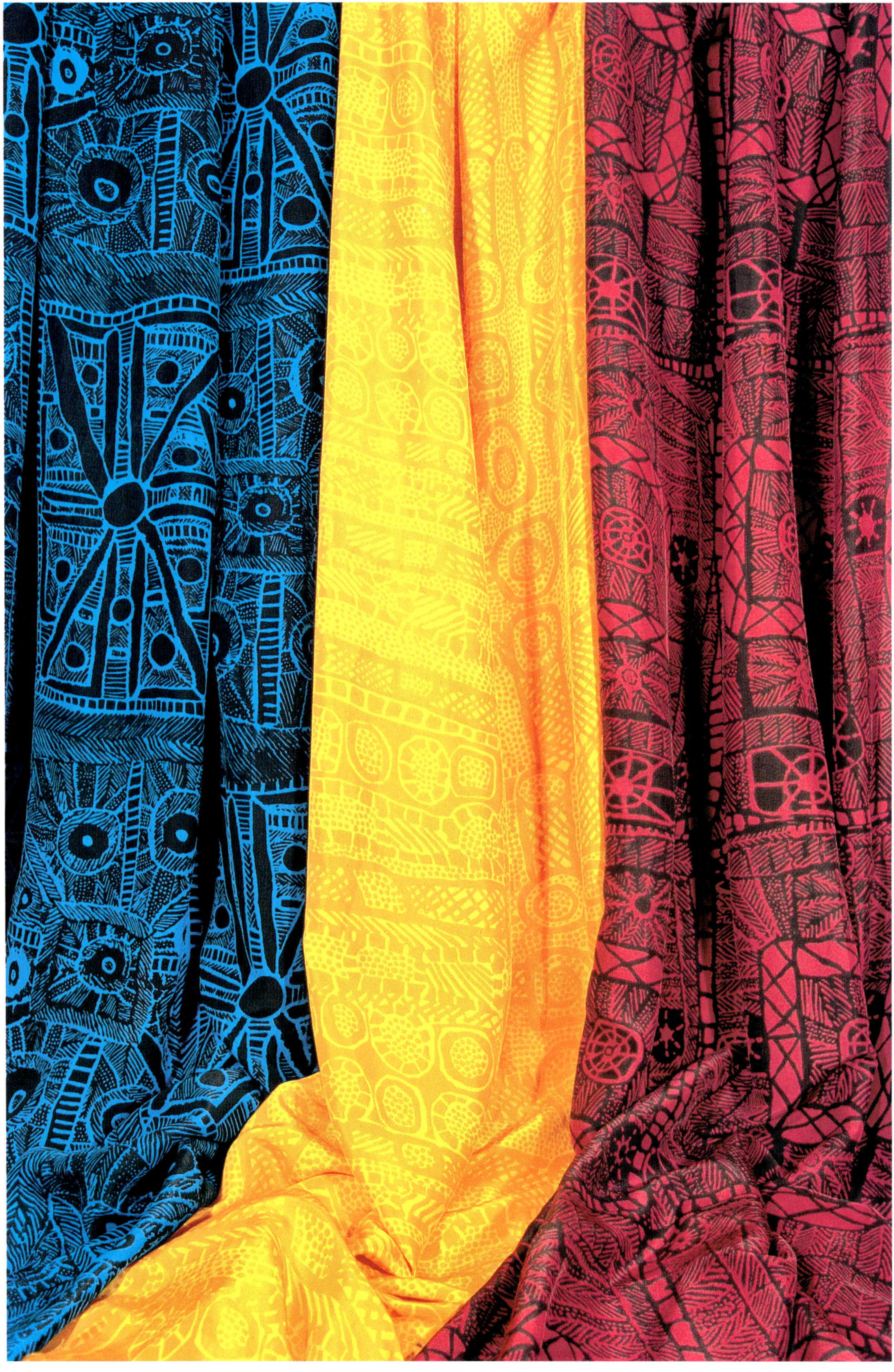

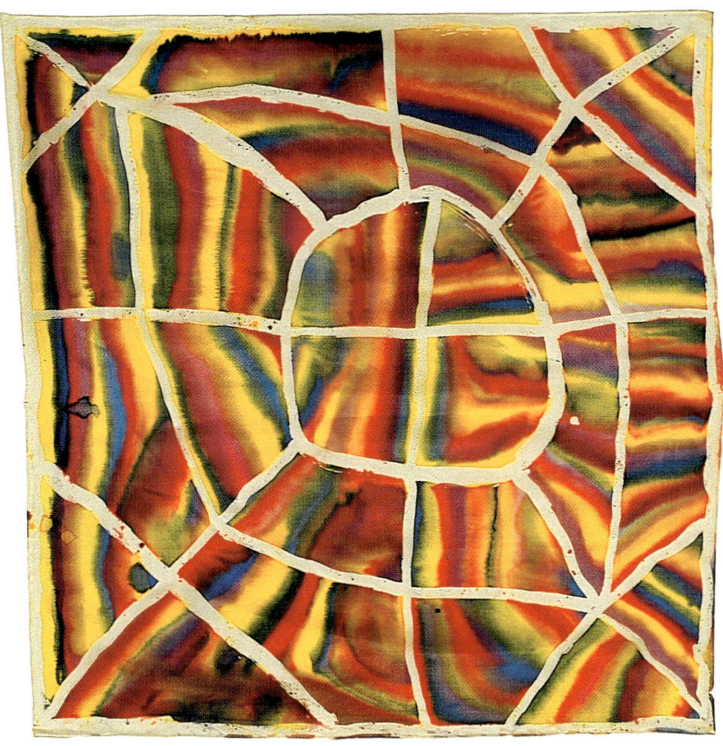

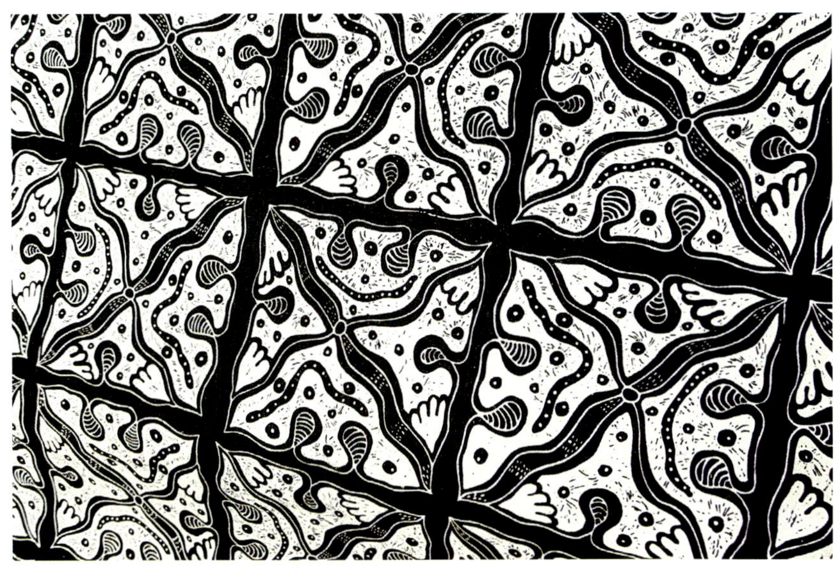

25 (Left to right)
Ngini Parlini Jilamara (from old designs *Crocodile* and *Spider Woman Dreamings)*, **Untitled, Untitled,** Jilamara Arts and Crafts Association
Screenprinted cotton

26 *Untitled*, Peggy Napangardi Jones
Julalikari Arts and Crafts
Handpainted silk scarf, 90 cm x 90 cm

27 *Untitled*, Marita Baker
Kaltjiti Arts and Crafts
Screenprinted cotton length, design based on a lino-block print on paper

28 *Lizard and Bush Medicine*,
Lena Apwerl
Utopia
Silk batik with brush and canting
design, 500 cm x 115 cm
Collection: Powerhouse Museum
(Photo Penelope Clay, courtesy
Powerhouse Museum)

29 *Yilinginga (Dance)*,
based on a 1979 bark painting by
Paddy Henry Ripijingimpi,
screenprint developed by
Ray Young
Tiwi Design
Screenprinted cotton,
400 cm x 150 cm
Collection: Powerhouse Museum

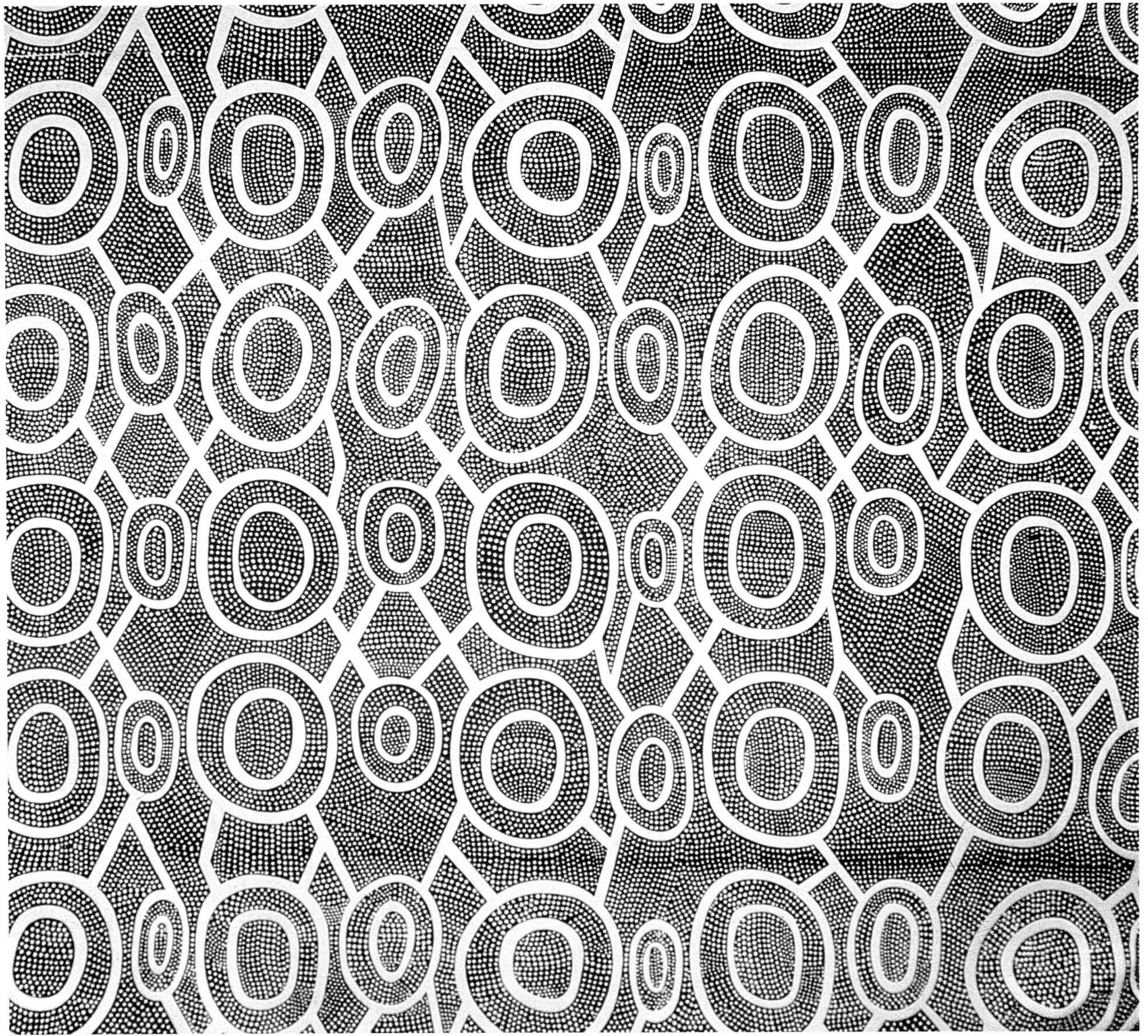

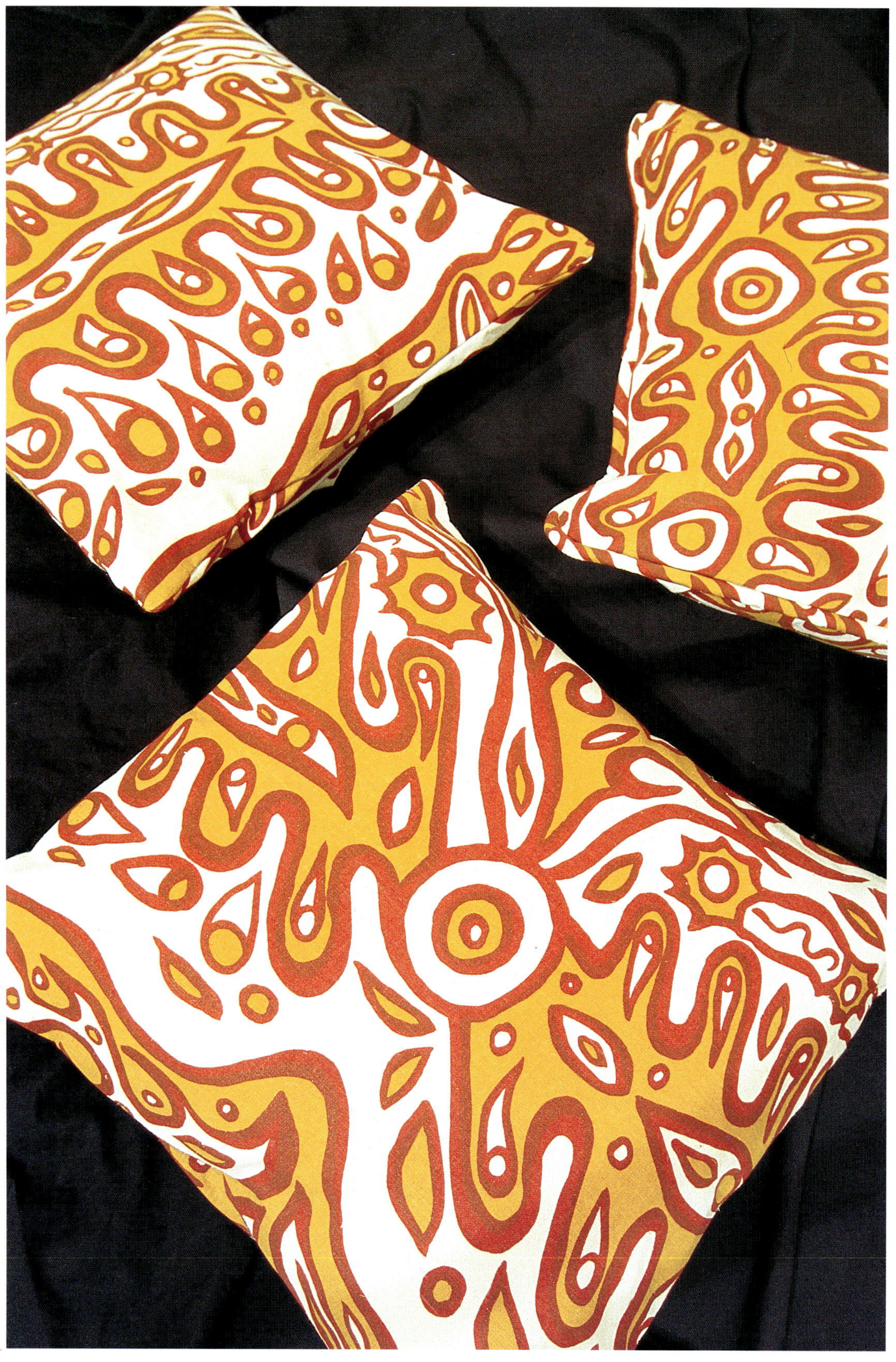

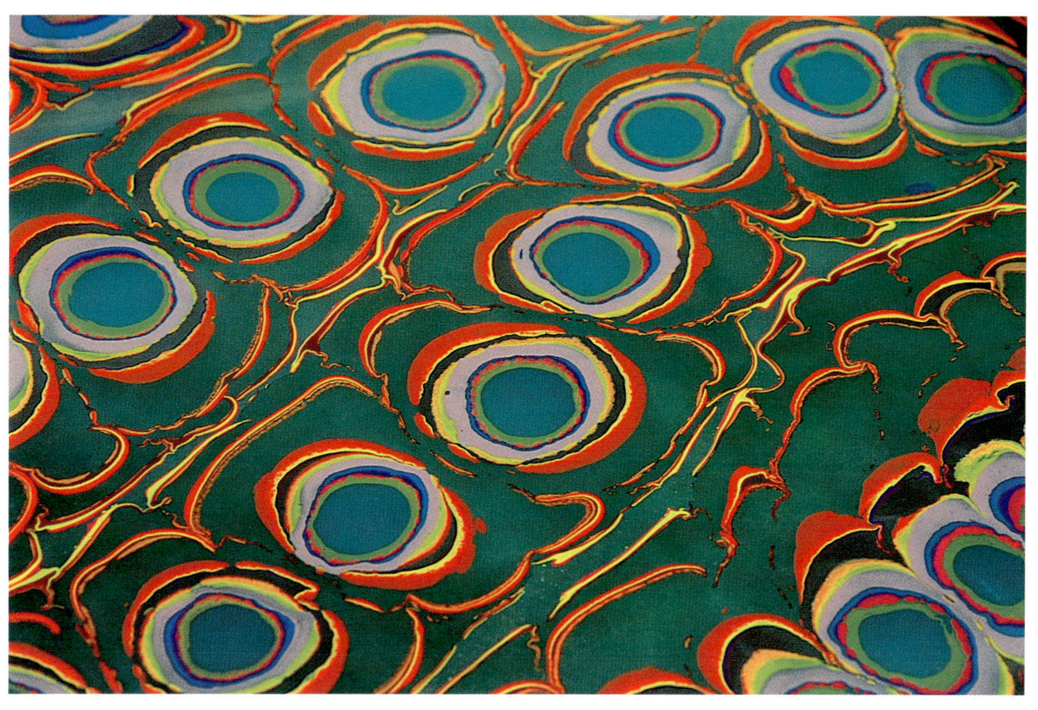

30 *Cushions*, Yanyi Wells
Kaltjiti Arts and Crafts
Screenprinted cotton hemp

31 *Untitled*, Kelli Bruce
Dunnilli Arts
Marbled cotton, 150 cm x 120 cm

32 *Lampshade*, Mona Mitakiki
Minymaku Arts
Cotton batik, lampshade 75 cm high

33 *Jilamara (Design)*, **based on three
paintings by Marie Josette Orsto,
screenprint developed by
Osmond Kantilla**
Tiwi Design
Screenprinted cotton, 400 cm x 150 cm
Collection: Powerhouse Museum

Next page:
34 *Untitled*, **Marie Young**
Keringke Arts
Handpainted silk

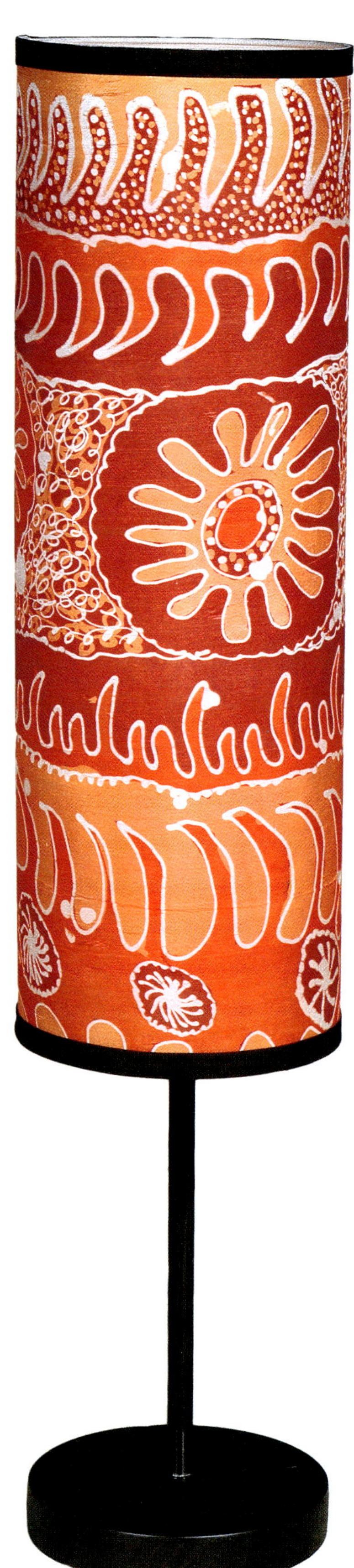

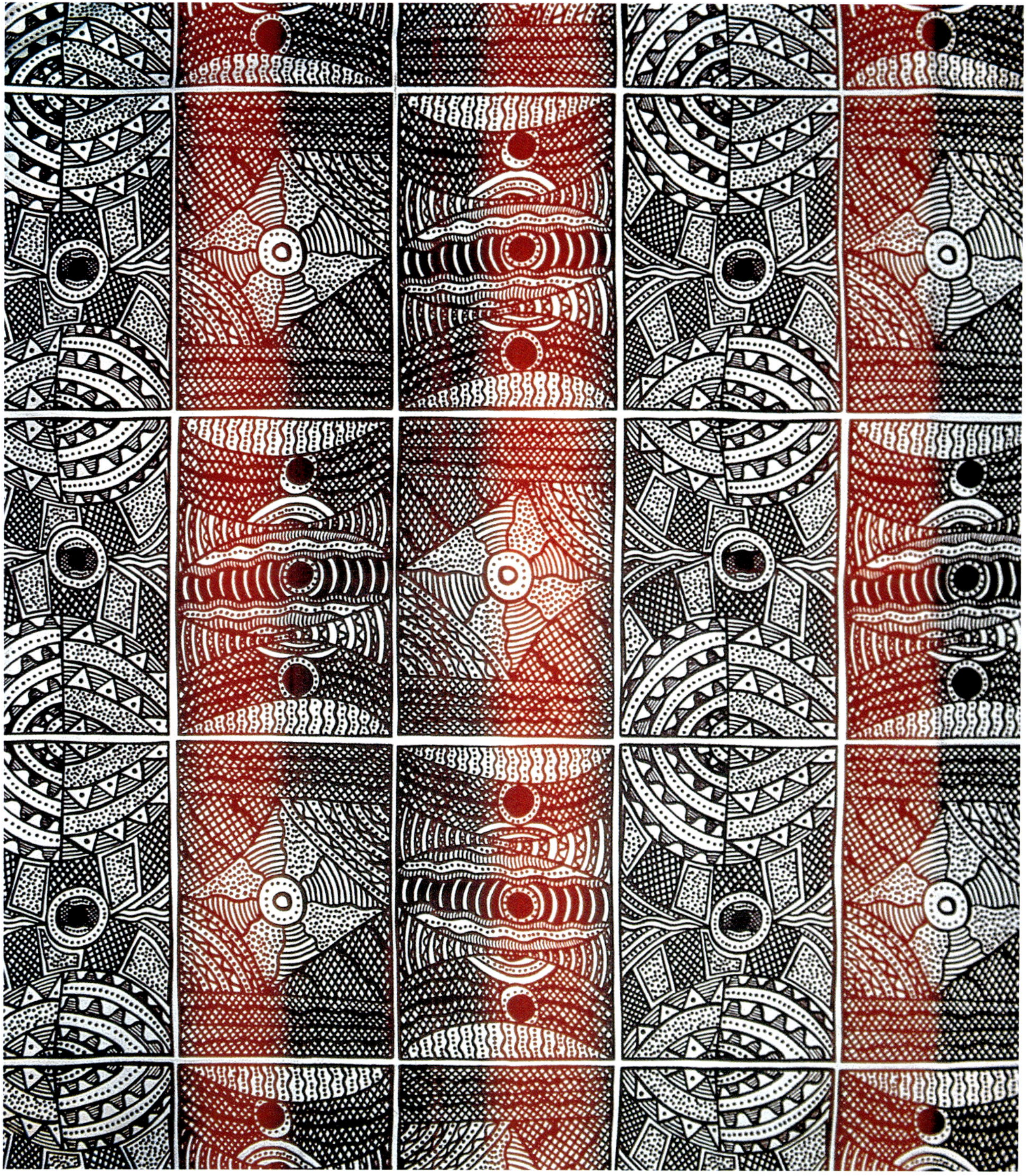

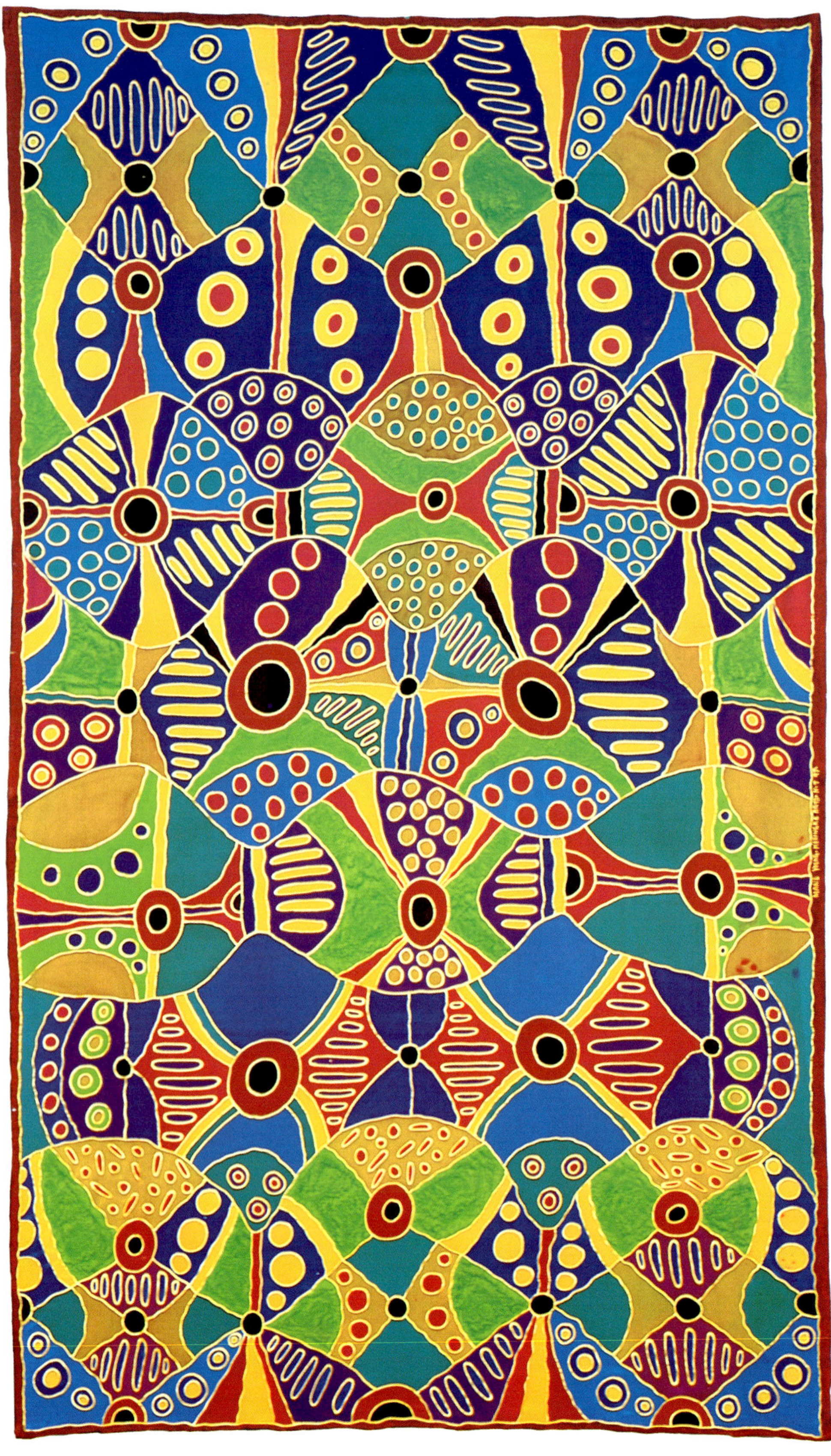

we started batik a long time ago

the introduction of textiles to Aboriginal art centres

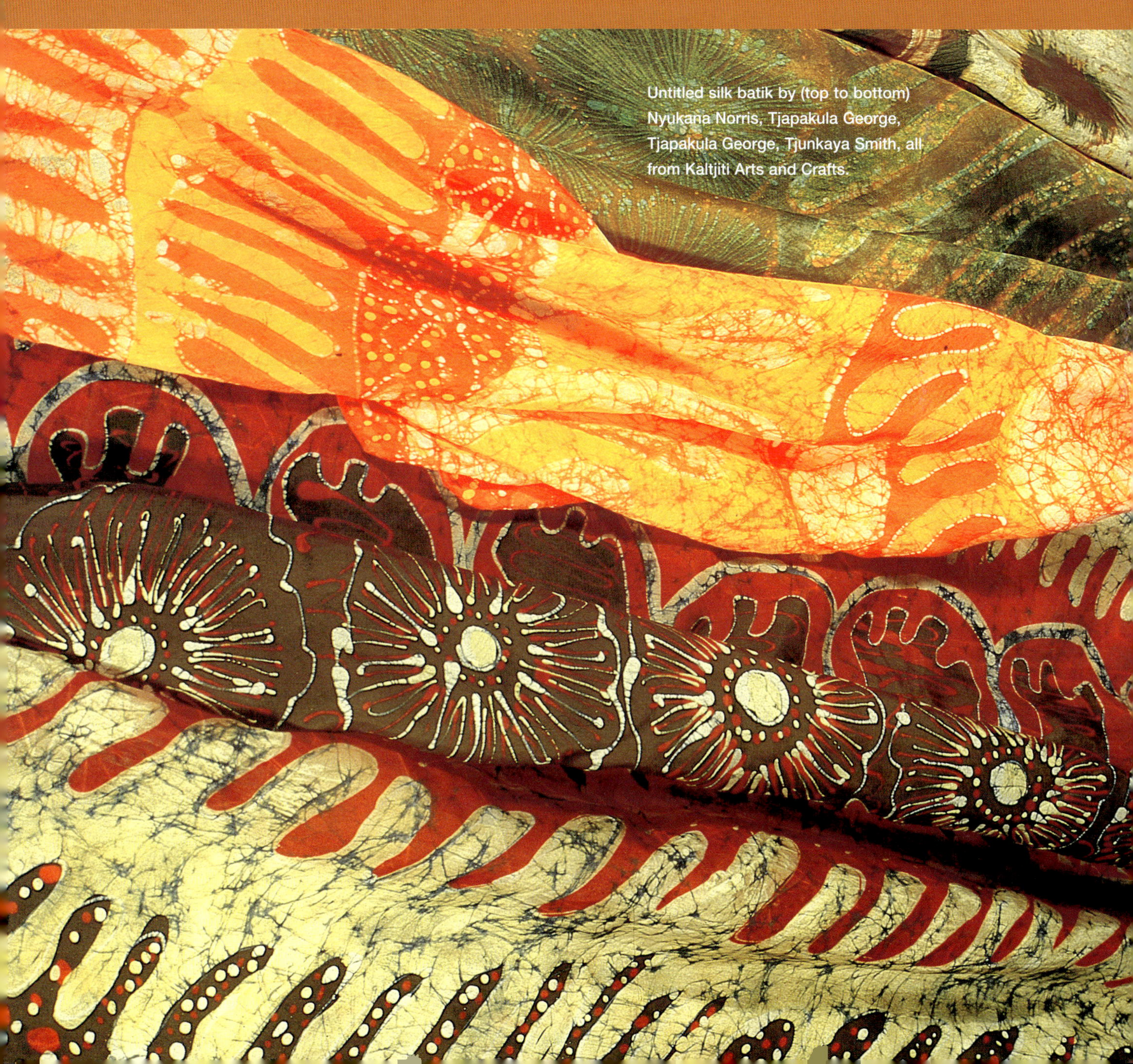

Untitled silk batik by (top to bottom)
Nyukana Norris, Tjapakula George,
Tjapakula George, Tjunkaya Smith, all
from Kaltjiti Arts and Crafts.

Ernabella textiles:
The early days

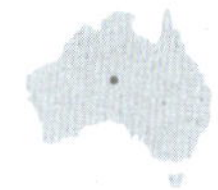

Daisy (Nyukana) Baker

Ngayulu iriti kulangka nyinara tjitjingku walka palyalpai mununa paintamilalpai. Mununa palulanguru kula wiyaringkula ngayulu kuliningi craftroomangka waakarinytjikitjangku mununa pitjangu nyanga palula kutu munula tjinguru paintamilaningi card kulunypa tjutangka.

Ka Win Hilliardanya nyanga palula waakaringi nganampa craftroom nyangangka palu craftroom nganmanyitja nyarangka ngarangi nyara punu tjuta kuwari ngaranyi palula.

Palula malangkana kula wiyaringu mununa craftroomangka pitjala waakaringi, ngayulu waaka kutjupa tjutaku mukuringkunytja wiyatu panya clinicaku munu walingka warkarinytjaku kulu palu ngayulu ngurkantanu waaka nyangatja paintamilantjikitjangku munu floor rug tjuta palyantjikitjangku. Mununa 1963ngka anu New South Walesala kutu weaving nintiringkunytjikitja nyara palulana waakaku nintiringangi weavemilantjikitja munu waaka kutjupa tjutaku kulu. Win

Untitled, Atipalku Intjalki, Ernabella Arts, crepe-backed silk batik, 3.2 m length.

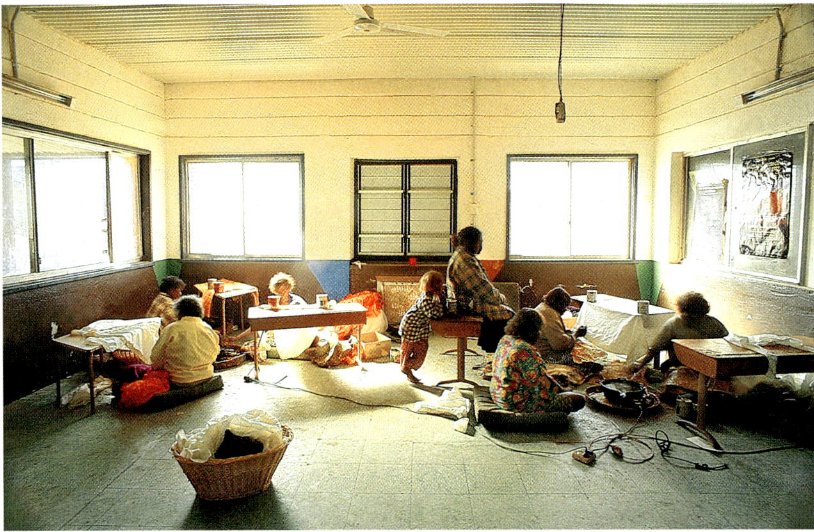

The batik room at Ernabella Arts, 1997.

Hilliardanya ngali nyara palula kutu anu munuli wiki mankurpa manyinangi nyura nyara palula.

I first started drawing and painting at school. After school, I came to the craft room. And I worked in the craft room, maybe painting small cards.

Win Hilliard was working in the craft room, it used to be over there where the trees are.

After I finished school, I started working in the craft room; I didn't take any other job, like working in the clinic or in a household. I chose to paint cards, and I made floor rugs, and— when was it?—in 1963, I went to New South Wales. For weaving. There was a workshop: weaving and tapestry. Winifred and I went together for three weeks.

Translated from Pitjantjatjara by Margaret Dagg.

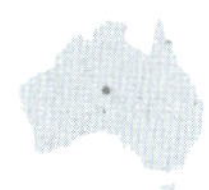

Winifred M. Hilliard

Ernabella art, as we now know it, had its beginnings in 1940 when a school was opened three years after the establishment of the Ernabella mission. The first teacher at the school, Reverend Ron Trudinger, discovered that his musical abilities gave him an immediate bond with his pupils, and he set out to discover what other abilities his students might have in the arts which could create a rapport between them.

Reverend Trudinger gave the children paper and pastels. Being a recent arrival at Ernabella, Reverend Trudinger had only a limited vocabulary

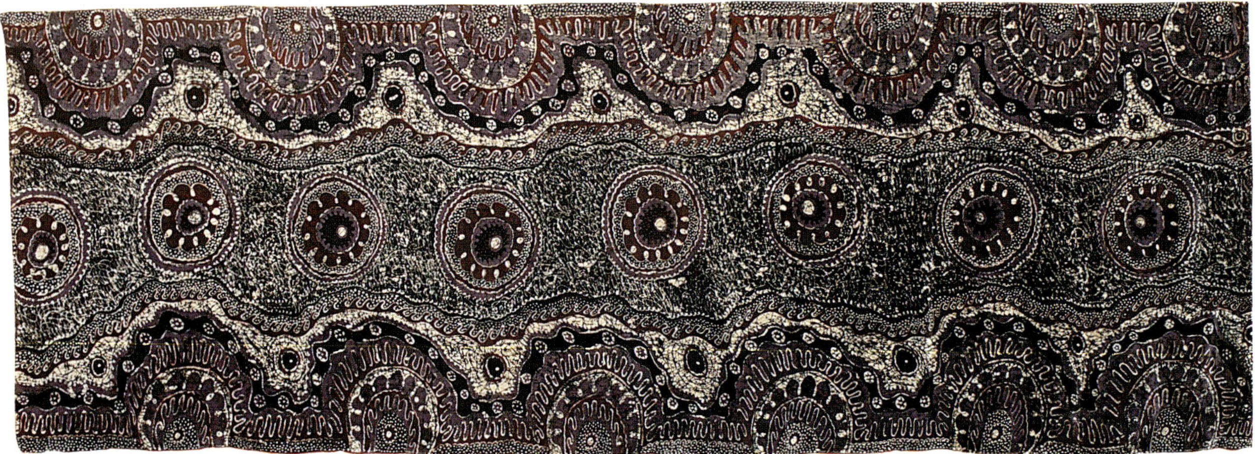

in Pitjantjatjara. He tried to instruct the children to draw anything they liked, but instead of saying 'anything goes' he actually said *'kurakura walkatjura'*, which means 'draw rather badly'. It was this confusing instruction that the artists were to later claim led them to draw wavy lines.

Some years later, towards the end of 1947, a visit to Ernabella by Mrs Mary Bennett of Kalgoorlie was the catalyst for the establishment of a craft industry in the community. Mrs Bennett set out to resolve what was becoming a serious problem: the lack of employment opportunities at Ernabella for women of all ages. Previously, the women carried out their traditional food-foraging activities while their husbands did fencing or stockwork, but, now settled in one place, small game and other foods had become scarce. Ernabella was a sheep station, and one solution that was put forward was to spin the wool produced there.

Mrs Bennett was aware of the role of spinning in traditional Pitjantjatjara life. She worked with four of the older women and discovered that terms existed for every stage of the spinning process. She had brought two looms with her. Four of the younger women learnt how to scour and dye the yarn spun by the older women, and to proceed to the next stage, woven fabric.

As well as weaving, the artists made small floor rugs and embroidered cushion covers incorporating designs chosen, at first, from the best of the pastel work created at the school. Eventually, specific designs were created by individual artists for particular items. This meant that each rug had an exclusive design and was locally produced and processed, resulting in floor rugs with costs far exceeding financial returns. However, for artists who worked in groups rather than as individuals, the positive aspects of the way they worked were more important than money. Rug making went on to become the mainstay of the craft enterprise at Ernabella until batik became firmly established.

Just prior to my arrival on the scene, my predecessor introduced handpainting on fabric, using fabric paint. This paint was intended to be thinned, but all the Ernabella artists liked to paint with strong lines, similar to those achieved when using poster colour on paper. As a result, the designs painted onto fine fabrics were rather stiff, taking away from the soft draping quality of silk scarves. Although this problem was never overcome, it wasn't altogether a handicap because only a limited number of scarves could be produced, and it was possible to keep up with the orders that were received. The fabric designs were not limited to scarves, however, and handpainted wall hangings, which were unaffected by the stiffness of the painted fabric, sold very successfully.

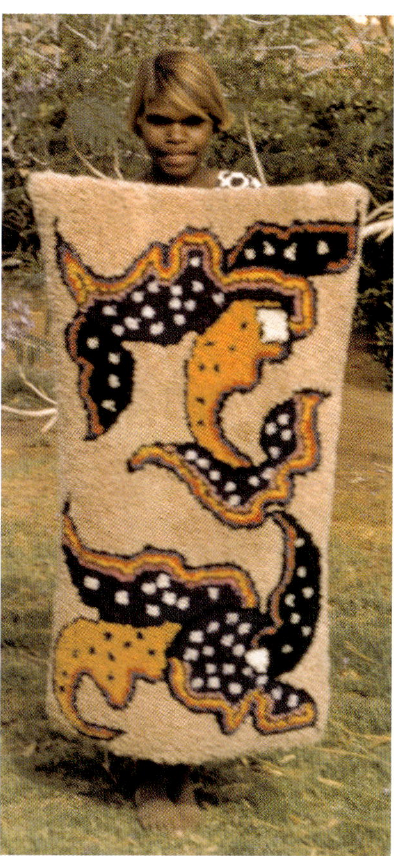

Daisy (Nyukana) Baker as a young girl with one of the floor rugs she made in the early 1960s (photo courtesy Ara Irititja Archive, Alice Peucker [Job] collection).

Despite the years of activity and development, Ernabella designs were still not seen to be 'Aboriginal': the colours were not considered to be the 'right' ones, and no bark paintings were produced! In order to generate a more successful enterprise it became imperative to find a new direction.

I had seen examples of batik cloth in Adelaide and, after a great deal of talk about the process, we received a visit by Mary White and Jenny Isaacs from the Aboriginal Arts Board. Back in Sydney, Mary White attended the exhibition of a young batik artist from New York, Leo Brereton, who had spent three months studying batik dyeing in Indonesia. It was soon organised through the Mission Board for Leo to spend two months working with the artists at Ernabella. In November 1971 the women began learning the skills that would enable them to produce world-class batik-dyed fabrics.

Ernabella artists have given many demonstrations of their work over the years and, on acquiring skills in batik dyeing, they extended these activities beyond the local Alice Springs region to travel and show their work throughout Australia and overseas. In doing this, though, the artists have never lost sight of their own people and have taught their craft at Ernabella to young students of a range of ages. They also visited other communities in Central Australia to share their new skills with friends and relatives, who could then do batik dyeing of their own, a process that the women accepted and shared, and made their own.

In 1975 three leading Ernabella artists visited Indonesia to spend time at the Batik Research Institute in Yogyakarta. The venture was a fruitful one, with the Indonesian and Ernabella artists expressing mutual admiration for each other's work.

Further travels undertaken by the Ernabella artists included two visits to Japan. On the first trip, a cultural exchange, the Ernabella artists, in addition to demonstrating their own skills, were taken to see some of

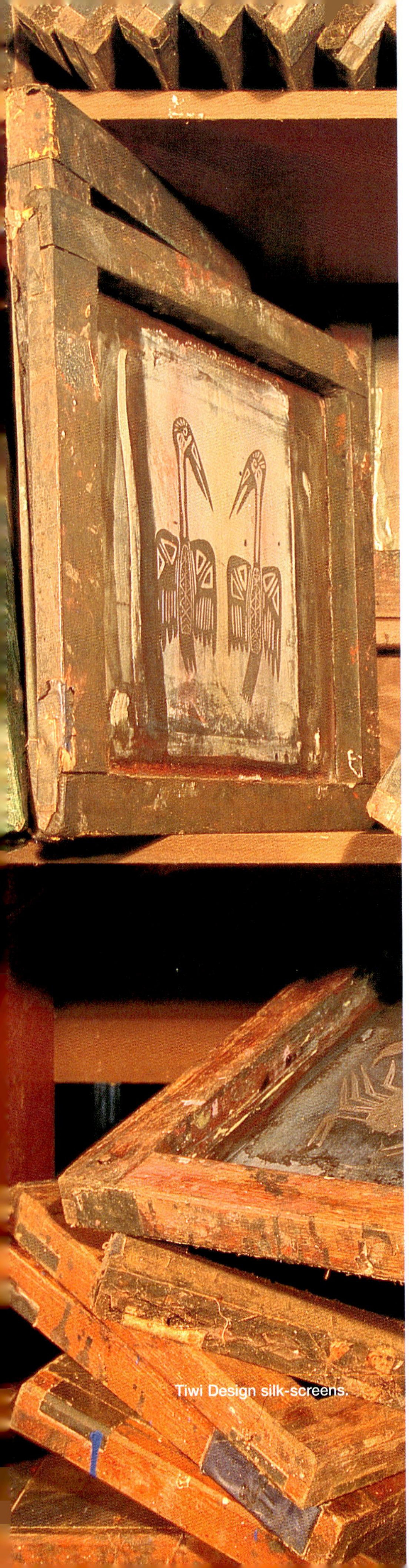

Japan's top artists and craftspeople at work. The second visit took place in conjunction with an exhibition of Ernabella art and included visits to schools, where the artists demonstrated their traditional wood carving.

Fine examples of Ernabella artwork, primarily batik work, have been included in numerous exhibitions, earning the artists growing recognition and ensuring the inclusion of their work in the collections of major art galleries in Australia, London, Indonesia and elsewhere. Ernabella Arts Inc. shows what can be achieved when people really work together and share with each other to produce works whose value is felt far beyond Australia's shores. Although the artists have made use of imported media and materials in their work, they have never departed from the foundations of the traditional artistry and skills that have sustained their people from time immemorial.

Tiwi Design

Margie West

When Tiwi Designs (now Tiwi Design) commenced at Bathurst Island mission in 1969, it was the only fully Aboriginal-run printery of its kind in Australia. It was, therefore, very much at the forefront of a changing art practice that was occurring at other community art centres, particularly later, in the 1980s and 1990s. Before fabric, the Tiwi people had been developing a market for the carvings, bark painting and other artefacts that they had been producing commercially at least since the 1950s. Irrespective of the artists' individual endeavours, the Catholic Church at Bathurst Island had no official policy for the promotion of Tiwi customary art which was sold on an *ad hoc* basis, mainly to the local market. This situation changed during the late assimilation period when the church began to work more closely with government on initiatives for greater community education and employment opportunities. In the belief that it would provide the Tiwi with a fresh approach to their 'tourist' art, the church gave precedence to the introduced technique of silk-screenprinting over traditional art production.

At the local Catholic school, Madeleine Clear (nee Drenth) was already teaching some of her students rudimentary wood-block printing when Bishop O'Laughlin discussed its economic potential with her. He was impressed after seeing some figurative wood-block prints by the Inuit of Alaska and, like Clear, believed that the Tiwi could do similar work. A print workshop was subsequently set up under the Old Presbytery where Clear instructed two of the school's most talented former students, Bede Tungatalum and Eddie Puruntatameri. Eddie subsequently went to work at the Bagot Pottery and was replaced by Giovanni Tipungwuti in 1969. Bede and Giovanni were then taught to print figurative wood-block designs onto rice paper as well as onto fabric, and in 1970 their printed linen placemats won the Design Council of Australia's Good Design Award. In the same year Bede and Giovanni founded Tiwi Designs as a legal partnership. By now they had a full-time arts adviser and eight young women working as seamstresses. Other major enterprises followed: Tiwi Pottery was formally established as a partnership in 1973; Tiwi Pima, the traditional art and craft outlet, in 1977; and Bima Wear, a clothing workshop for Tiwi women, in 1969.

By 1976 the Tiwi Design printery was relocated to a large tin shed opposite the palm-fringed beachfront on Apsley Strait. In 1980, when sales and staff began to increase, Tiwi Design was changed from a partnership to an incorporated Aboriginal association. Its aims were to be a business that promoted Tiwi culture, and to foster employment opportunities. These objectives have often been in conflict over the years due to a lack of funds and time for training, and an emphasis on attaining economic self-sufficiency. The situation was exacerbated in 1982 by the decision to abolish dedicated advisers for Tiwi Pottery, Tiwi Pima and Tiwi Design in preference for an overall manager responsible for all of the enterprises. By 1990 these enterprises also included Tiwi Batik and Tiwi Posters. Although there have been numerous training courses over the years and craft specialists have been brought in to refresh or develop skills in the pottery and printery, the bulk of management responsibilities have remained with Tiwi Design. As a result, human resources have been spread quite thinly.

In spite of these problems, Tiwi Design has not only maintained its output but has also developed and diversified its products over the years. The designers at the printery have always been male, although initially a number of women were employed when the emphasis was upon handmade individually produced items such as placemats, tablecloths, clothing and wall hangings. Occasionally women, like Francine Tungatalum, were also paid for design work, but mostly women did the sewing and hand fraying of the placemats and ponchos. A few of the men also carved wall-hanging supports shaped like grooved fighting clubs. Making such items was quite labour intensive, so a move was made to increase production for the fashion market with the installation of longer print tables in 1976. About this time the women at Bima Wear took over the sewing of garments made from Tiwi Design fabric. By the late 1980s even larger print tables were installed that could easily accommodate the printing of 40-metre rolls of fabric. With this move Tiwi Design broadened its agenda to the furnishings arena.

During this period, Tiwi Design cotton T-shirts became extremely popular and included special themes for local consumption: reggae heroes, Tiwi football clubs, religious and other local events. With the introduction of batik in 1988, one-off silk batik lengths and colour painting were added to the repertoire. Individual fine-art pieces with combined silk-screened and handpainted imagery were also occasionally produced, along with fine-art prints on paper. Throughout this time, though, there have only been a few licence agreements with commercial printers for limited production of Tiwi Design designs onto fabric. The Tiwi Printers have wanted to retain the handmade look of their work.

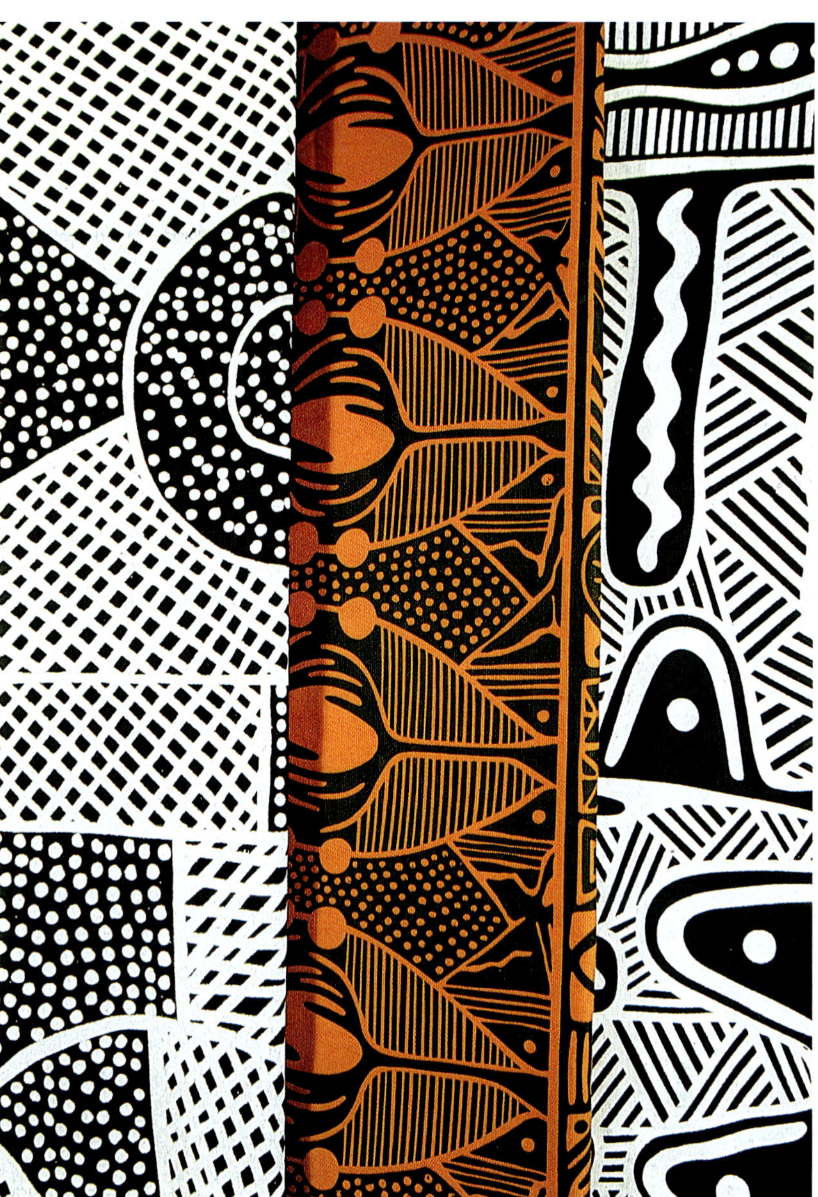

Tiwi Design fabric: (left to right) *Snake Design* Bede Tungatalum, *Yam* Bede Tungatalum, and *Kurlama* Marie Josette Orsto, screenprinted cotton.

The items produced at Tiwi Design have often developed out of creative interchanges with artists who have worked there as advisers or short-term instructors. Especially in the first decade when the emphasis was more on skills development, a special bond was forged with young printers who were attracted to the islands by the growing national awareness of Indigenous rights. These included Ray

Young, Colin Little and, later, Marie McMahon, artists who had cut their teeth at political poster collectives like Earthworks in Sydney. Other artists and designers, like Diana Conroy, Linda Jackson, Jack Frawley, Rose-Marie Schulz and Kathy Barnes, are just some of the people who have also left their creative mark on the printery. Over the years, changes in Tiwi Design imagery have included a move from isolated figurative motifs to all-over symbolically-based designs, the layering of motifs, use of splatter backgrounds (mercifully only short-lived!), production of multicolour separation prints, combining handpainting and silk-screening, and the distinctive Tiwi Design multicoloured striped effect achieved by mixing inks directly on the screen.

The artists' designs combine naturalistic motifs with symbolic elements that refer to their *jilamara,* or customary patterns, that people painted—and still paint—onto their bodies and ceremonial objects. Normally, these are constructed from conventionalised elements like dots, lines and so on. By custom, Tiwi ceremonial designs are non-sacred and rarely relate to an ancestral narrative, so typical of mainland Aboriginal groups. They can, however, operate as symbols for a range of subject matter, though often they are simply called *jilamara,* or body paint designs, with no further explanation being given. This seeming lack of circumscribed ancestral meaning allows the artists a degree of freedom to experiment, within the conventions of their art style. The development of the repeat-motif patterns, so suited to the print medium, is a case in point. Over the years, the designers have created approximately 150 images that provide the printers with a diverse repertoire to work from. Some patterns have become popular classics: the Sun, Pukumani Poles, Snake, Bark Painting, Spider Web and Tiwi Bird Body Print to name a few. Some artists complain, though, that the rote work

generated by fixed customer orders doesn't give them enough time to design new prints. When they do develop a new print design, it is a challenging process of peer-group assessment before the design is finally accepted and adopted by Tiwi Design.

The artists say that to be accepted, the image has to look Tiwi. It can't be 'too crowded'. It must include some recognisable element of Tiwi culture: an artefact, animal, mythological figure, or a symbolic element representative of the *jilamara.* Cloth is seen as another skin that can also be imprinted with marks, and it doesn't matter that the designs are made with fabric paint rather than with ochre. Like body paint, the wearing of Tiwi Design clothing is now an important marker of Tiwi identity. It is another vehicle for

creative expression that provides one of the island's few economic exports. With the diminution of ritual life, especially at the former mission of Nguiu, an enterprise like Tiwi Design can never be underestimated for the self-esteem that it fosters among the community.

After two decades of operation, Tiwi Design is now one of the oldest community art enterprises in remote Australia. Currently, there are a range of artists who work across a number of mediums, including long-term printers like Osmond Kantilla, artists Cyril James Kerinauia and Alan John Kerinauia, and potters John Patrick

Tiwi Design printer Osmond Kantilla (photo by Gillian Dallwitz).

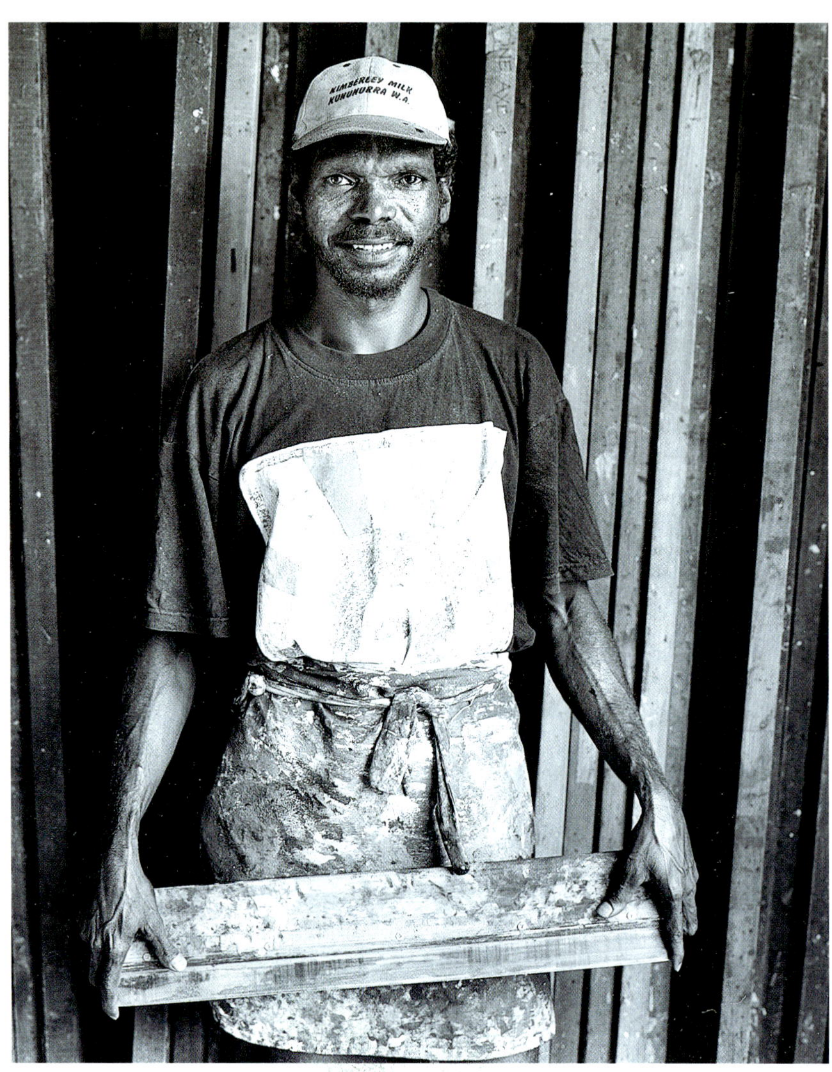

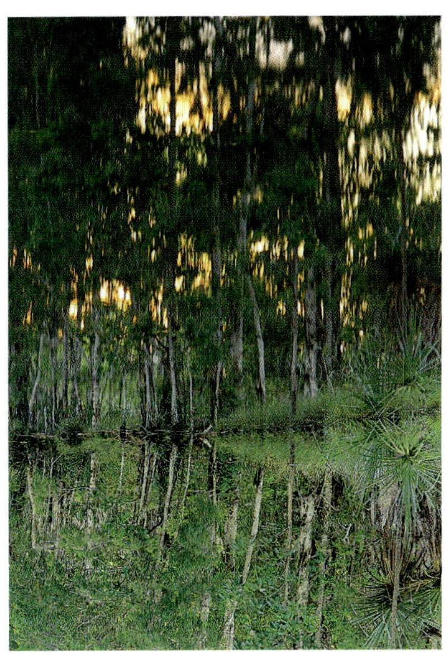

Billabong, Tiwi Islands.

Kelantumama and Mark Pautjimi. The printery has become an integral part of daily life on the island and symbolises the many changes that the Tiwi have endured since the mission was established there in 1911. In that same year, long ago, the anthropologist Sir Baldwin Spencer visited the island to document the unique cultural attributes of the Tiwi, including their distinctive art and material culture. He recorded one of the Tiwi's first encounters with cloth. He was collecting artefacts destined for the museum in Melbourne and for these he bartered a range of Western goods including sixty yards of red cloth, a highly coveted item at the time. Spencer could never have foreseen then, that eighty years later, the Tiwi would be using their own printed fabric as a significant item of economic exchange with the outside world.

Urapuntja Artists: The early days

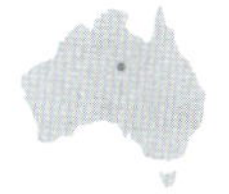

HILDA APWERL

Kel start-irrekaleng, kel sewing machine anem anwekantherrenh anek.

War amperel thenarl ingkel then ulthetyamel. Shirt-arlk mpwaretyam, skirt mpwaretyam. Anwern sew-em-ilemel. Alakenh anwantherr anek. Arrpenhem anwantherr tie-dye yanh-ulker mpwaretyart. Mpwarerlanem, ayernemel, white one-ek-amparr, apwert inemel tie-dye, tie-em-ilemel kel marbles map ayernepernerl apwert apek, akwernemel yellow one-warl, kel weth renh-anteyarl ineynemel, iylweynemel, arrpenh anemarl ayernepernem, ayernemel-antey, kel akwernemel atyetyek-warl apek. Tie-em-up-anteyarl ileynem, kel dark one red one yanh-ulker, yanh-warl akwernemel last one. Alakenh anek. Ankerrapw caravan-el start-irrek yanh.

Well, we started then—we had our treadle sewing machines that we worked just by pressing them with our knees and feet. We sewed up shirts and skirts. That's how we were. Then another thing we used to do was tie-dye. The fabric was white at first, and we used to get stones or maybe marbles and tie them up in the fabric, then put it in the yellow dye, then get it and tie it up again, then put it perhaps in the red dye—tie it up again and then put it again in a dark colour like red, the last colour. That's how it was. We started in the caravan there.

Translated from Anmatyerr by Jenny Green.

Keringke Arts: Finding silk

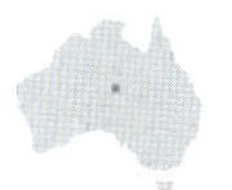

TIM ROLLASON

There is a story about a women's business ceremony held at Keringke Rockhole in early 1997.

The ceremony, which lasted many days, was attended by women from all over Australia. Each group of women brought with them ochres from their own country to paint their bodies for singing and dancing. Everybody present agreed that the ochres of the Eastern Arrernte women were the brightest of all. Perhaps this is a factor in the evolution of the highly colourful, contemporary silk textiles produced by the women at Keringke Arts at Ltyentye Apurte, Santa Teresa, today.

The artists are renowned for their handpainting of silk. The fusion of colours and the luminosity of the silk surface have resulted in a brilliant contemporary cultural expression which has its roots in ceremonial body painting. While the combination of

The women batik artist of the Utopia area congregate around a shared wax pan: (left to right) Roese Apwerl, Amy Napangardi, Gracie Nangala, Tania Nangala and Lena Apwerl.

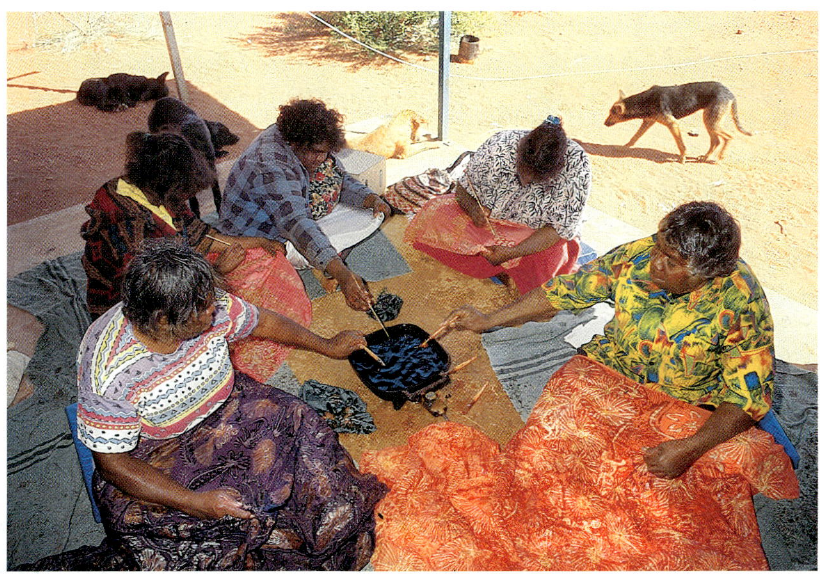

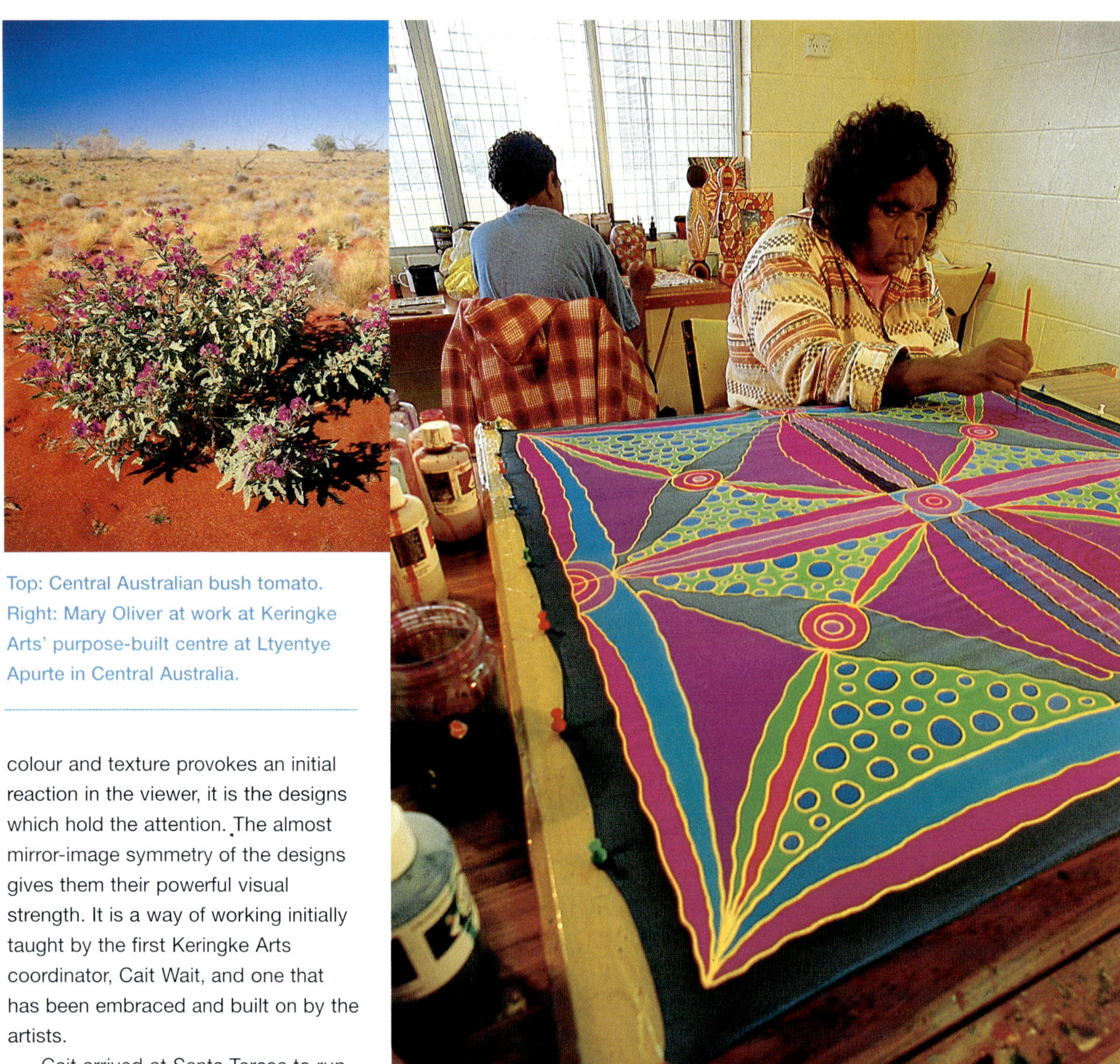

Top: Central Australian bush tomato.
Right: Mary Oliver at work at Keringke Arts' purpose-built centre at Ltyentye Apurte in Central Australia.

colour and texture provokes an initial reaction in the viewer, it is the designs which hold the attention. The almost mirror-image symmetry of the designs gives them their powerful visual strength. It is a way of working initially taught by the first Keringke Arts coordinator, Cait Wait, and one that has been embraced and built on by the artists.

Cait arrived at Santa Teresa to run a short fabric-painting course in 1987. She worked with a group of women who were, at the time, mainly training to be teachers. The women were introduced to aspects of colour theory, and began printing fabric with lino block. The fabric was then made into simple garments and tablecloths. Handpainted T-shirts were also produced, a practice which was to continue for the next five to seven years.

Cait Wait worked with the women for the next five years, teaching them design and silk-painting techniques. During this time, a purpose-built art centre was established, giving the women the space required to produce works as long as five metres. The

women wanted to give the new art centre and fledgling enterprise a culturally significant title. The men in the community were against using a name connected to traditional life and Aboriginal ways, but Keringke artist Kathleen Wallace stood up to them and named the workshop 'Keringke', the name of the sacred rockhole close to where the art centre now stands.

At the time of Cait Wait's arrival at Santa Teresa, artists often used Western-influenced imagery, particularly from the Western landscape tradition. However, after the opening of the Keringke Arts centre, imagery from

Aboriginal culture began to emerge. The women began to paint images telling the story of their country.

Silk painting has continued as the main focus of Keringke Arts. Designs have evolved from simple to highly complex structures, with colour combinations becoming brighter and richer with the years. The development is evidence of an increasing sense of self-esteem among the artists, and the forging of a strong cultural identity within the Aboriginal and wider Australian community.

I got better and better

learning the craft

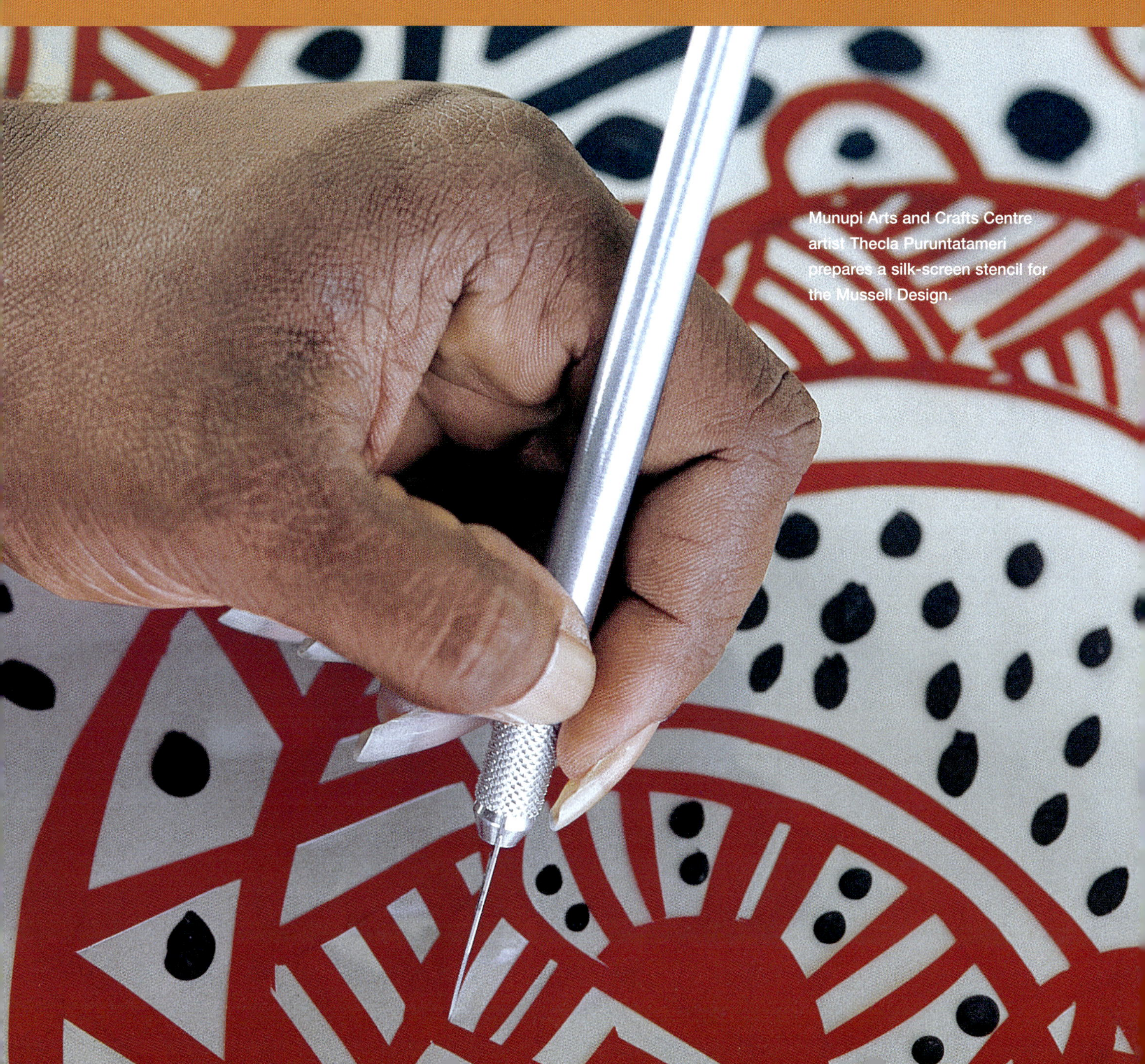

Munupi Arts and Crafts Centre artist Thecla Puruntatameri prepares a silk-screen stencil for the Mussell Design.

We didn't know what we were doing at first

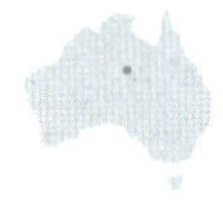

GLORY ANGAL, URAPUNTJA ARTISTS

Akalty-irrenh ayeng arrurl, arrurl innga ayeng akalty-irrek, anwantherr ingkerrek batik-ek. Station-el. Jenny-el akaltyel-anthety-alpek, kwey awenk-ankel. Batik anwantherr ingkwernetyart tie-dye. Ayernemel anwantherr kel colour-ek akwernerliwerretyart, kel colour-penh tekewerretyart, kel iylwemel renh, aweth renh ayernemel, colour ingwerek anem akwernemel, green one-ek apek. An arwerl akely-akely-arlek anwantherr ingkwernetyart, wire-elarl arrtyekel, wire-el amperneynek amperneynek mpwaremel pretty flower-artek arrernetyek. Toly-el anwekantherr mpwaretyart—arwerl-rnem aketyart anwekantherr Toly-el. Kel anwantherr wire-el arrtyetyart kel renh-rnem irrkerrkewem stampem-ileynemel anem, mwerrangker colour ingkernem.

Kel anwekantherr apetyemel Suzy Bryce ra anem, kwey anyent then, ratherr akaltyel-antherlanetyek. Ratherr akaltyel-anthek, wax-ek—'Brush-el ingkwernenherr-arey cotton one nhenh-rnem kwenh!' Kel ikwerel anwantherr ingkwernetyart akalty brush-el anem wax-el then, wax then akngetyekarl anem. Colour-ek anem renh akwernetyart, kel renh tekewemel, aweth renh ingkwernemel brush-el, ingkwernemel renh colour-rnem-warl arrerneynemeley. Kel ingkwernenty-penh aweth renh colour-ek akwernem. Kel ingwereley ulhewemel clean-ilemel, proper clean-irrenhetyart mwerrangker colour-rnem show-irrenhety-alpem— amern-rnem, arlewatyerr akely-akely kaperl akely-akely.

Mwerr anem mwerr anem arlkenyan irreynetyart akeng-akeng imerntarl ingkwernerretyart-penh. Apal-apal war imernt. Mwerr anem mwerr anem irntwarr-ulker iterlareynerliwenh anem arratyam arraty. Aleth ra anem akalty-irrek batik-ek ingkwernetyek marl ingkerr anem—learn-irrerliwerrek anem.

Silk one-ek anwantherr start-irrek apmer Three Bores-el-antey. Silk one anem anwekantherr arwem-irrek.

Cotton one anwantherr ingkwernetyart, kel anwantherr light one anem ingkwernetyart. Mwerrangker anem. Silk one aleth ra anem start-irrek. Machine-el apmer ikwerel atantherretyart dress skirt-rnemek, shirt silk one-rnem mpwarem. Machine-el atantherretyart akalkew-akalk. Kel ingwerel ingkwernepernem ingwerel machine-el atanthetyart, kel ingwer anem apetyanemel ingkwernetyek, ingwer-rnem machine-warl alhetyart atantherretyart. Skirt akely-rnem an trous-rnem mpwarerliwerretyart. Arlewatyerr-akert-rnem Pip Duncan-kenh-amperlan anetyart— ingkwernetyart ikwer trous-rnem. Julia-kenh trous ingkwernetyart arlewatyerr-rnem-akert arrpem. Mwerrangker ingkerrek. T-shirt mwerrangker-rnem arrpemarl ingkwernerretyart.

I was learning a long time ago—it was really a long time ago that we all learnt batik at the station. Jenny Green [the first arts and crafts teacher at Utopia] came back and taught it, when she was younger. We used to make tie-dye. We tied it all up and then we all

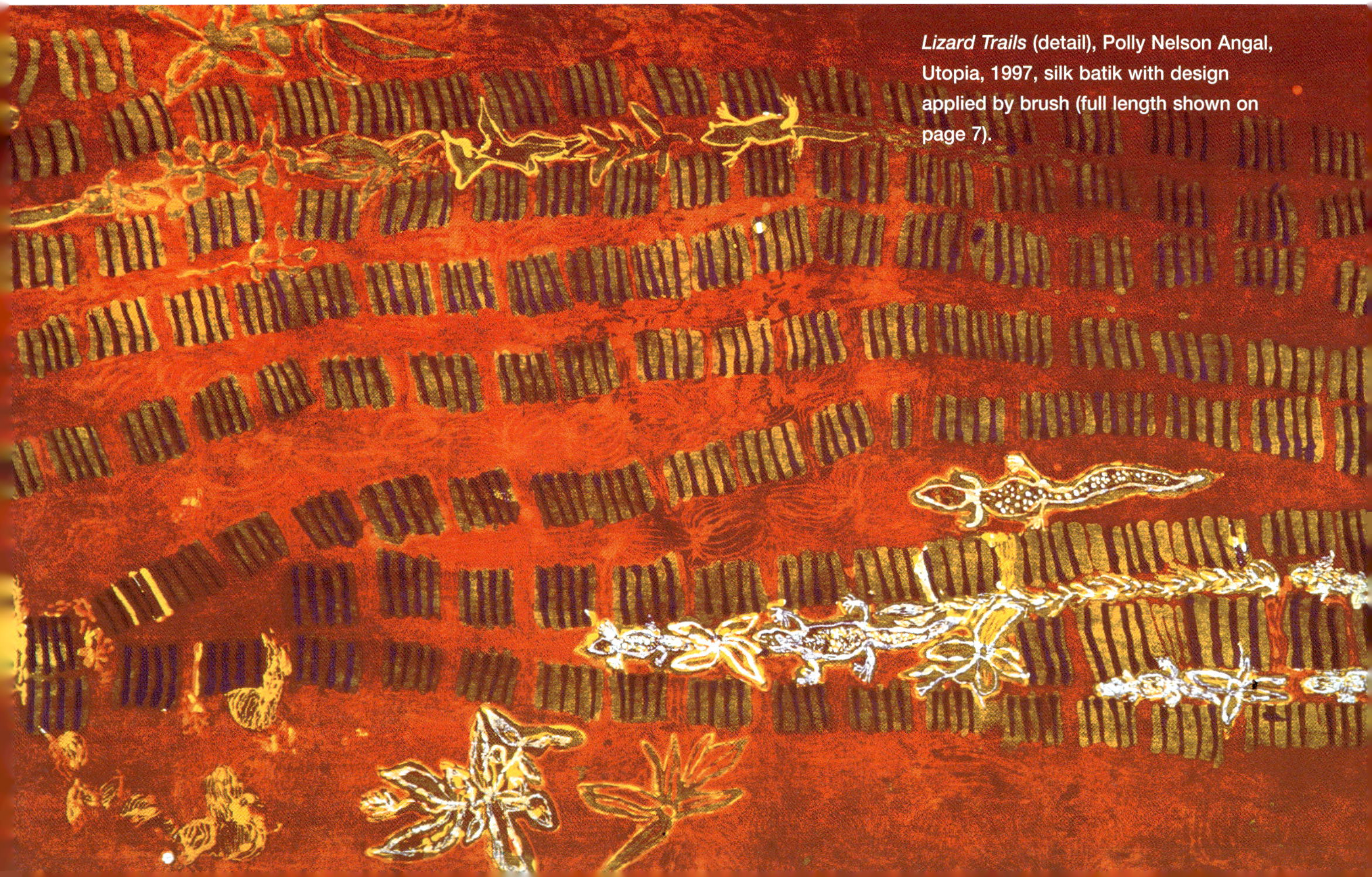

Lizard Trails (detail), Polly Nelson Angal, Utopia, 1997, silk batik with design applied by brush (full length shown on page 7).

used to soak it in the colour, then after dyeing, hang it out, then untie it, tie it up again, then put it in another colour, perhaps green. And we used to make patterns using small pieces of wood that we had burnt with hot wires. We used to burn the designs into the wood with hot wire, and make designs like 'pretty flowers'. Toly Sawenko [schoolteacher at Utopia] used to make wood blocks for us—he used to cut the wood. Then we used to burn them and then stamp or press them onto the fabric and apply the lovely colours.

Then Suzy Bryce [who introduced batik to Utopia] came to us, and another woman, to teach us. The two of them taught us about wax—'All you lot, paint these cotton ones with the brushes!' That's how we learnt to do batik, with the brushes and wax that they had brought with them. We used to dip the batik in the colour, then hang it out to dry, then wax it again with a brush, paint it and then put it in the colours. Then, after waxing it, put it in the colour again. Others would be washing the batik to get the wax out, and when it was really clean all wonderful colours would become visible—all the bush foods, and the little goannas and other small lizards.

The designs progressively got better and better, after the early ones which we used to do which weren't so good. We didn't know what we were doing at first. We kept on improving as we went along, learning how to do it properly. Then, once and for all, the women had learnt to do batik—we had all learnt.

Then silk came on the scene. We started with the silk at Three Bores. We used to only work on cotton, and then we started doing batik on this lighter fabric. It was really good. Once silk started we kept going with that. At Three Bores some would sew up dresses and skirts and silk shirts on the sewing machines, while others did batik, in separate groups. Some did batik while the others would go and do sewing, and then they'd come and do batik while the others went to the

machines to sew. We used to make little skirts and trousers. Dear old Pip Duncan [a nursing sister at Utopia] had goannas on her jeans—we used to batik her trousers. And Julia Murray [later the arts coordinator at Utopia] had goannas on her trousers as well. They were all really flash. We used to make really good batik T-shirts as well.

Translated from Anmatyerr by Jenny Green.

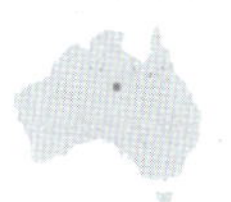

Apwert anem atha arertnenh apwertel anem tie-em-up-ilek, arlewatyerr yanh-warl ayeng apwert-penh turn-irrek. Marbles anemarl arernenh, like angwenh-warl, arlter-antey-warl marbles-areyarl tie-em ilenh. Kel colour-warl anem-warl akwernemel. Yellow-one-warl anem akwernek renh. Kel ikwer-theyan angkeparl angwenh anem, iylwemel iylwemel kel colour-penh, iylwekek kel colour-warl akwerneyamel, 'Ah, mwerr akngerrart atyenh kel akalty-irrek anem ayeng kwenh!' Mwerr akngerr iyterrty anem atyenh-amperl nhak arernekarl kwenh. Kel marbles arlka anem apwert akely-akely kwetyerretyam, arrernetyam,

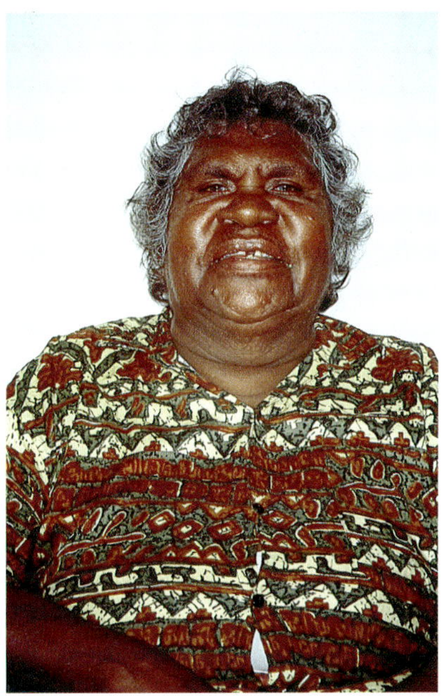

Lena Apwerl, Urapuntja Artists (photo Jenny Green).

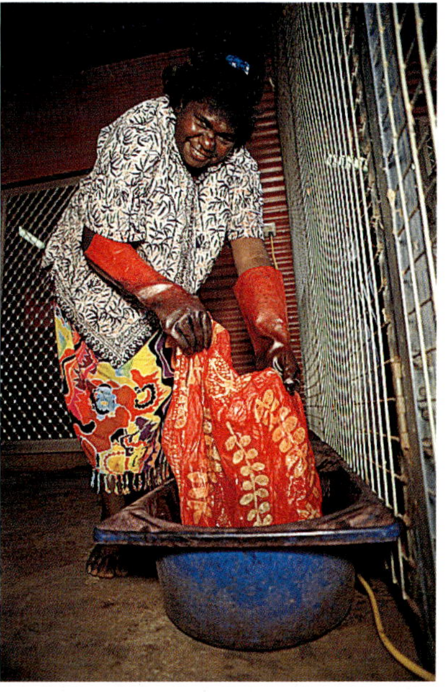

Roese Apwerl of Utopia dips a waxed fabric again and again to build a rich patina of colour for her batik cloth.

---

arertnem tie-dye, rag-el ilekarl string arertnek tie-dye. Ikwerel anem anwantherr akalty-irrenh. Caravan school an kitchen-el anwantherr kitchen-ek arriwek mpwarerliwerretyam. Kitchen ikwer arlperr ikwerel arelh arrepanenh. Arelh akaltyirrenh kwa akutn map. Lyetant.

I used to tie up the fabric with rocks, and after that I changed over to that goanna. Marbles were tied into the white cloth, then it was soaked in the dye. Then it was put into the yellow dye. Then after that it was untied again, after being in the dye. 'Oh, mine's really good, I've learnt how to do it! Poor old me has really tied it up well!' Then we'd gather up marbles and little rocks, and make tie-dye, with string. That's how we learnt. We used to work outside the door of the school kitchen caravan. There were lots of women under the whitewood—women who were just learning.

Translated from Anmatyerr by Jenny Green.

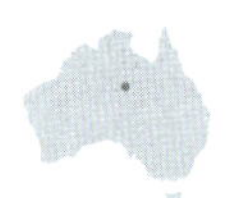

Hilda Apwerl, Urapuntja Artists

*Arwerlan mpwarek an atywerety
yanhwelker apek, saw-em-ilemel, kel
pretty arrernetyek, arna renh war saw-
em-iletyek, akwek war akwek war, kel
brandem-ilemel. Wire-el war item arna
renh. Mpwaremel mern apek bush-
areny apek. Kel paint-el anem
apernemel arna weth stampem-ilemel
anem, white-one material yanhwelker.
Alakenh anem anwern anetyart start-
irrekarl.*

*Arrwekelan anwantherr
mpwaretyart saucepan frying pan apek,
akeng-akeng war arrwekeleny inemel.
Mpwaretyart. Wax arrernemel. Wax
yellow one arrernemel, wax arrpenh
yanh arrernemel candle-artek. Wax
urrperl arrernemel brown, urel anem
arrernem iterlanemel, kel brush-arl
inemel, brush-el mpwarerlanemel.
Brush. Canting-ek arrwekel. Urrek.
Brush-elek-amparrarl mpwaretyam.
Mpwarerlanemel myall-wart start-
irrepirrerl anwantherr. Kel canting-ek
ant anem start-irrem—canting anem
canting anem arratek. Ikwerel anem
mpwaretyart—brush-el then
mpwarepwarerl atherram atherramel.*

We made wooden stamps from bean-
tree wood, sawed it up into small
pieces and then decorated it by
branding it with hot wire. We made
designs of things from the bush—
maybe foods. Then we rubbed paint
onto the wood block and stamped it
into the fabric, that white material.
That's how we were when we started
off.

In the beginning we used to do
batik—we'd get a rubbish old
saucepan or something to put the wax
in. We'd put the yellow wax in, then the
white wax which was like candles, and
the brown one, and then heat it for a
while over the fire. Then we'd get
brushes and keep on painting with
them. Brushes. This was before
cantings [traditional Indonesian tool for
applying wax]. They came later. We
used to do batik with brushes at first.
Of course we were really ignorant
when we started off doing it. Then we
started using *cantings*—*cantings* came
along then, and we used to do batik
with them—with both *cantings* and
brushes.

Translated from Anmatyerr by Jenny Green.

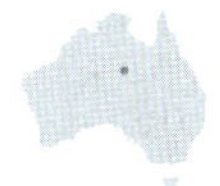

Mary Akemarr, Urapuntja Artists

*Ayengan Ingkwelayel akalty-irrew.
Kalty anem akalty anem ayeng
irreynenh, Ingkwelayel anem.
Amwamwam-tangkwel atha
ingkwernenh, thap mwerr anem
mwerr anem alyelk anem mpwarenh.
Arenh-tangkwel atha, arenh-tangkwel
atha, aytarrenh-tangkwel, ingwerel-
rnemarl mpwarenhan. Kalty-anthenh
anem ayenh rernem, ayengan ament
anem akaltyerrew. Kalty anem akalty
anem ayeng irreynenh. Ament anem
atha pwerlpeweynenh atha ament
anem.*

*Colour-warl anem akwernenh,
yellow-one-warl, red-one-warl, ingwer-
rnemel, mpwarenh, akwerneynenh,
irrpwerl-warl-tangkwel. Kel ra
artwerretyerrenh, arternpel-antey anem
renh mpwarenh, angkep-antey
arrpemarl. Bush-el anem ratherr
akaltyanthenh. Jenny Green-el atherr
Julia-el atherr kalty-anthenh. Akalty
anem akalty anem mwerr anem ra
arenh. Julia-el. Julia-el inkwer anem
ilenh, 'Eh, akalty anem rernem irrew.'*

I learnt at Ingkwelay. I learnt bit by bit
at Ingkwelay. At first I batiked badly,
but I got better and better. Initially I
watched the others making batik.
They taught me and then I learnt how
to do it myself. I learnt more and
more.

Then we put the batik in the
colour—in yellow, red—did some more
batik and then put it in the dark colour.
Then it got dry, and then, carefully it
was waxed again. Those two taught us
in the bush. Jenny Green and Julia
[Murray] taught us. As we learnt more
and more, Julia saw the work improve
and she'd say enthusiastically, 'Hey,
they've all learnt.'

Translated from Alyawarr by Jenny Green.

Then we changed over to silk

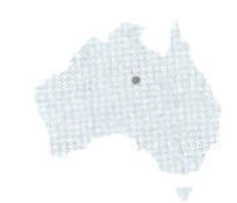

Violet Apetyarr, Urapuntja Artists

*Batik anwantherr mpwarek, tie-dye
imernt akaltyirrek, tie-em-up ilek,
anwantherr tie-em-up iletyart, kel
ikwer-they akwernetyart colour ingwer-
warl. Kel anwantherr batik-ek anem
mpwarek. Jenny Green-el first arrwekel
akaltyelanthek, Jenny Green-el
akaltyelanthetyart anwenantherrenh.*

*Kel silk-warl-irrek anwantherr. Silk
anem anwekantherr apetyek, silk-an
anwantherr mpwaretyart
angwenhakwey, brush-el. Kel
anwantherr, kel canting anem
anwekantherr apetyek. Canting-el then
anem mpwaretyart brush-el then
mpwaretyart atherrel. Canting, Julia
time apetyek canting, canting an
mpwaretyartey, canting-el then brush-
el then atherrel mpwaretyart*

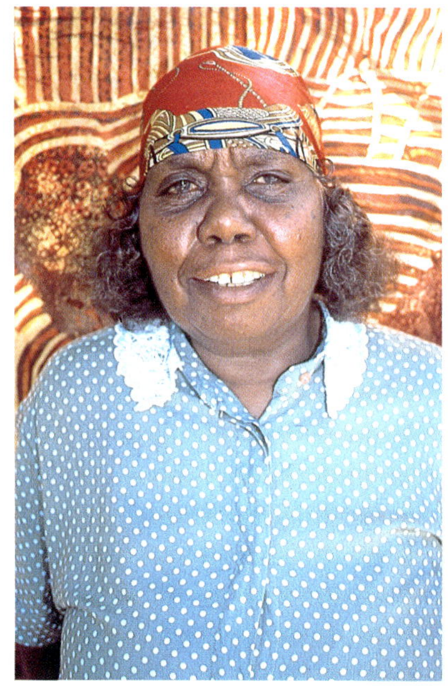

Violet Apetyarr, Urapuntja Artists
(photo Jenny Green).

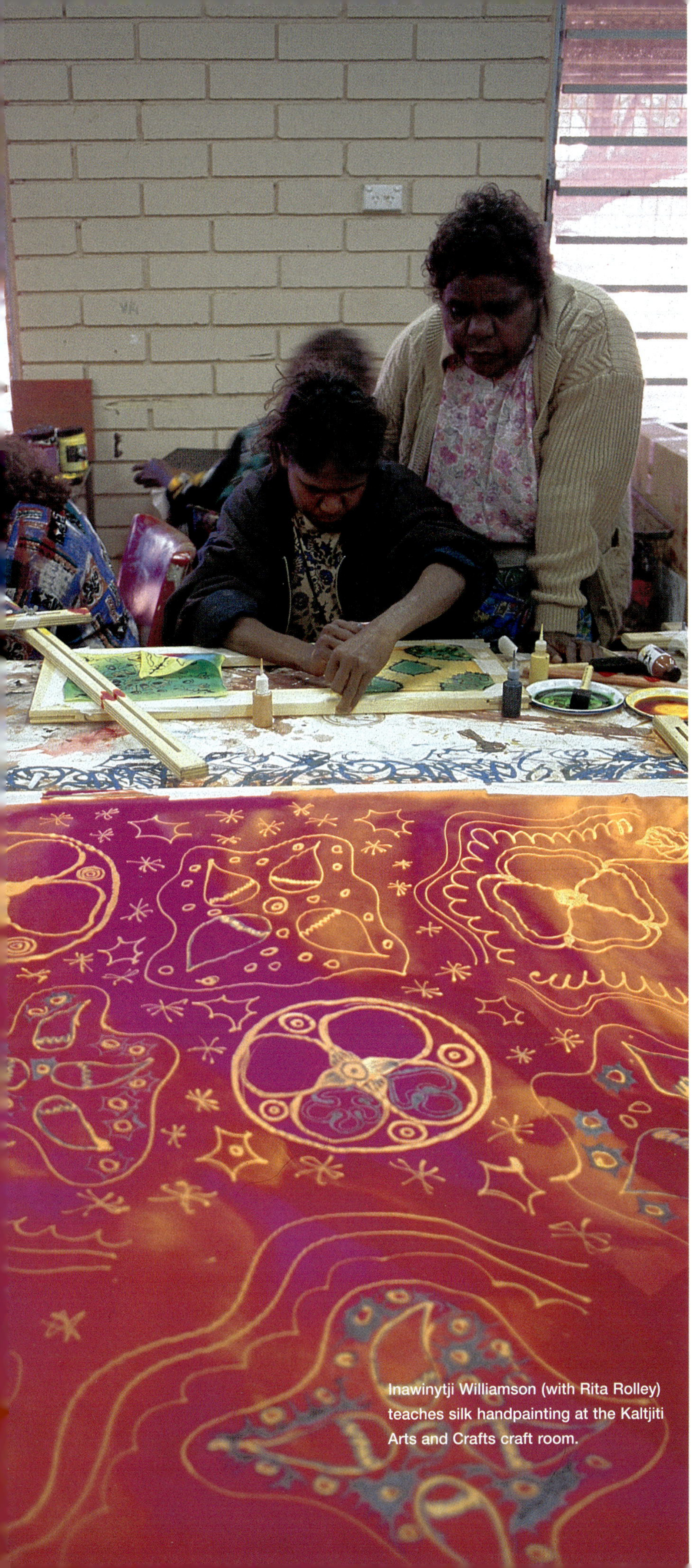

anwantherr. Sellem-iletyart anwantherr, good money-arl ap anwantherr silk-iperr inetyart anwekantherr petyalhetyart, mayl-angkwarr. Good money anwantherr inetyart silk-they.

We made batik—at first we learnt to do tie-dye. We tied up the fabric and then dipped it in the dye. We made batik then. Jenny Green taught us first, she taught us.

Then we changed over to silk. Silk turned up and we batiked on silk using brushes. Then we got *cantings,* and we made batik using both brushes and *cantings.* The *cantings* arrived during Julia [Murray]'s time, and we used both the brushes and the *cantings.* We used to sell the batik, and we got good money from the silks, in the mail. We got good money from silk.

Translated from Anmatyerr by Jenny Green.

We ended up knowing all about it

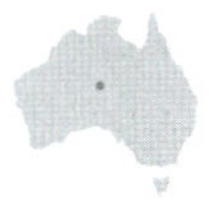

ALISON (MILYIKA) CARROLL, ERNABELLA ARTS
Batikikula nintiringanyi ngura nyangangka, panya minyma mankurpa anu, ngura nganalakutu, Indonesia-lakutu munuya nintiringu nyara palula, munuya malaku pitjala, nintingkulta, minyma kutjupa tjutala nintinu. Ka kuwari nganananya nintinu, malatja tjuta kulu, munula nintingku kuwari palyani batiki tjuta raiki tjuta, scarf tjutala palyani, T-shirt, tjutala palyani.

We learnt batik here at home in Ernabella, but a few women did go to a different place, to Indonesia, and they learnt over there. They came back with their knowledge and taught a lot of women. Now us younger ones have been taught as well. We make batik with a lot of skill, we make many lengths of cloth and scarves and T-shirts.

Translated from Pitjantjatjara by Suzy Bryce.

Inawinytji Williamson (with Rita Rolley) teaches silk handpainting at the Kaltjiti Arts and Crafts craft room.

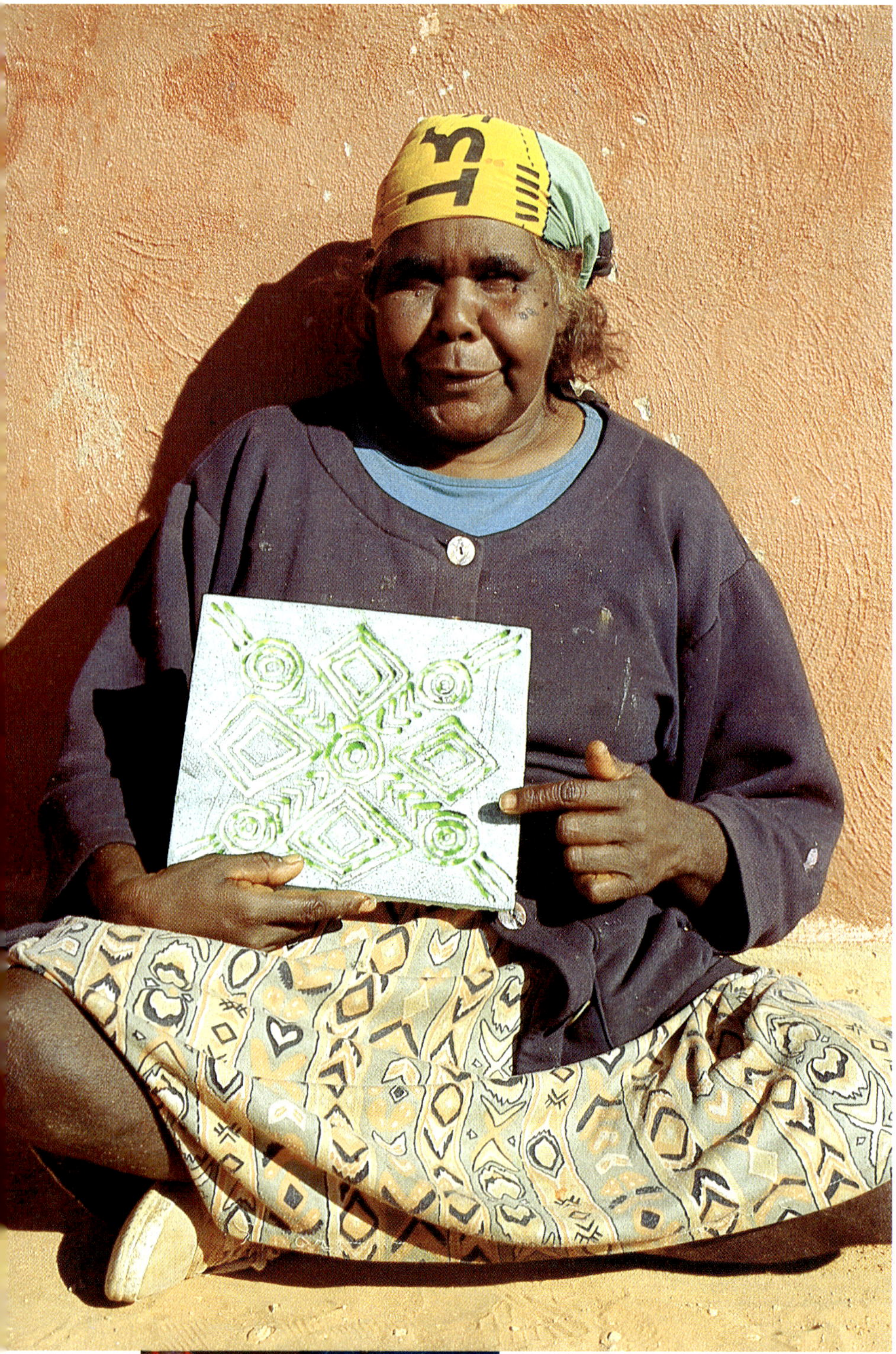

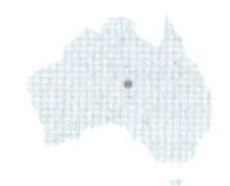

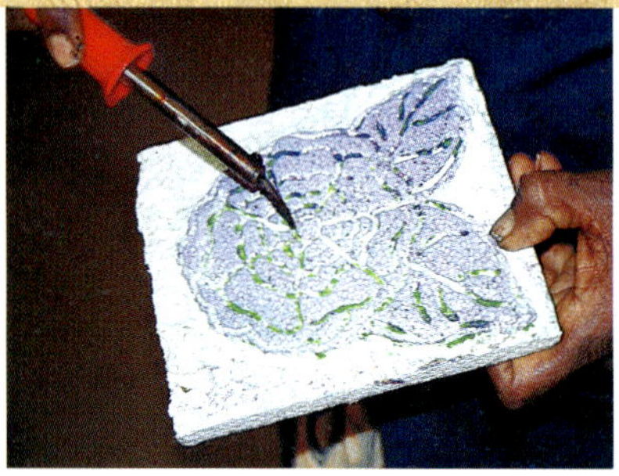

DORIS THOMAS,
TITJIKALA WOMEN'S CENTRE

[Holding a polystyrene tile] *Idea kulira, nganana palyani, nyaangka?* We think of an idea and we make it.

That thing, branding with that hot electric one. On that big sheet you know? It's at Araluen [Centre, Alice Springs, for the Desert Mob Show].

Kutju kutju palula tjunanyi, every corner, munu kutjupa tjunanyi, pretty flower tjunanyi, palula wanu, nyakula ngayulu pukularinyi, wirunya ngayulu palyanu.

We put the tile on one print at a time, every corner, and put others on as well, like the pretty flower one.

When I saw [my work] I was really happy, I made something lovely. We put it on paper and try it out and if it's right, we finish it off.

Translated from Pitjantjatjara by Suzy Bryce.

MATJANGKA (NYUKANA) NORRIS,
KALTJITI ARTS AND CRAFTS

Nganana panya Fregon-ta nintiringangi batik. Palu nganmanpa nganana paint-ngka waakarinyi. Munu nyara palula nintiringanyi. Munula nintiringkula, nintiringkula arkaralta batik palyaningi raikinguru, munula palyara palyara nintiringangi.

Panya minyma ninti tjutangku nganananya nintiningi Maylenelu tjana. Maylene Russell, Mantuwa Treacle, Nola Roly, paluru tjana nganananya nyanganka nintiningi. Ka nganana nyara palulanguralta nintiringangi tjana tjunkula nintinangka panya kala tjuta. Nganana paura, patalpai, palumpa tjanampa ka paluru tjana nganananya nintilpai, kala tjunkula. Ka nganana kuwari nintiringkula, waltjakulta palyani kutjungku kutjungku. Kala waltjangku palyani munula palyara tjuta mulapa tjunkula, iyani, panya piranpa kutjupa

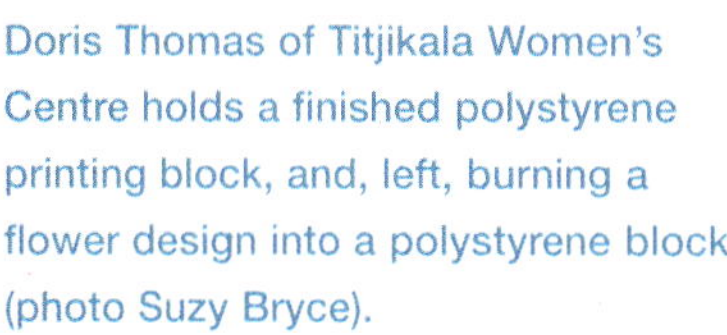

Doris Thomas of Titjikala Women's Centre holds a finished polystyrene printing block, and, left, burning a flower design into a polystyrene block (photo Suzy Bryce).

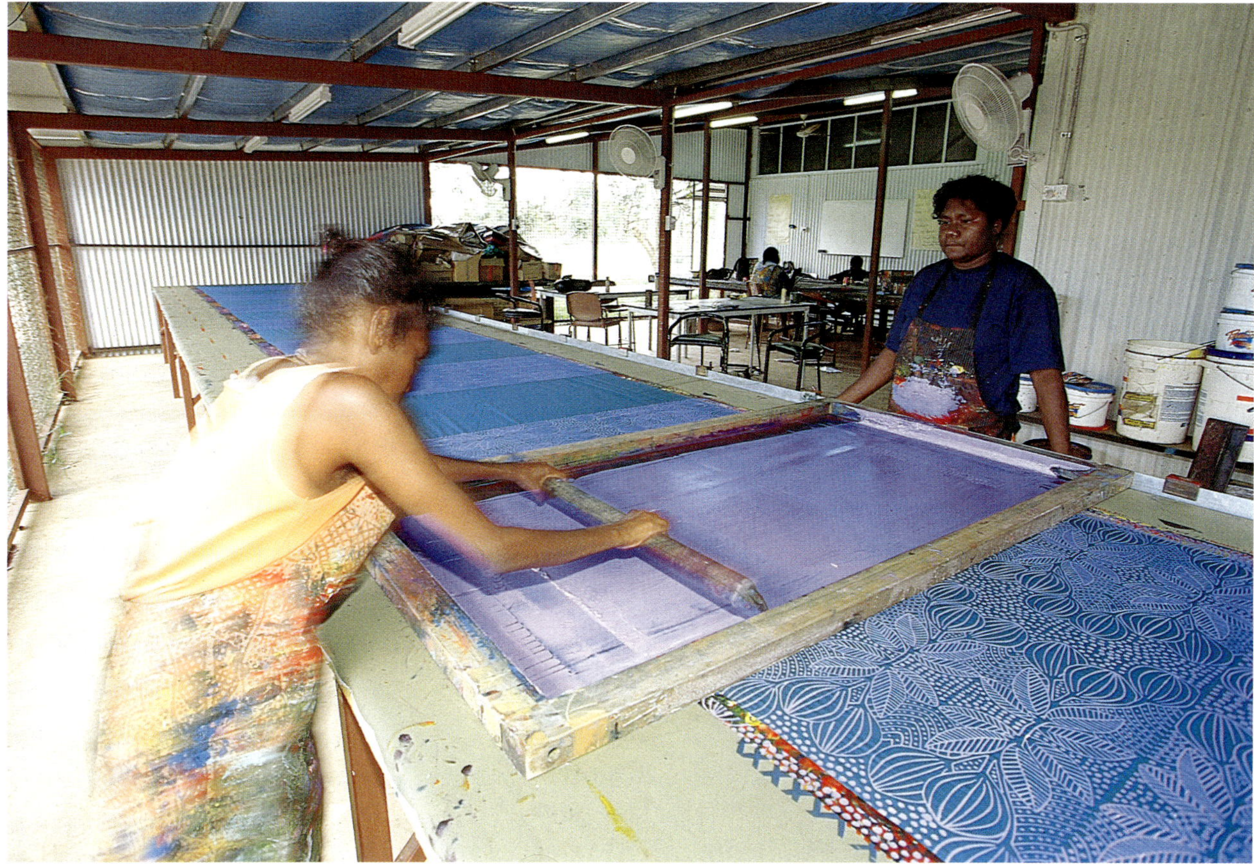

Francesca Puruntatameri (left) and Thecla Puruntatameri print fabric at Munupi Arts on Melville Island.

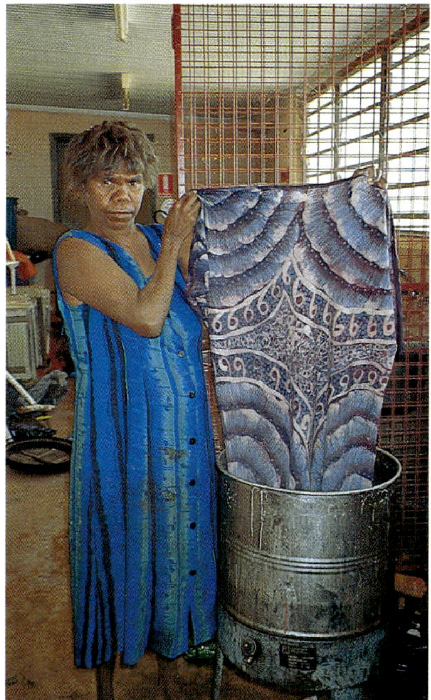

Mrs Norris in the Kaltjiti Arts and Crafts art room dyeing a piece in progress.

tjuṯa payamilantjaku . . .

Nganaṉa anu. Hamilton Downs, munu nganaṉa nyara palula batik kuḻu kuḻu palyaṉingi, munula raiki tjuṯa batikingka palyaṉi, T-shirt munu material. Ka tjana nyarakutulangurungku nganaṉanya nintiningi, munu urilta kataṟa tjuṯa, kala tjuṯa palyaṉi, ka nganaṉa nyara palula nintiringanyi urilta ngarala. Tjana bucket tjuṯangka palyaṉu munu tjunanyi, ka nganaṉa kala nyara palumpa tjanampa nintiringanyi. Tjana wangkangu, 'Kala nyangatja puḻka mulapa tjunama, mankuraṟa, ka nganaṉa nyara palulanguru nintiringkula. Kuwari kala nganaṉa mankuraṟa tjunanyi. Panya paluṟu tjanaya nganaṉanya nintintja—Hamilton Downs-ta tjana nintiningi. Uwa three aṟangku tjunanyi. Ka kala wiruṟa pakani, kala puḻkaringanyi. Ka nganaṉa nyara palula kuliningi. 'Ai, nganaṉa nyapartji Fregon-takutu kati, munu nganaṉa nyanga palu puṟunypa palyaṉingi.'

We learnt about batik at Fregon. Before that, we worked with paint. We learnt a lot from doing painting, until we were ready to try our skill with batik. Then we practised and practised to develop our skills.

Maylene and other women who were skilled in batik taught us. Maylene Russell, Mantuwa Treacle, Nola Roly, these women showed us here, and that's how we learnt about dyes. We would put on the hot wax, then wait for the older women, and they would show us about putting on the colours. Now we've learnt all that, we do our work on our own. We make the colours ourselves, and we have quite a considerable output which we send away. White people buy the work . . .

We went to Hamilton Downs and we made some batik with T-shirts and material. Those women from way up there at Utopia taught us. They made up a lot of dyes in buckets and cut up pieces of cloth. We stood outside learning about their use of colour. They told us to dip the cloth three times in the dye, and we learnt from that. Now we dip our fabrics three times. The colours become more intense. We thought then that we should take this technique to Fregon to use it. That's what they had to teach us at Hamilton Downs.

Translated from Pitjantjatjara by Suzy Bryce.

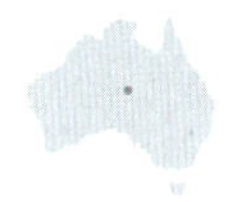

MARLENE BOKO, TITJIKALA WOMEN'S CENTRE
I've been an artist for a few years. I do silk painting and lino and canvas and necklaces. I was doing a course at the Institute for Aboriginal Development in Alice Springs for lino and batik.

I cut one of those plastic boards and get one of those soldering irons. I make my own design and I put the white sheet on the table and paint a colour on with a roller and put the tile

Kelli Bruce of Dunnilli Arts at Nungalinya College in Darwin prepares marbled ink for printing on cotton (the finished fabric is on page 25).

on the material and press it with my hands. I like doing lino-block printing and silk painting and canvas—I'd like to do more. I'd like to learn about pottery, I've never done that before.

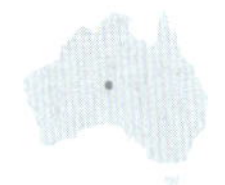

KATEY CURLEY, KALTJITI ARTS AND CRAFTS
Ka nganana nintiringu tjuku tjuku pauni, ngurpangku paunu munu nganana ninti pulkaringu malangka.

We would do a bit of waxing without really knowing what we were doing , but we ended up knowing all about it.

Translated from Pitjantjatjara by Suzy Bryce.

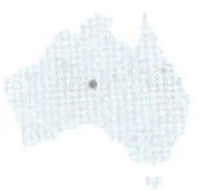

DAISY (NYUKANA) BAKER, ERNABELLA ARTS
Munu 1974ngka Jillian Daveynya Carolku ngunytju munu ngayulu anula ma-nyinangi Indonesiala kutu panya batikaku nintiringkupai ngarangi Jakartala.

Ka batikaku panya nintiringkupainya wali pulka alatjitu, kaya wati tjuta munu minyma tjuta kulu tjungu waakaripai nyara palula. Ka ngura nyara Indonesiala tjana raiki wara pulkangka alatjitu palyalpai waaka wiru mulapa. Ka nyara palula ara ngayulu ngurpangku. Putu nguwanpa palyaningi batik putu alatjituna kuwaripatjarana palyaningi.

Nyara Indonesiala, palu ngura nyara katu kuluya wati tjuta waakaripai batikangka munuya tjatangka kulu walka tjunkupai munuya paintamilalpai ka ngayulu putu kulini nyaakula panyatja minyma kutju waakaripai craftroomangka.

Uwa ngayulu kuwaripatjarana mulapa nintiringu Anapalaku walka palyantjikitja tjitji kulitja mununa milpatjunkula mantangka walka palyalpai tjukurpa wangkara.

Ngayulu rawangku Anapalaku walka palyalpai ka ngayuku panya walka kutjuparingu munu ngalya wiruringangi yiya panya nyara malakitja tjutangka palu minyma uwankarangkula walka kutjupa kutjupa katangku kanyini walytjangku walytjangku.

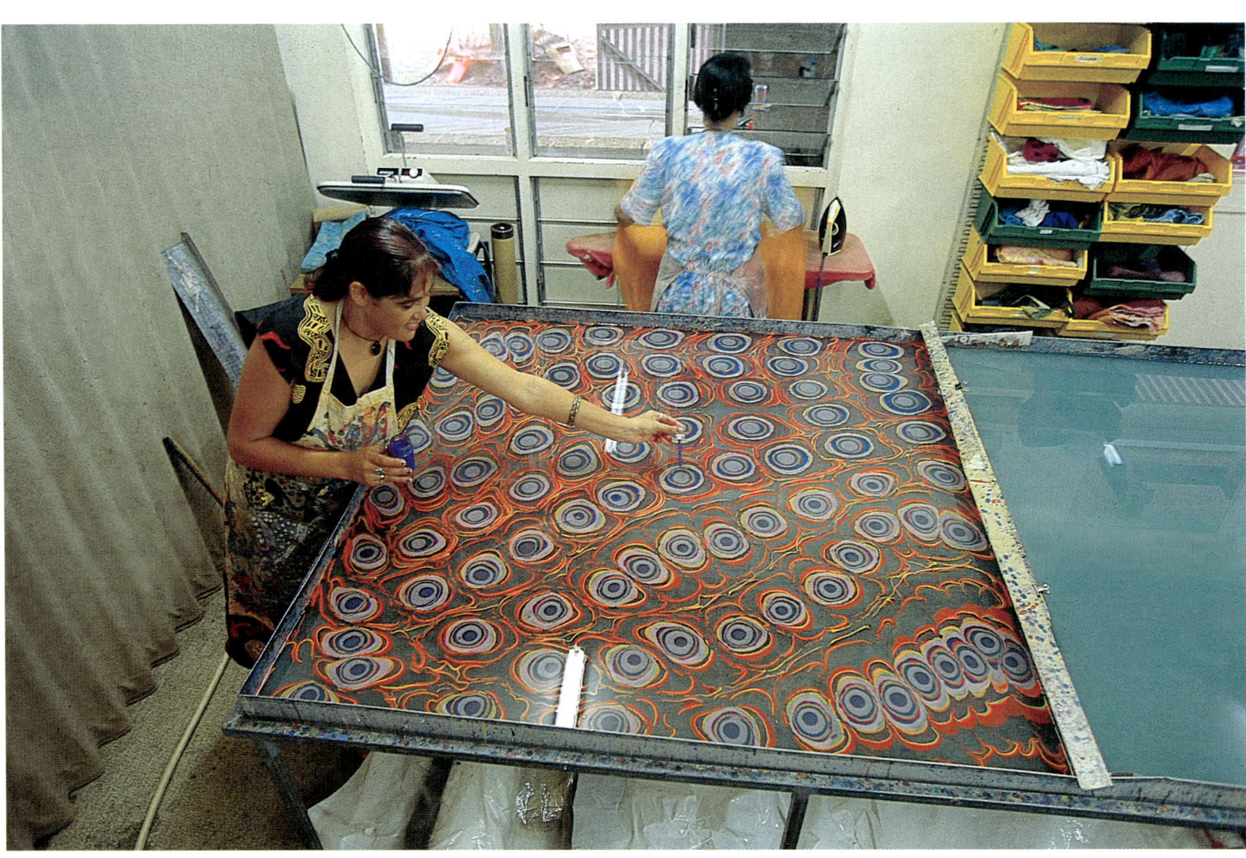

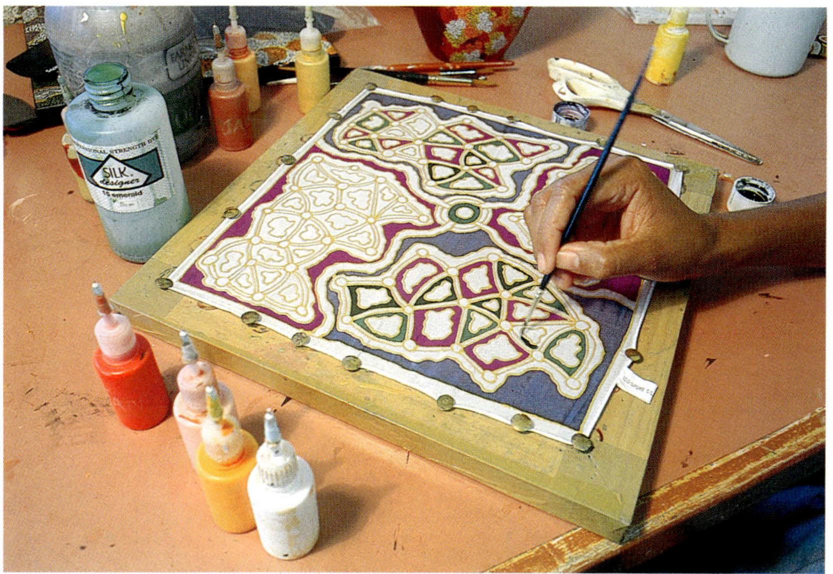

Jane Oliver of Keringke Arts in Central Australia handpaints a silk square.

Palu walkatjunkunytja kuwaripangkana kulilpai tjanpi munu kililpi palyanyangka palku palu wiya.

Ngayulu iriti Fijilakutu anu munu Japantakutu kuḻu munun̲a nyangu panya tjanayanku walka walytjangku palyantjantjanungku kanyini ngura nyara palula tjanala. Palu Anapalaku walka kutjupa alatjitu. Munu walka paluṟu kutjuparingu yiya panya nyaranta palu kutjuparinytja mulapa wiya panya walka palunyaya kutjupangka kutjupangka palyalpai. Panya ngayulu mukuringkunytja wiyatu nguratjara walkatjunkunytjikitja.

Munu ngayulu walkatjunkula tjukurpa purunypa tjakultjunanyi. Palu minyma pampa tjuṯangkuya walka tjunkupai wiya, kungkawara tjuṯangku munu minyma malatja tjuṯangku kutjuya palyalpai palu iritiya palyalpai wiya.

In 1974, Jillian Davey, Carol's mother, and I went to Indonesia [to the batik research centre in Yogyakarta]. The batik workshop was big: many men and women took part. The Indonesian materials are huge and they make beautiful batik. At that stage, I didn't know how to make batik. I couldn't do it.

In Indonesia, but also in the Top End of Australia, men work with material as well. They make T-shirts and screenprints. I don't know why only women work in the Ernabella craft room.

I first learnt the Ernabella design as a schoolgirl, by telling stories in the sand—*milpatjunanyi*—the storytelling game.

I have always made the Ernabella design and my own design has changed only a little bit over the years, and yes, each artist has got her own design.

Before I draw the design with wax on the scarf, I have an idea. Yes, some people think this is spinifex, or stars, something, but *wiya* [no], it's not.

I also travelled to Fiji and to Japan, and yes, they've got their own design. But the Ernabella design is different. It has changed over the years, and with different mediums, but yes, it's still the same. I have never wanted to paint something totally different.

Painting a *walka* is like telling a story in your mind. Old ladies don't do it, only girls and younger women. They didn't do it in the old days—*iriti wiya*!

Translated from Pitjantjatjara by Margaret Dagg.

We all help each other

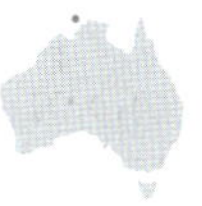

Angelo Munkara, Tiwi Design

When I was a schoolboy, we had an art competition which I won. Giovanni Tipungwuti and Bede Tungatalum, printers at Tiwi Design, saw the design. Michael La Pont, the craft adviser, said, 'Do you want a job?' and I said, 'Yes.' So I started work with Tiwi Design. I made new designs and screens—Giovanni taught me how to make a frame for the screens. Today, I'm on my own here, but we all help each other here.

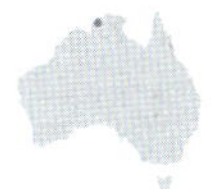

Djankawu Garrawurra, Dunnilli Arts

I like it here at Dunnilli Arts where everyone helps each other to learn all different kinds of printing. When I go home to Milingimbi, I want to show all the community how to do this tie-dye and printing too.

The weather is a problem

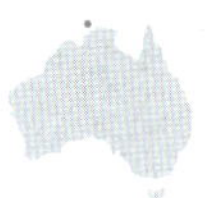

Bernadette Puruntatameri, Munupi Arts and Crafts association

We mainly concentrate on screenprinting and lino-block printing on cotton. We draw the designs onto paper and then cut out the design in rubylith film. We then put the designs onto the screen using photosensitive emulsion [see glossary on page 87] and expose them in a darkroom. We find this a very good way to make our screens, exposing them in sunlight has not been very successful.

I am the main printer and the artists' supervisor. I have been working in this position for three or four years. Rappie Osto is another main printer here. I usually work for one or two days a week, just on the printing. This is very hard work and I need to take a rest. We also teach young girls, but they often don't stick at it because it is such hard work. But it's good for these young girls to learn, though. I will finish doing it one day and it is important for this place that we keep going.

The weather is a problem here also, and the water. Sometimes we have no water at all. The people who do the power come in and turn off the water, and we can't wash the screens.

Training on the ground

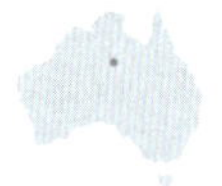

Penny Watson, Batchelor Institute of Indigenous Tertiary Education

An appropriate and relevant training structure is essential to the development of art production in Aboriginal art centres. Tennant Creek's Julalikari Arts and Crafts is a model example of a successful community-based training program. Its success is based to a large degree on the effective partnerships between the organisations and individuals involved: between Julalikari Council and their arts and crafts program, Julalikari Arts and Crafts; between training provider Batchelor Institute of Indigenous

Tertiary Education and the arts and crafts program; and between individual artists and staff members within these organisations.

The Pink Palace is the workplace of artists employed by Julalikari Arts and Crafts. I first began working there at the start of 1996, as a lecturer in Batchelor Institute's Certificate II in Art and Craft. Batchelor Institute is a Northern Territory-based tertiary education provider for Indigenous people that has a number of campuses but also, as in this instance, conducts courses in the workplace. The Certificate II in Art and Craft has been designed to give Aboriginal people experience in a wide range of art techniques, as well as developing skills to increase the artists' involvement in the Aboriginal art industry. The course has been successful at the Pink Palace both in terms of the specified outcomes of the certificate and also in what I understand to be the aspirations of the artists working there.

Having the course brought to the artists in their own workplace has worked extremely well. Being on-site ensures that the specific needs of the art centre are known and met, and that the opportunity for flow-on momentum from workshops is maximised. Quite often it has simply provided the impetus for artists to get working on something new.

Top: T-shirt detail by Inawinytji Williamson, Kaltjiti Arts and Crafts, cotton batik (photo Mary-Lou Nugent).
Middle: Edna Rupert of Ernabella Arts applying a wax design with a *canting* to a silk length.
Bottom: Lena Apwerl of Utopia applies a wax design with a *canting* to a silk length.

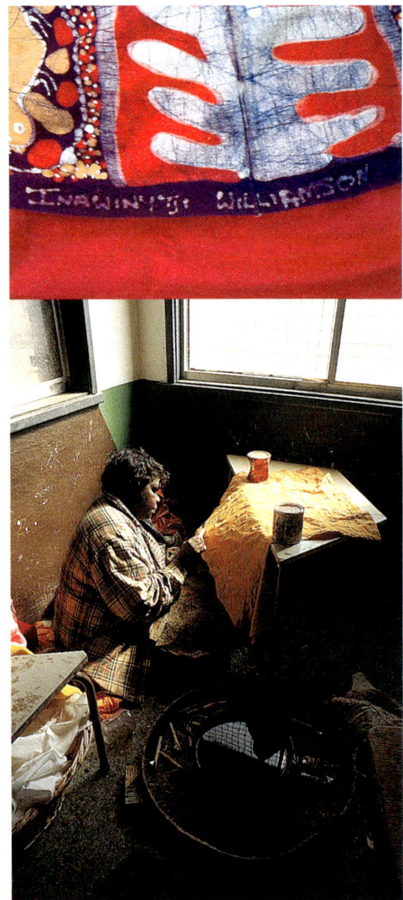

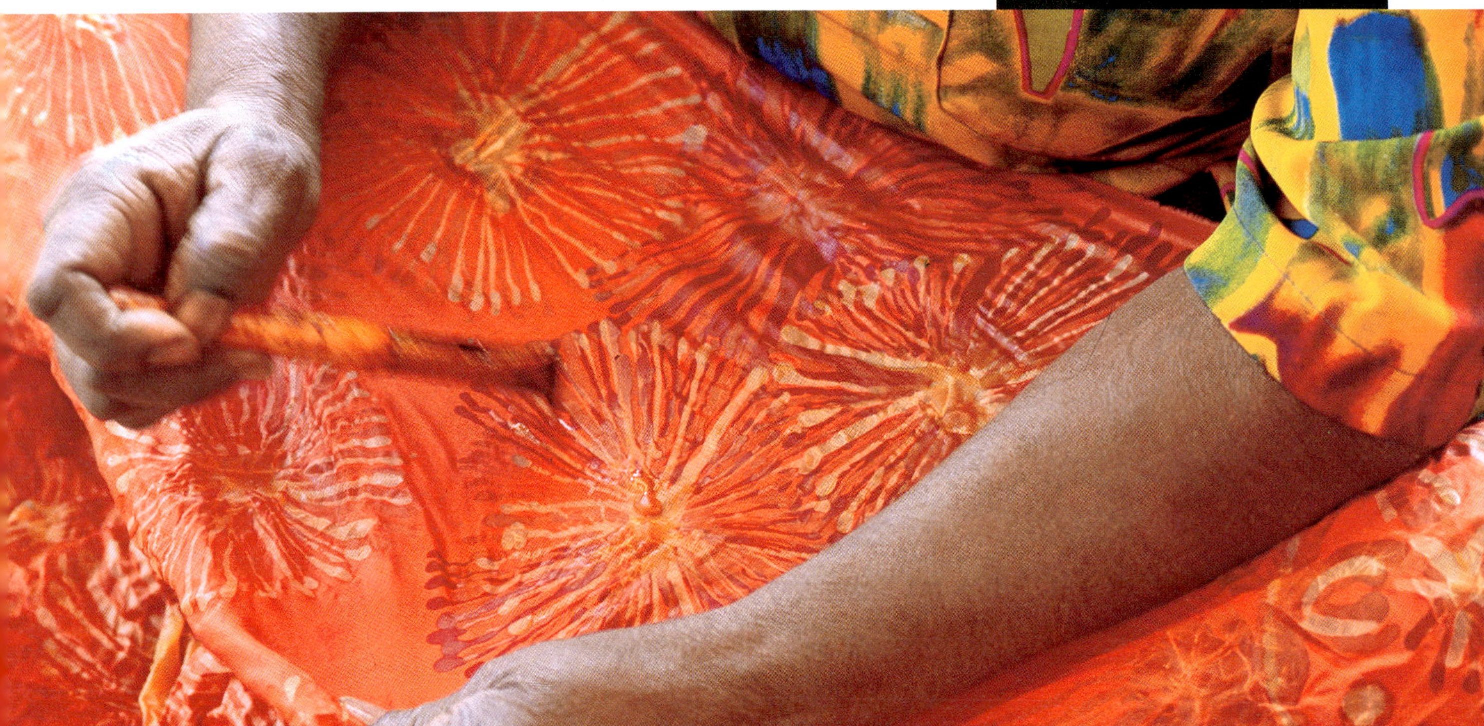

The certificate's workshops are generally run in fortnightly blocks, during which time a technique, for example silk dyeing, is introduced and demonstrated. Then artists have the opportunity to experiment with the medium. Artists can continue working in that medium if they so wish after workshops have concluded. When interest is strong the centre has acquired the necessary materials and equipment.

This is what happened as a result of the course's silk-dyeing workshop held at the Pink Palace in September 1996. Julalikari artists went on to produce, exhibit and sell extremely high-quality handpainted silks. Rather than replicating the style of silks made by Aboriginal artists from other centres, the Pink Palace artists have developed their own individual styles.

Batchelor Institute works with several art centres across the Central Australian region. Many of the art centre coordinators at these centres have skills in the areas in which workshops are run, but lament the fact that they are so caught up in administration of the centre that they lack the time or energy to practise an art form or pass on skills. For most art centres, there are insufficient funds available to risk introduction to a particular medium or technique which artists may not be keen to continue.

Introductory workshops offered through the Certificate II in Art and Craft provide an excellent environment for experimentation. The focus is on techniques which don't require huge amounts of 'high-tech' expensive equipment, and we also endeavour to maintain a high standard of health and safety in the workplace. The certificate also introduces the artists to current art industry issues. Exposure to a number of techniques and ideas helps broaden the artists' approach to their work and makes them aware of the possibilities available to them.

I have heard people (never the artists themselves!) express the fear that formal training will spoil the

'natural' or perhaps 'traditional' style which Aboriginal artists have. However, I would argue that it is patronising to think that Aboriginal artists, in particular, should be 'protected from external influences', as if this were even possible for any contemporary artist, whether they live in Tennant Creek or Sydney. Artists can be exposed to new ideas without compromising traditional knowledge or an artist's individuality. Good arts training should give artists the opportunity to think about their work and provide them with the freedom to experiment and find the best means of giving expression to their own ideas and style.

Training should be flexible enough for students to take from it what they want or need. There are a number of issues which particularly affect Aboriginal artists and their place in the art market. An awareness of these issues can only help to strengthen the artists' ability to control that market, protect their own rights, and to make their own choices and informed decisions.

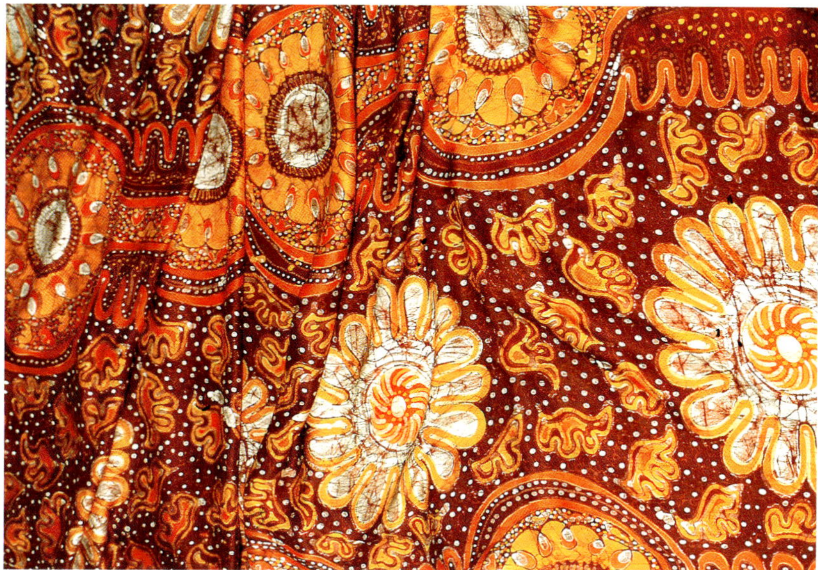

Untitled, Alison (Milyika) Carroll, Ernabella Arts, silk-satin batik, 3.5 m length.

Keep doing this work after we are gone

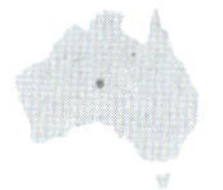

Inawinytji Williamson,
Kaltjiti Arts and Crafts

When I finished school at Ernabella I went to work doing paintings in the craft room. The women taught us how to make floor rugs. Some of us learnt weaving. We learnt to do the crafts that were being done in those days. As kids we were told stories by someone drawing in the sand—*milpatjunanyi*—and those stories stayed in our minds and we were able to remember them later when we wanted to make designs. In school in Ernabella we were given crayons and we learnt to draw designs on paper. So we had drawing in school and sand-drawing storytelling, and we practised and practised, and so we learnt.

At Fregon the craft room was small. It wasn't much bigger than a little shed and the TAFE building stood close to it. We worked there sewing

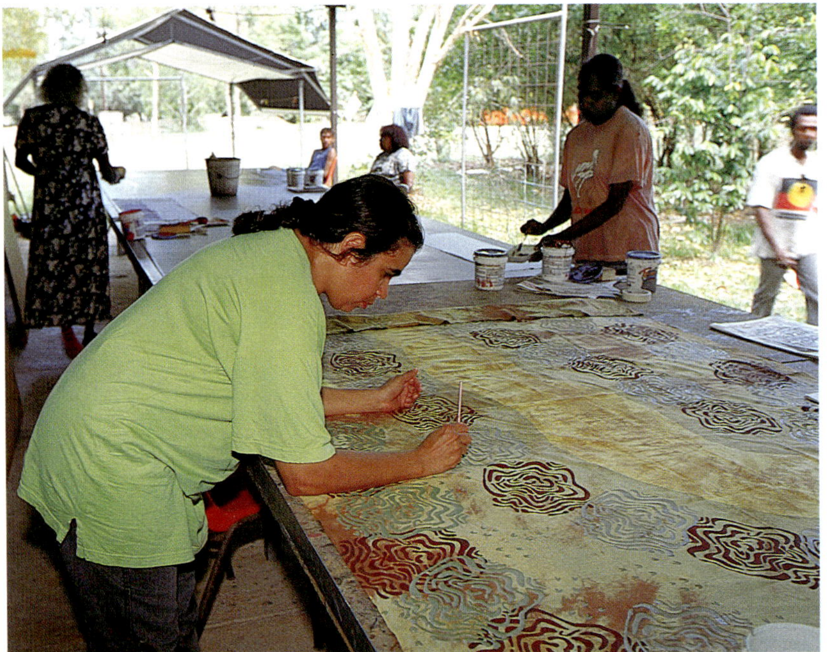

were women from Titjikala and Ikuntji and other places and we all enjoyed learning together from the Utopia women.

They hold the *canting* with the bowl slanting upwards and then direct them downwards onto the work. They put cardboard inside their work and we thought, we can't do it that way! We use a table to hold the work in place as we do the design. We had a few goes at it and by the next day we could do it too!

moccasins with kangaroo skins. Diana James had come to teach us. She was a young girl from Sydney and she came to manage the craft room. We didn't make a lot of money in those days. When we were starting off, we made very little. We kept working and we learnt a lot of different things, doing craft from the early days and learning things that were new. We have done painting for a long time and continue with canvas and dot painting. We learnt batik at Ernabella and then we were able to do it well.

Other women, like Kunytjitja Brown, were taught by Margaret Tischler at the Institute for Aboriginal Development in Alice Springs. Then Suzy Bryce from the Institute for Aboriginal Development and Kunytjitja Brown went around teaching women how to make batik. Margaret Tischler came to Fregon and the women learnt sewing and tie-dye and other things. They were able to add these new skills to the range of things they were already able to do.

When teenage girls are leaving school, they come to the craft room to learn. They paint cards and they might learn dot painting. Sometimes they practise batik. They like to come in and learn—girls like my daughter. I teach

her batik when she has finished her other work. We tell these girls, 'We'll be getting older sometime, and our eyesight won't be very good. We want you to keep doing this work after we are gone. Keep this work of ours strong and always maintain a high standard. Never let it slip, because if it does, then our work could be finished.' We really love our artwork, and we value the continuity of it which goes back a long way. We want this work to extend into the future, too. Sometimes we teach our children, and sometimes the school kids come in to do painting or batik.

We went to Hamilton Downs to learn from the women from Utopia and their craft adviser, Jan Ross Manley. They do batik a bit differently there. They use a piece of cardboard and they put it inside the T-shirt. Mantuwa Treacle and Matjangka Norris and I were there and we enjoyed the workshop, seeing how these other artists do their work. They taught us about colour. Jan would talk about colours. She explained about repeated dipping in the dye pots. Dye it twice, and then do more wax, and dye it again, twice. This is the way to get really strong colours and make the designs stand out really clearly. There

all kinds of designs

the fabric imagery

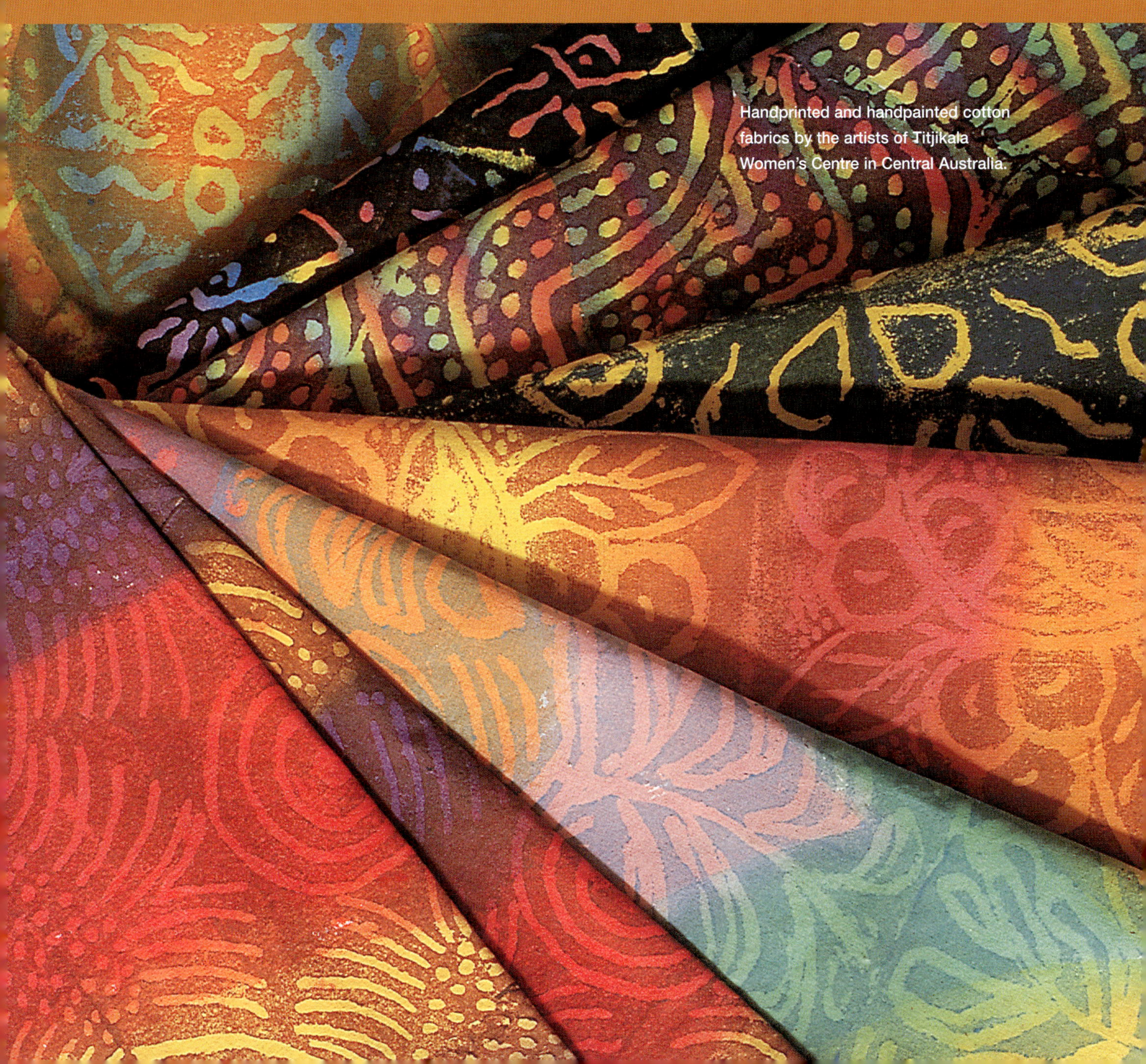

I do bushtucker

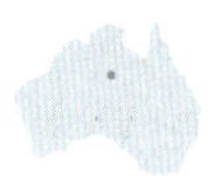

PEGGY NAPANGARDI JONES,
JULALIKARI ARTS AND CRAFTS

I do bushtucker, like *parpada* (bush potato), *ngamukurtu* (bush banana), *kurtinja* (bush turkey), *yawirri* (kangaroo), *kaluwurru* (goanna), *yakajirri* (bush sultana), *nyinawurtu* (porcupine), *karnanganja* (emu), *nyingka* (lizard), *palyupalyu* (blue tongue), *ngarlu* (sugarbag—wild honey), *nganjawarli* (bush tomato), *parntali* (bush orange) and *ilatju* (witchetty grub).

I remember stories from my mind.

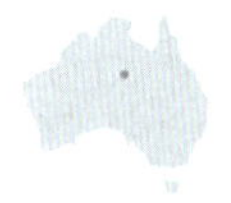

MYRTLE APETYARR, URAPUNTJA ARTISTS

Mern akely akely, mern akatyerr, alperr yanhwelker, antywer, mern alkwarrer akely-akely arrenpernerl. Mern bush-areny yanhwelker-rnem. Alkwarrer, akely-akely, antywer renh, akaperl, akarntetyarntety akely-akely renh. Ker-kweny pang wethwelker, paytey akely-akely. Athan awelyan mpwaretyart. Proper way anwekingkerrenh-antey.

I paint little food plants: bush tomatoes, those leaves, grass and bush bananas. I paint all those sorts of bush foods. Bush bananas, grasses, *kaperl* lizards and little *karntetyarntety* lizards. That one is not edible—a small cheeky thing. I used to paint *awely,* women's ceremony, designs, the proper way, the one belonging to us.

Translated from Anmatyerr by Jenny Green.

VIOLET APETYARR, URAPUNTJA ARTISTS

Alkwarrer anwern ingkwernem batik-warl. Still mpwarerretyel aley, amern nhanyem. Amern akatyerr then, yellow one, amern nhanyem, painting-ek canvas-ek an silk one. Amern alakenh anwantherr idea-el iterlaremel

arrernetyel. Anwenekingkerrenh. Arlewatyerr mpwarenh, akatyerr mpwarenh, amern akely-akely bush-areny mpwarenh, alangkw, an kaperl akely-akely anwantherr mpwarenh. And sometimes dreaming arrernem awely alakenh. Arlkeny awely, canvas-warl anem.

We paint bush banana designs onto batik. That's what we still do. Foods such as the bush tomatoes, the yellow one, are painted onto silk and canvas. That's how we get our ideas about

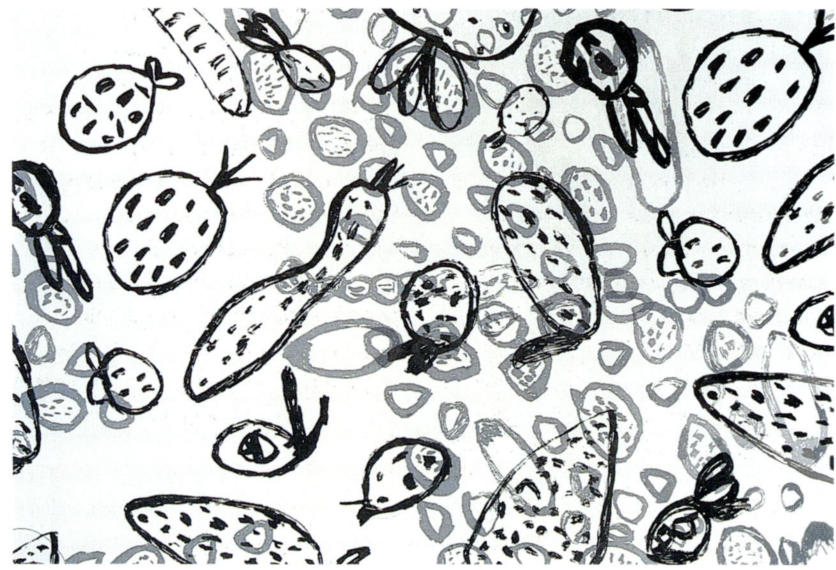

Untitled (detail), Peggy Napangardi Jones, screenprint placement print on cotton twill, 5 m length (photo Mary-Lou Nugent).

what to paint, from our bush foods. We've painted goannas, bush tomatoes, bush bananas, all sorts of little edible plants, and little dragon lizards. And sometimes we paint dreamings and *awely,* the designs from the women's ceremonies, onto canvas.

Translated from Anmatyerr by Jenny Green.

To hold onto our country

KATHLEEN APETYARR, URAPUNTJA ARTISTS

Arelh ampwety-ampweynengel awenh-awenh mapel then, kwey aler-aler mapel then, well, ingkerrekel anwankerr arrernanem, awely anwekakerrenh, apmer anwekakerrenh antwerrkerlanemel. Arrpenh angketyangel. Arelh angwenh apek ra petyemarl kwertengerlel aretyek, 'Kel kwenh mwerr, arrakerr ingkwernetyek, apmer arrekakerrenh. Kel arrakerr antwerrkerlanetyek.' Arrengel antherlelpek inngarl. Aperlelarl antherlelpek. Kel kakel apek aretyek,

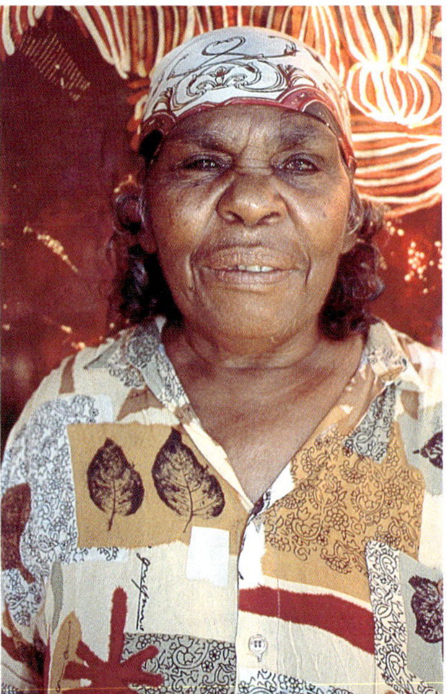

Myrtle Apetyarr, Urapuntja Artists (photo Jenny Green).

kelikw imernt aremel, 'Ah, apmer anwekingkerrenh mpwarepwenemaw ntwa, batik-warl.' Kel aremel ra, 'Kel kwenh apmer antwerrkemel ntwa ingkwernepernerl.'

Awely ingkwernetyart arelh ampwel-rnem werlaty-angkwarr arrernemel, iltyel arrernemel, arrernemel iltyelek-amparr werlaty arrpenh-angkwarr, and inweng-angkwarr arrernemel iltyel, an tyepalel arrernemel. Iyleperek atherr arrernem, white one atherr iltya atherr arrernem, iltyel ingkwernem iyleperek, kel tyepalel anem ingkwernemel. Urlpa then arrernem ngwenty-ngwenty then, alakenh arrernemel, kel iyleper aketh imernt urntemel. Kel arelh ampwa pwath urntemel, kweter-akert, arrkarlp-akert, urntemel kweter ingkernemel ra. Arelh ingwer-rnem akenh aylelhanerleng. Aperl-aperl atha aretyart, aperl-aperlel akalty-anthetyart urntep-urnterleng. Well, ayeng aperl atyenh-apeny anem akalty-irrek.

Anwantherr arrernem awely batik-warl story anwekantherrenh, arrernem anwenanantherrenh aperleyel akalty-anthek. Well, anwantherr arrernetyel anem renh story ingkerrek anem, arreng-kenh arrernemel. Batik-warl arrernetyek awely mwerr, anwenekantherrenh, marl-kenharl yanh, awely arrernem, atey-kenh self again-arl ikwerareyenh atywerreng, rarey apek arrernetyek, self again anerlanem. Anwantherr self again awely anwekantherrenh, arelh maparl. Pmer anwekantherrenh antwerrkeman anwantherr arrernerlanem arelh mapel. Ingkerrekel arrern anem, arelh ampwetyampweyneng, awenh-awenh mapel then, kwey aler-aler mapel then, well ingkerrekarl anwakerr arrernerlanem, awely anwekakerrenh. Apmer anwekakerrenh antwerrkerlanemel.

All the old women, the aunties and the young nieces, well, all of us do our *awely* ceremonies to hold onto our country. Nobody else can say anything about it. Whoever is the *kwertengerl* woman will come and have a look and say, 'That's really good what you are all painting—your country. You are all holding onto it.' That's the country that our grandfathers and grandmothers handed on to us. Then their brother might have a look, and when he sees it say, 'Oh, you're doing our country designs on the batik.' He'll have a look and say, 'So, you're holding onto the country by doing that painting.'

The old women used to paint the ceremonial designs on the breasts, first with their fingers, on the breasts and chest, and then with a brush called a *tyepal,* made from a twig. They paint the thighs with white paint, with their fingers and then with the *tyepal.* They paint up with red and white ochres, then they dance, showing their thighs. While the other women are singing the

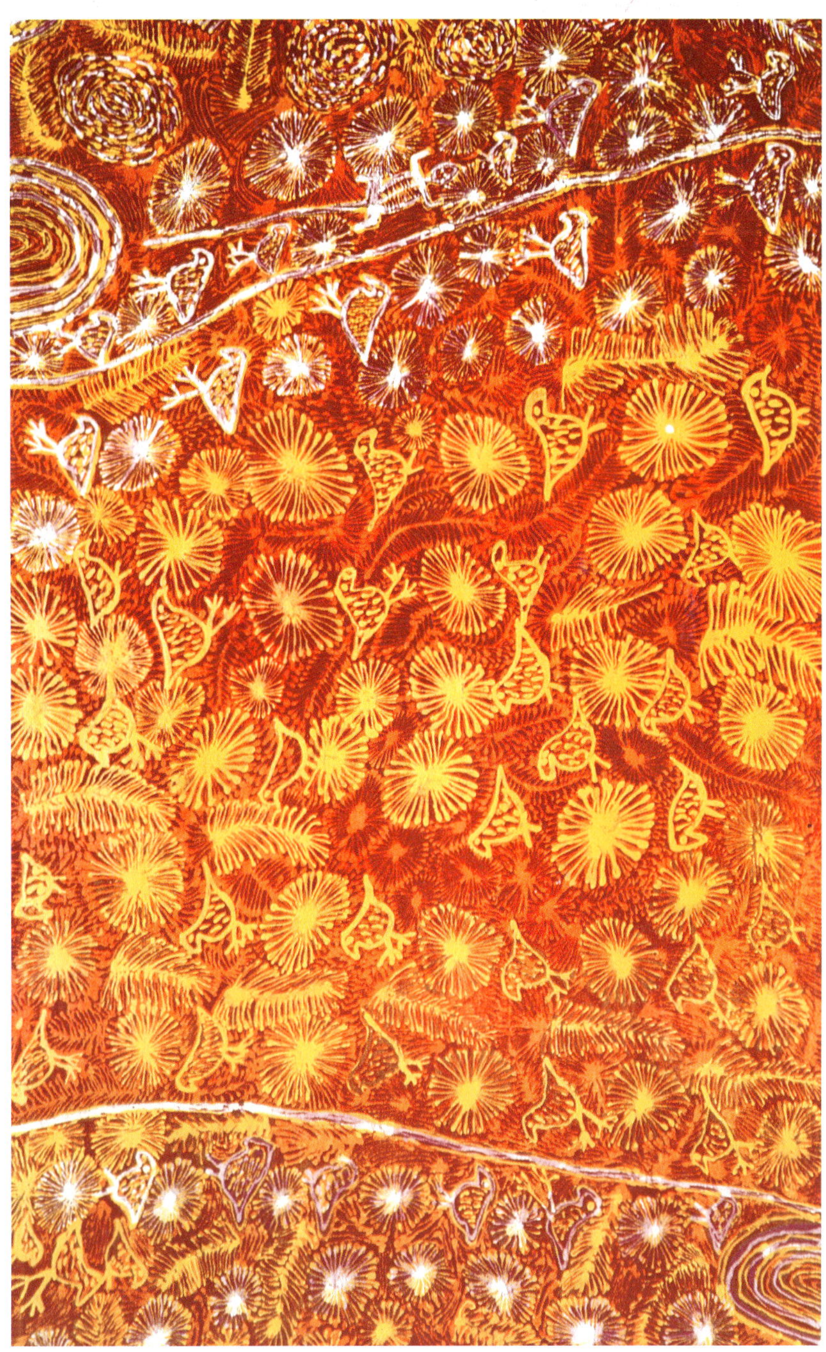

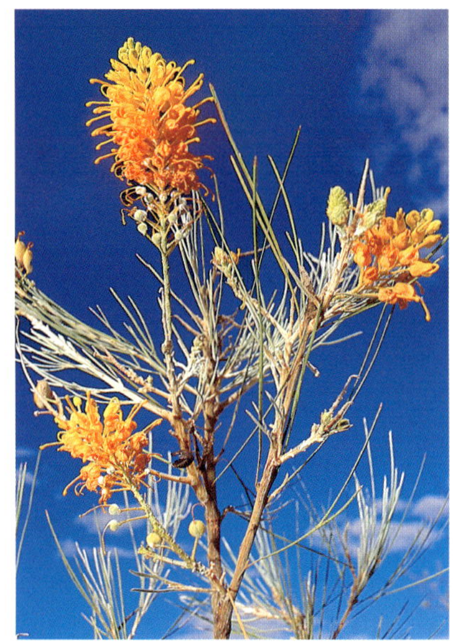

Western Desert honey grevillea.

old 'boss' woman dances with a ceremonial stick and a headdress of feathers, and she places the ceremonial stick in the earth. I used to watch my father's mother, and she used to instruct me as I was dancing.

Well, now I have learnt about it, like my father's mother.

We paint the *awely*, the women's ceremonies, on the batik, the stories that our fathers' mothers taught us. Well now, we put all these stories on batik, our grandfathers' stories. It's good to represent our ceremonial designs on batik. That's women's business that *awely*—men have their own business— *atywerreng* or sacred objects. They might paint these things themselves; they've got their own business. We women have our own separate ceremonies. We women paint these designs to hold on to our country. All of them do it: the old women, the aunties and the nieces. Well, all of us paint our *awely* designs, to look after our country.

Translated from Anmatyerr by Jenny Green.

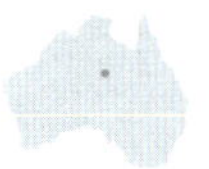

Mary Akemarr, Urapuntja Artists

Apeng anem tha arrernenh, mern altwerr-rnem then, atyenharrp atha mpwarenh, ment, pmer atyenharrp- penh an mern ngkweyang tha mpwarenh, apeng-penh mern. Ment anem tha iterlarenh, arlanty tha ikwer mpwarenh, ker arlanty. Apengelarl aneyelan irrwerl, jump-irrerl-anem ra. Arlanty tha arrernenh silk one-warl, arlanty anem arrernew.

I use the kurrajong tree as a design, and the wild orange as well. I paint my own things myself, things from my country. And I also paint *ngkweyang,* the seeds from the kurrajong tree. I think of these things myself. I also paint the bicycle lizard that lives high in the kurrajong tree and jumps down to the ground and runs along. I paint the bicycle lizard onto the silk.

Translated from Alyawarr by Jenny Green

Kaltjiti Arts and Crafts screenprinted cottons by (left to right) Yanyi Wells, Marita Baker, Maria Curley, Inawinytji Williamson, and Inawinytji Williamson.

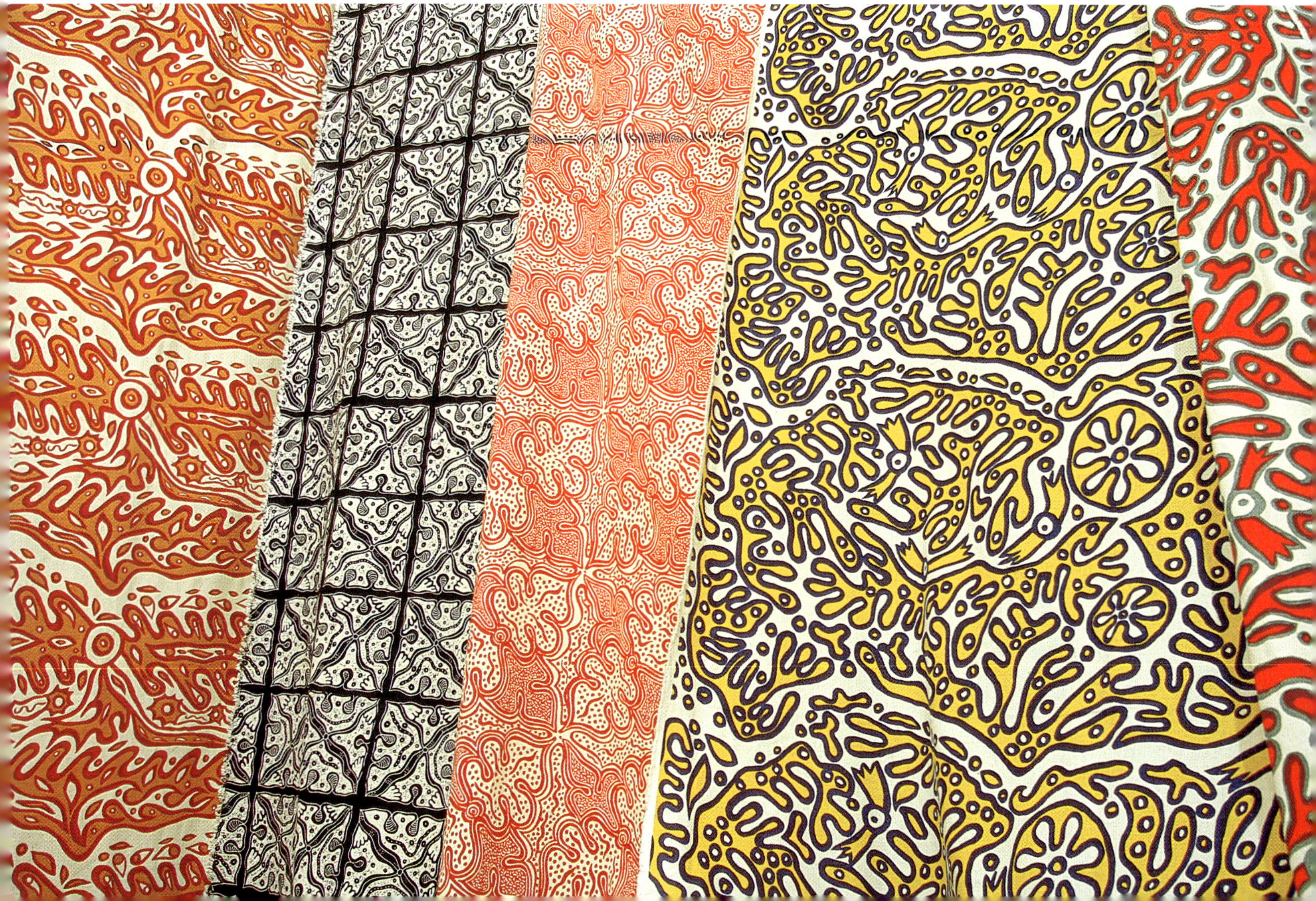

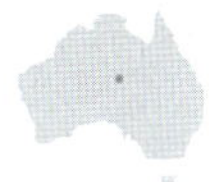

KATHLEEN WALLACE, KERINGKE ARTS

The stories I paint on the silk come from what I see on rock carvings and what our ancestors used to do a long time ago. My stories are about dancing and ceremony, about the country here and about how to look after the land. It's all my country around Santa Teresa. This is my grandfather's country, my mother's father. The dreaming place for Santa Teresa is where they have now built the water tanks, on the hill behind the community. This place is called Tyerenepe; it's a very special place. It's the Rainmaking Dreaming and we call it Irelampe. The Keringke Arts centre is just nearby—we wanted to put our art centre next to that place. Keringke Rockhole, after which the arts centre is named, is a sacred site and it is my dreaming place. It is the place where my mother's life started. Keringke means kangaroo tracks, and that's why there are kangaroo tracks on the Keringke logo.

We paint our dreamings

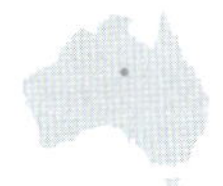

HILDA APWERL, URAPUNTJA ARTISTS

Aknganenty anwekenh anwantherr ingkwernem arlewatyerr, aker arlewatyerr. Tyap atnyemayt, ingkwernerlanem. Atnyemayt arrpantey. Tyap ankerrayt, akeng-artek war mpwarerlanem. Tyap aylperlayt, aper-areny, yanh-areyarl. Caterpillar akeng weth anem ingeth. Yanh-areyarl anwekantherrenh ingeth, like anwekakerrarl aknganek. Anwenekakerrarl aknganek map. Anwantherr sellem apek ilem anwekantherrenh nhelkwer anwantherr warrk-irreperremel, sellem-ilemel, well anwantherr ngkwelty apek inem anwekantherr. Iterrek anwantherr alakenh. Anwantherr apmer anwekantherrenh-angkwarr,

anwekantherrenh altyerr-angkwarr mpwarerlanetyek, aknganekarl-angkwarr. Akwetant anwantherr mpwarerlapetyek.

Ingkwernetyart batik-warl ker arlewatyerr, ker apmwa, ker apmwa weth, arlkwenh-arlkwenh kwang ker war. An, ker arlkwenh arlkwenhan apmwan, arrwepel, utney, ker, batik-warl arrpenhemelan ingkwernerlanem. Tharl ingkwernem kel-anteyarl apmwa ahelengkw ahelengkw yanh-welker. Like mer apmwa anwekantherrarl aknganekarl. Anwenekantherrarl aknganekarl. Ker arlewatyerr too

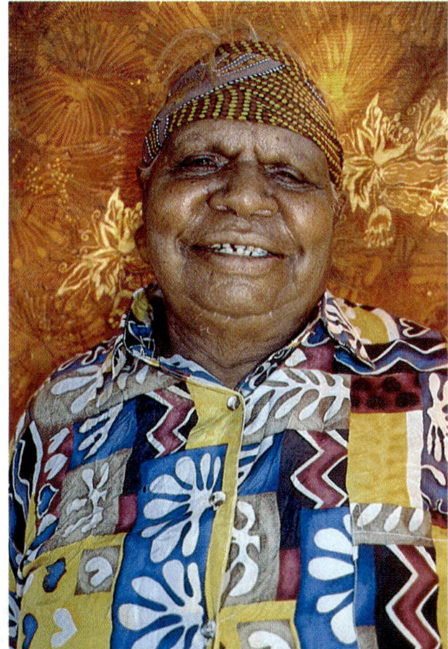

Hilda Apwerl, Urapuntja Artists (photo Jenny Green).

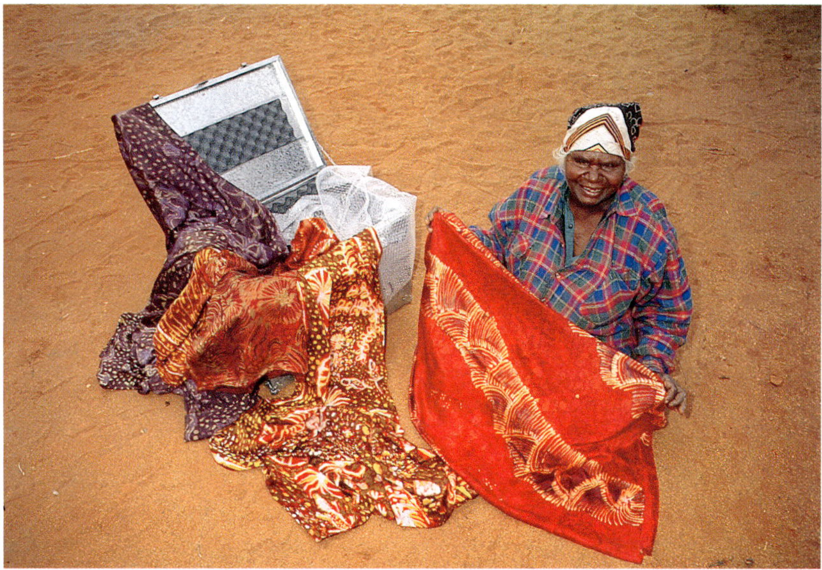

Ada Bird Apetyarr of Utopia packs a case with silk batiks ready for exhibition.

---

anwekantherr aknganek. Rap mentyel intepinteman. Sometimes tha ingkwernerlanem—arlewatyerr, ker arlewatyerr arwerr-areny yanhwelker. Iterrek, alakenh anem mpwarerlaney akwetant kwenh. Ker anwekantherrenh Law anwekantherrenh, anwekantherrenh law anwantherr mpwarerlapey awely apek, ker arlewatyerr apek tyap anyemayt apek, batik nhenh-warl, arrernerlapem tyepety apek. Arrernerlanemel, mern alangkw apek. Mern arrutneng apek, lakenh arrernerlapem pretty flower apek arrernetyek, mern akwek akwek.

We paint our dreamings, for example, goanna, and we also keep on painting witchetty grubs—they look like witchetty grubs. We also paint grubs from the coolibah tree, and other grubs from the river red gum tree. We just do it, that's all. And that awful caterpillar—the itchy grub. We try to represent those things. All of those things such as the itchy grub belong to us—they are our dreamings—that were created for us. And we might sell the things that we are working on—we might make ourselves some money. That's what we thought. We've got to keep on painting the things that are related to our country and to us through the dreamings of our mothers and our fathers—the things that were created. We've got to keep on doing it.

I used to paint goannas on the batik, and that edible snake. And others painted the carpet snake. The one that I have painted is that cheeky snake, like the one that came from our country. Goannas as well came from our country, but I leave it be, although sometimes I paint them—goannas, which live in burrows.

We thought that we would keep on making batik like this. Our animals and our Law—we'd paint our Law—*awely* [women's ceremonies], or maybe goannas or witchetty grubs or *tyepety* [stories drawn on the ground by women], onto the batik. That's what we'd keep on putting on the batik— maybe bush bananas, or wild passionfruit, or other pretty flowers or little foods.

Translated from Anmatyerr by Jenny Green.

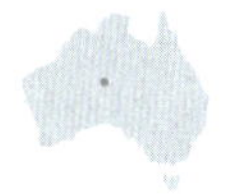

NYURPAYA KAIKA, MINYMAKU ARTS
Kutjupa tjuta batikingka waakaripai, kutjupa tjuta floor rug-ngka nganana palyani, kutjupara ngayulu kulu batiki palyapai mununa palula batiki palyara ngayulu tjukurpa palyapai. Ngayulu kulilpai panya ngayuku ngura, ka

ngayuku ngura Mount Connor-la itingkapanya 'Seven Sister-ku ngalya pitjantja', ngayulu kulilpai. Ngayuku ngurangka tjungu palu ila.

Ka ngayulu nyara palula kulilpai munu material-ngka tjunkupai, nyakuntjaku panya. Kulintjaku tjukurpa, tjana nyakuntja ngaranyi. Ka nyara palunya tjanaya palyapai munu kulilpai mununa ngayuku tjitjingku nyaparti wangkapai, 'Ngayuku ngurangka tjukurpa nyangatja ngaranyi, Seven Sister panya Pitjantja.'

Some of the women work on batik, others on floor rugs. I do special dreaming designs on my batik work. I think about my country which is around Mount Connor, where the Seven Sisters travelled through. My place is very close to Mount Connor.

I think about my country and the dreaming for that place and put it onto the fabric in my work so others can see it. My ideas about my dreaming are on the fabric for people to see. This is what we do. My child says, 'The dreaming of my country is here on this design, the place where the Seven Sisters came to.'

Translated from Pitjantjatjara by Suzy Bryce.

A series of bushtucker designs on tea-towels, Kaltjiti Arts and Crafts, cotton batik.

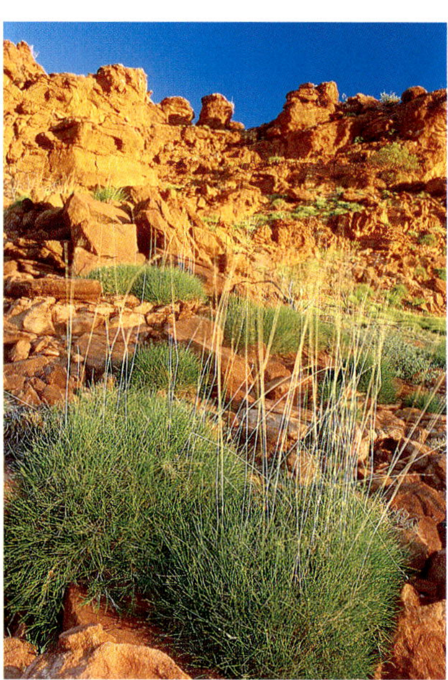

A rocky Central Australian hillside.

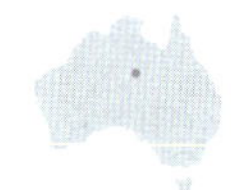

ROSIE KUNOTH KNGWARRAY, URAPUNTJA ARTISTS
Batik-warl atha ingkwernetyek mern aknganenty atwakey, merelarl aknganenh, alakenh ingkwernerretyart wethey. Merelarl akngananek-antey tha ingkwernetyart. Mer nhel-anyem. Mer atyenh-ampenyel-anteyarl aknganek country-ek.

I paint the Wild Orange Dreaming on batik. I used to only paint those things that came from the country on the batik. From this country. The dreamings that came from round my country area.

Translated from Anmatyerr by Jenny Green.

We have our own style

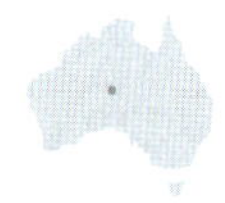

MATJANGKA (NYUKANA) NORRIS, KALTJITI ARTS AND CRAFTS
Nganampa Ernabellaku purunypa. Kutjupa way nganana palyapai— maratjara munu tjinatjara. Mara tjunkulala munu nyara palulanguru kala

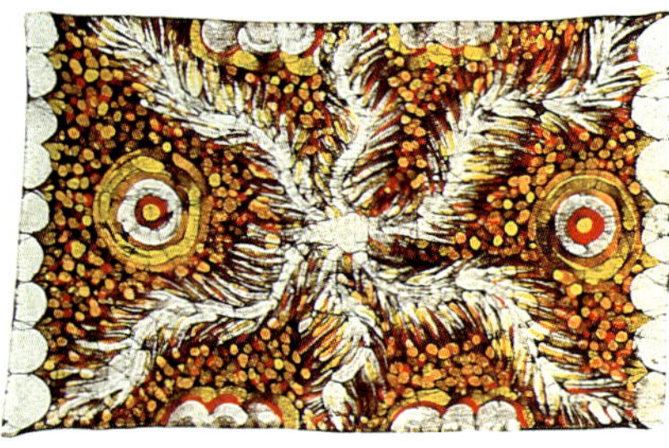

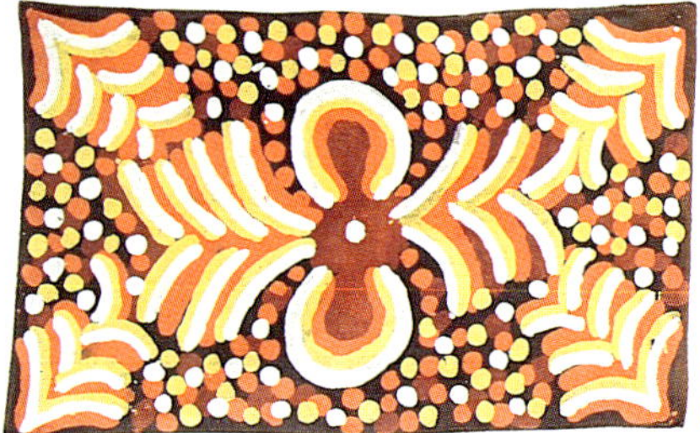

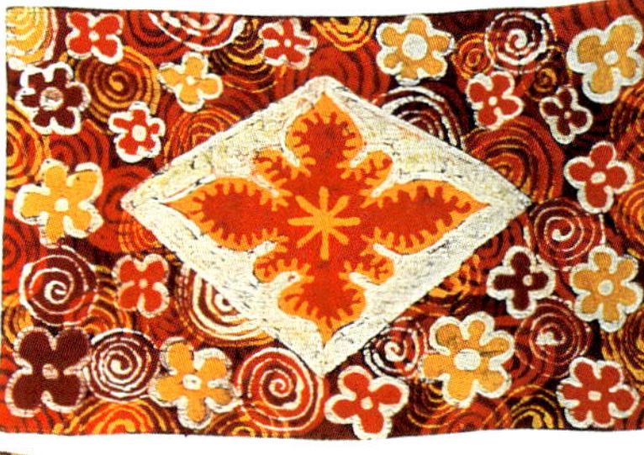

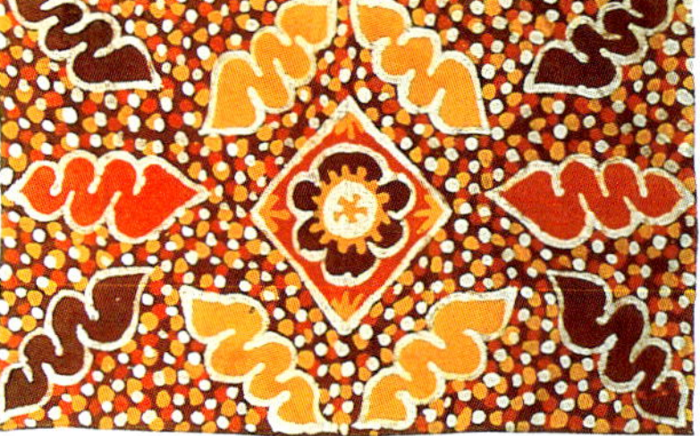

tjunanyi, T-shirt tjutanguru. Tjina tjunkula walkatjunanyi munu nyara paluru kala wiru tjunanyi kutjupa. Pretty flower, tjinangka itingka. Arkara nganana kutjupa, kutjupa palyani. Tjina kutju nganana palyani. Tjukurpa wiya. Papa tjina, anangu tjina munu mara tjunkula palyani. Ayinayini tjutala palyani. Ka piranpa tjuta mukuringanyi nyara palulanguru, maratjara urantjikitja, tjinatjara urantjikitja, munu papa tjinatjara. Tjana alatji nyakula payamilanyi. Uwa alatji nganana tjunkula, pen-ta walkatjunanyi. Munu palulanguru palyanilta. Ka nyara palulanguru kala wiru ngaranyl . . .

Nganana nyanganguru palyani, panya nyaangka, painta malangka piruku batik-ngka palyani. Munu walkatjura palu purunypa, batik-ngka tjunanyi. Munu kuwari batik walka, batik tjinguru palyani.

Our work is similiar to Ernabella, but we have our own style, which includes hand and footprints. We put on handprints and footprints and then dye the T-shirts. We build up designs with footprints and flower shapes. We try out lots of different ways, using dog paw prints and human footprints. We use the footprint motif but not the story from the Tjukurpa [see glossary on page 87]. We make unusual designs and our customers seek out the hand- and footprint designs. They take a look and buy them. We just trace around our hand to make the shape, and then dye it a good colour…

We have moved from painting to making batik. We used the designs we developed doing painting. Now we are taking these batik designs and making paintings like batik.

Translated from Pitjantjatjara by Suzy Bryce.

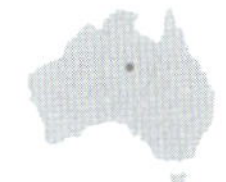

GLORIA APETYARR, URAPUNTJA ARTISTS
Three Bores-el, akalty-irrenh, akelyarl ingkwernenh. Ingkwernenh awely an arnkerrth arrernenh, akely-akely wethwelker mern-rnem then. Kel

awetharl ingkwernem imernt aremel. 'Mwerrangker kwenh.' Areynenh. Colour-warl akwernepwernemel. Kel awetharl ingkwernemel aremel, mwerr, awetharl ingkwernemel kel ingkwernemel aweth batik, colour ingwer-iperr anem. Atyetyek might be atherr apek colour apek. Yellow one. Red one.

Mern akatyerr, arlkwenh-arlkwenh-rnem ant, ingkwernenh. Arlewatyerr ingkwernetyang than ingkwernetyam angwenhant, awely. Awely Atnangker-areny, atyenhant. Anwekingkerr self-arl ingkwernem, anyentek. Story ingwer-kenh iletyang, arrangkw. Anwekingkerrekenhant iletyel. Apmerareny-antey country. Violet, Myrtle-arey ingkerrek, same story. Anwingkerr ingkwernerlanem. Ntang alyatywereng an akatyerr anem mern

akatyerr. Aknganekarl. Apmer Atnangkerel. Akatyerr, alyatywereng, ingkwerrm mixed up-awatyel. Arnkerrthan main one rarl story.

Anwantherr ingkwernemel aretyek. Antwerrketyek apmer, apmer antwerrkerlanetyek. If anwantherr ingkwernetyang anerlanem, well, whitefella-el apayutnhem, 'Unta apek ingkwernetyek anything apmer ngkwenh kwenh?' Rntertel aretyel, 'Yeah, awely anwekingkerr anwingkerr urntetyel thenarl kwenh.' Arlkeny

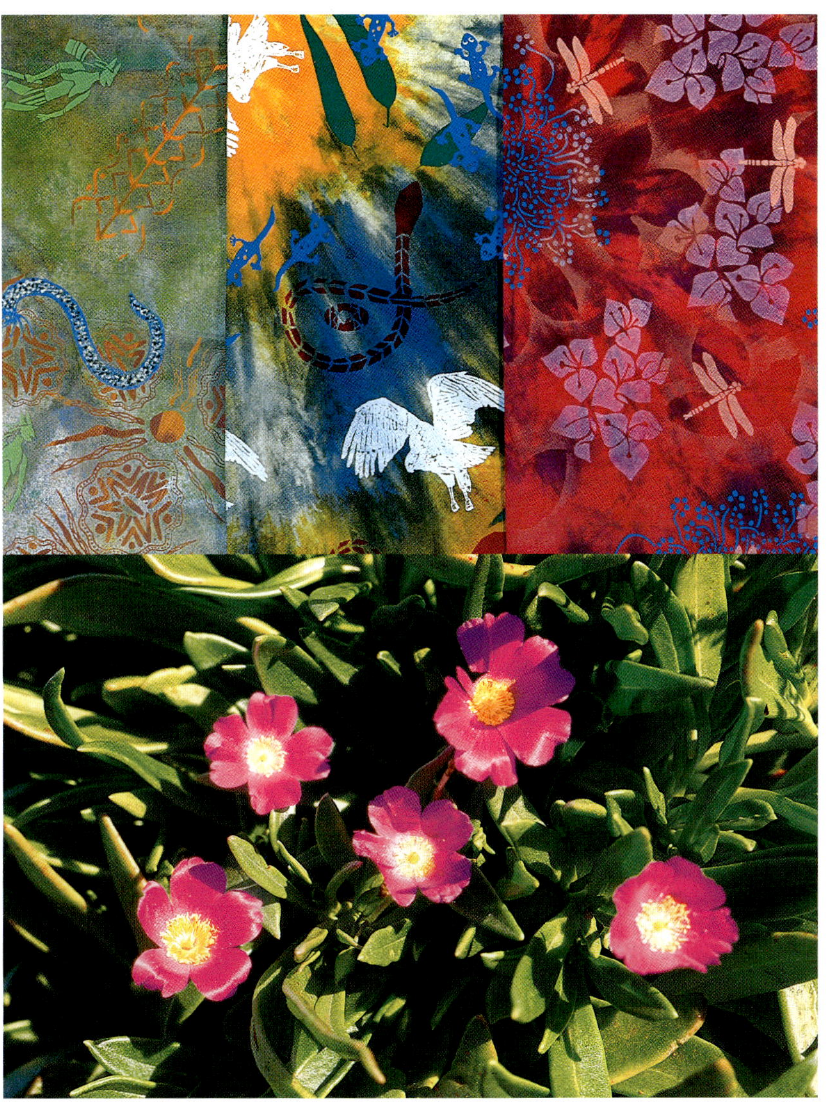

*iwelhem, anthepirrerlanem. Awely
yanh-antey batik-warl arrernem.*

*Ampel ingkwernetyart arlkeny renh.
Arrwekelenyekenh ap yanh arlkeny. Still
anwenantherr ingkwernerlanem
ahernek ilelhepelherl, arlkeny anem
alanh arrernem, atyetyek, yellow one
arrkeyt arrkeyt. Ilelherlanem inngart
war. Awely anem yanh iwerretyel,
amultek then unengek.*

I learnt batik at Three Bores. I batiked
a bit there. I painted *awely* [women's
ceremonies], the mountain devil lizard
and other sorts of little bush foods.
Then I'd wax it again and then look at
it to see if it looked okay. Then put it in
the dye, wax it again, then put it in
another colour—maybe red or a couple
of colours.

I was painting bush tomatoes—

Puti (Bush), designed by Vera Mbitjana
Williams and Daisy (Nyukana) Baker,
Ernabella Arts, screenprinted cotton,
printed by Marie Warren.

those edible ones. I didn't use goanna
designs in the batik—I only painted
awely—that *awely* from Atnangker
country—just mine. We paint that one
thing ourselves. We don't tell other
people's stories. We just tell ours, just
the ones from the country. Violet
Apetyarr and Myrtle Apetyarr and the
others have the same story. We sisters
keep painting that. The woollybutt
grass seed and the bush tomato.
These things come from that country—
Atnangker: the bush tomato, the
woollybutt grass and mistletoe berries
as well. The mountain devil lizard is the
main story.

We paint these things so that they
can be seen, and to hold on to the
country. If we just sit down and don't
paint, well, the whitefellas might ask,
'Are you painting anything from your
country?' 'Yes, the *awely* ceremony
that we dance to as well.' We paint up
and dance. Well, that *awely* design is
put onto batik.

We used to draw those designs
when we were kids. Those designs

belong to the olden-time people. We
still draw on the ground and tell the
stories, and paint the design—red and
yellow—just telling ourselves stories.
Then we paint ourselves up for the
awely ceremonies.

Translated from Anmatyerr by Jenny Green.

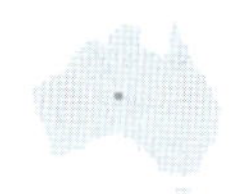

Inawinytji Williamson,
Kaltjiti Arts and Crafts

Ernabella batik is different to Fregon.
They think about their work and their
designs come from their imagination.
They make many varied designs.
Nyukana and the other artists at
Ernabella do their work in a different
way. They have been to Indonesia and
they spent time learning over there.
Their work reflects that influence…

We are still making batik, and we
are doing paintings in a new style
which has emerged out of the way we
conceptualise batik. Both the paintings
and the batik are happening together.

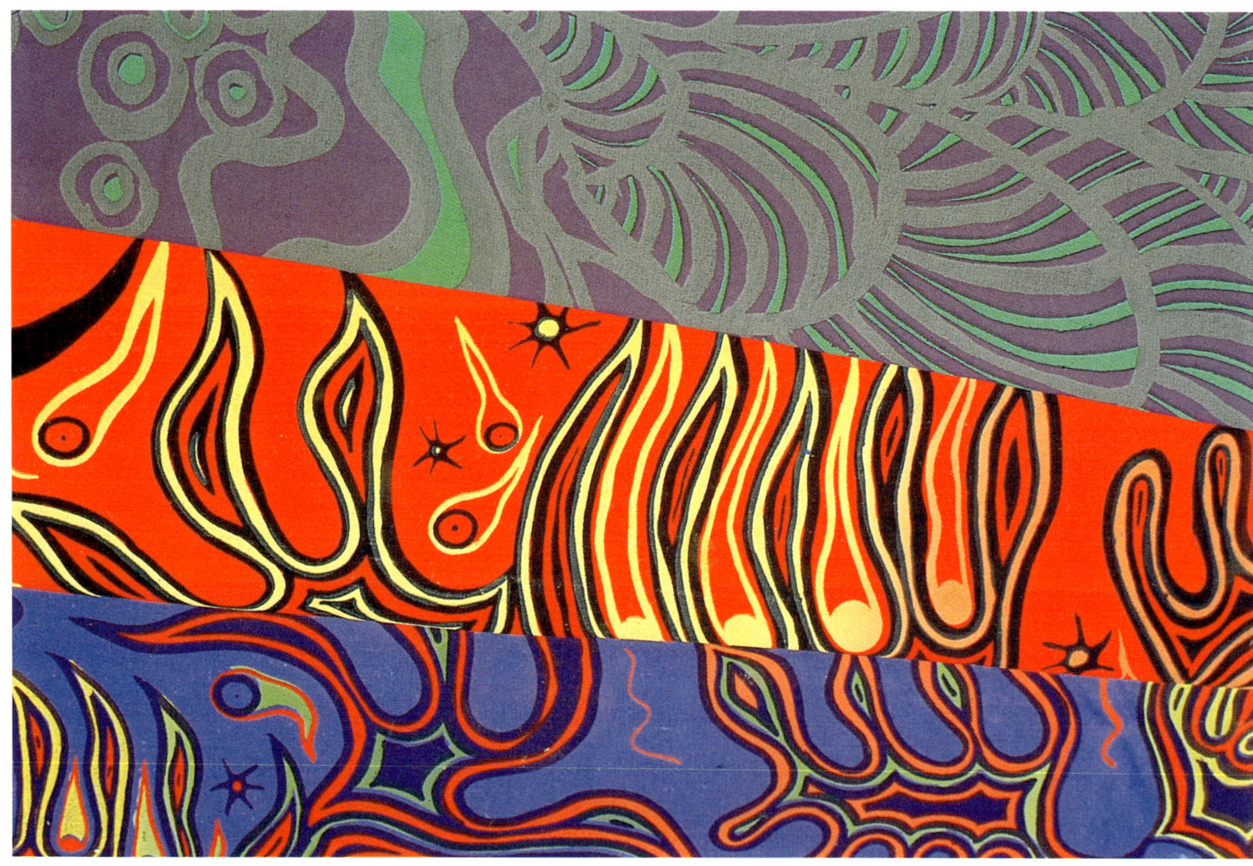

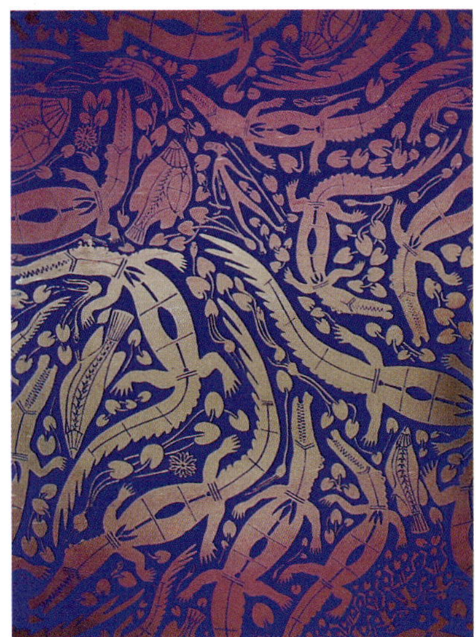

Kinga (Saltwater Crocodile), Danny Djorlum, Injalak Arts and Crafts Association, 1990, screenprinted cotton twill, 8 m length (photo courtesy Injalak Arts and Crafts Association).

We want to have access to both new and existing art forms. One form will feed another…

When I think about making batik I ask myself what kind of design I want, and what kind of motifs I will use, like bushtucker and all the things in the bush. It just flows onto the material as I think about it.

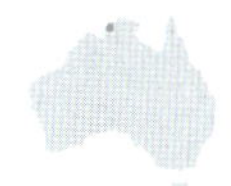

Kelli Bruce, Dunnilli Arts

After becoming a mother, I hated seeing plain white nappies and wanted to see colour and designs on them. I started at Nungalinya College in 1992: marbling, tie-dyeing and screenprinting nappies and singlets, as well as other fabrics.

I feel that I'm most relaxed when I'm creating a piece of artwork which, in turn, helps me to release my energy and emotions into creations that reflect this.

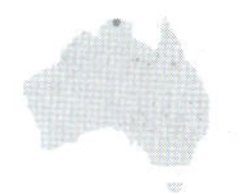

Isiah Nagurrgurrba,
Injalak Arts and Crafts Association

That *mimi* [spirit] design—Kennedy made that design. He drew that from his own head. The barramundi was Gabriel [Maralngurra] and Ray Young [the first trainer at Injalak]. The first designs were small ones. That first workshop was too small. We couldn't make big designs. We made them when we came here. We asked old Lofty [Bardayal] if we can get his designs. Ray was really interested in Lofty's painting, and we asked Lofty and he said, '*Kamak*—okay, you can get my design.' So we did. And then we paid a royalty to him, and he was really happy, and he is still happy because that's his design, that *ngarrbek* [echidna].

That turtle design was Gabriel, he made it in his own mind. That *kinga* [saltwater crocodile]. We asked Danny Djorlum, we gave him paper [to paint on], which is the same they're doing now. We gave him that paper because Ray was really interested in Danny's painting. So, we took Danny's painting and put it on screens, like old Lofty's painting. We paid him a royalty. He was quite happy. He did four *kinga,* facing different ways, and we got barramundi from Injalak hill. And we put a little Injalak logo on, so no-one can steal it. If anyone steals that design, that logo is there so we know

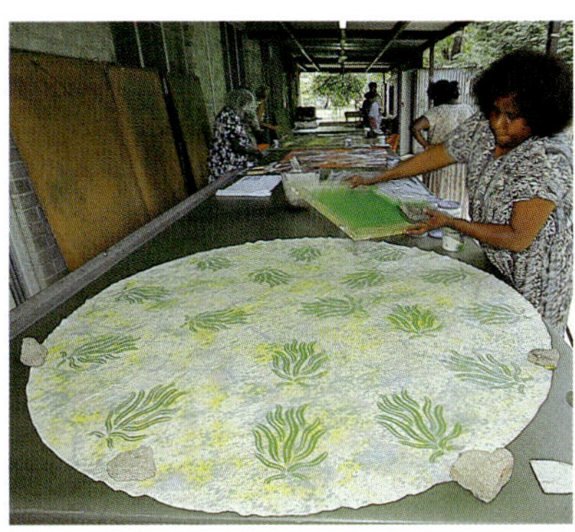

Lanita Numina of Dunnilli Arts in Darwin at work screenprinting a cotton tablecloth.

that's Injalak's design. And Ray cut that up and made it right.

We got that rock art design from Nourlangie Rock. We didn't go there and take photographs, we got it from a book. We asked the traditional owners and they said '*Kamak.* These Bining people—Aboriginal people—can get those designs. That's *kamak.*' So we did. We got that rock art and put it on screens.

All the same—Kakadu and Nourlangie and Gunbalanya—you can see that rock art. They all the same. Same picture. My children, my grandchildren in the future, they might see this rock art. That's really important for us. Keeps culture alive and strong, in fabrics, T-shirts, painting—everything. We got fruit bat from a book, from [— —] from Ramingining. We asked him and he said, '*Kamak,* it's all right.'

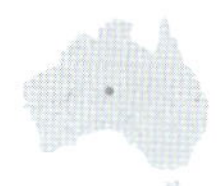

Katey Curley, Kaltjiti Arts and Crafts

Kutjupa kutjupa alatjitu palyapai. Nyaatjara, tinkatjara munu papa inura, ngintaka, tinka—tjukurpa tjutala wangkapai. Tjukurpa tjuta tjunkula kulira raikingka. Paluru tjanaya nganampa raikiku mukuringkupai, wiru tjuta tjunkunyangka.

I do all kinds of designs. It might be sand goanna or perentie or wild dog— we tell all those stories. Elements of the stories are put onto the cloth. A lot of people want to buy our material because of all the wonderful designs.

Translated from Pitjantjatjara by Suzy Bryce.

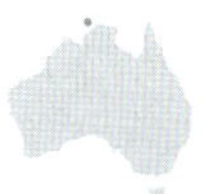

Janice Murray,
Jilamara Arts and Crafts

I get a lot of ideas for designs from Leon [Puruntatameri Snr], one of the senior carvers at the art centre. I also get them from books with old Tiwi designs in them.

Designing the Tiwi way: An element of spontaneity

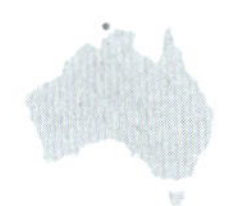

JAMES BENNETT

It is not accidental that amongst the Tiwi of Melville and Bathurst islands fabric printing has become a significant craft form. Of all black Australian cultures, the Tiwi historically had perhaps the richest tradition of bodypainting. The word *jilamara* nowadays means any type of painting or design, but originally referred to the complex decoration applied to the body during ceremonies. It is important to remember that, in the past, this living body art provided a significant source of inspiration for the other forms of Tiwi visual arts, such as the *tali pukamani* poles erected around graves during the important mortuary ceremony, and the wide variety of figure carving produced since European contact. Even today at Milikapiti, the younger generation of Tiwi artists prefer to commence with a black ground, suggestive of the colour of skin, when painting on the introduced medium of canvas or paper.

As the dynamics of Tiwi society change, ceremonial art is produced less and less. Yet the essence of ceremonial designs is being transferred to screenprinted fabric; not just as the core vocabulary of existing surface design motifs, but also in the depiction of traditional ceremonial artefacts now only rarely or perfunctorily made. The wide variety of armbands and body ornaments—ritual weapons once essential to ceremonial regalia—and richly-carved funeral poles are all favoured themes of contemporary Tiwi silk-screen designs. This is an important reason for the perceived 'authenticity' of Tiwi fabric prints, despite their modern medium and technique. Their art continues to be concerned with the decoration of the body, and its vitality is uncompromised.

Perhaps there is a second significant factor that has contributed to the success of Tiwi screenprinting enterprises: unlike the situation amongst most mainland Aboriginal cultures, the reproduction of many traditional designs is not restricted to certain totemic groups or those of a specific ceremonial or kinship status. Tiwi art, of all black Australian art, approaches closest to European

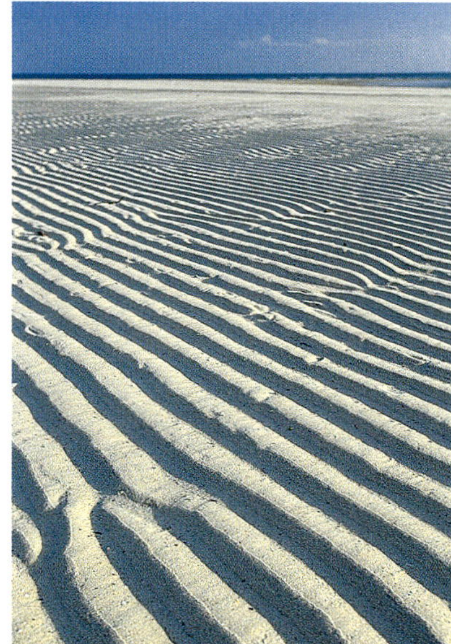

concepts of creativity, where individuality and innovation are valued as much as adherence to customary iconography. Thus, a wide variety of traditional designs may be used publicly in any appropriate context. This is reflected in the diversity of fabric prints produced in the three communities on Melville and Bathurst islands where Tiwi Design and Bima Wear have both been long established.

The distinct direction that Jilamara Arts and Crafts Association screenprinting developed in the early 1990s reflected the differences between the settlement of Milikapiti on Melville Island, home of Jilamara Arts and Crafts Association, and Nguiu on Bathurst Island, home of Tiwi Design. Given the strong sense of Tiwi cultural identity, and the close links between these communities, it is important to understand the differences between the communities and the influence those differences have had on the development of fabric designs.

Milikapiti is a small, comparatively isolated settlement that, unlike Nguiu, was never directly exposed to mission influence. As at Bathurst Island, screenprinting originally commenced at Milikapati as part of an adult education

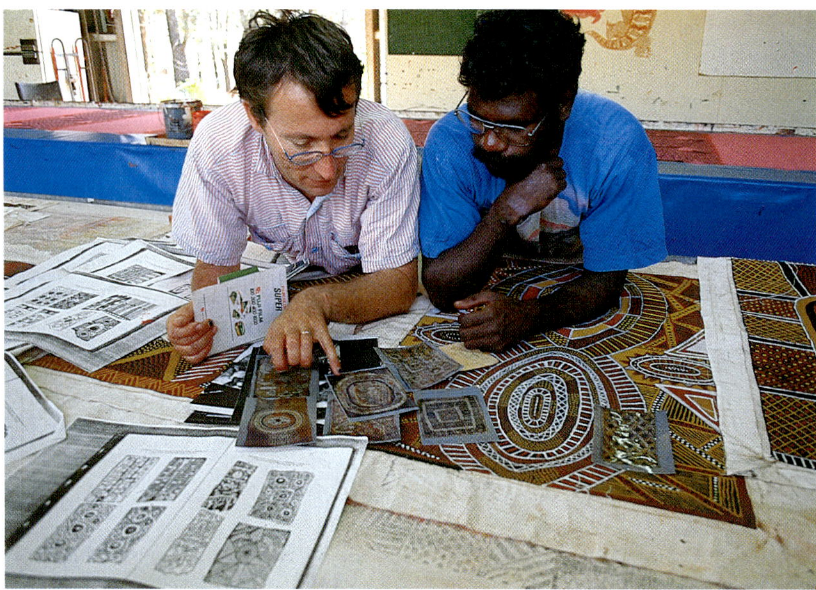

Mr Farmer (right) discusses old Tiwi designs found in various publications with then art coordinator James Bennett at Jilamara Arts and Crafts on Melville Island in 1991 (photo Grace Cochrane, courtesy Powerhouse Museum).

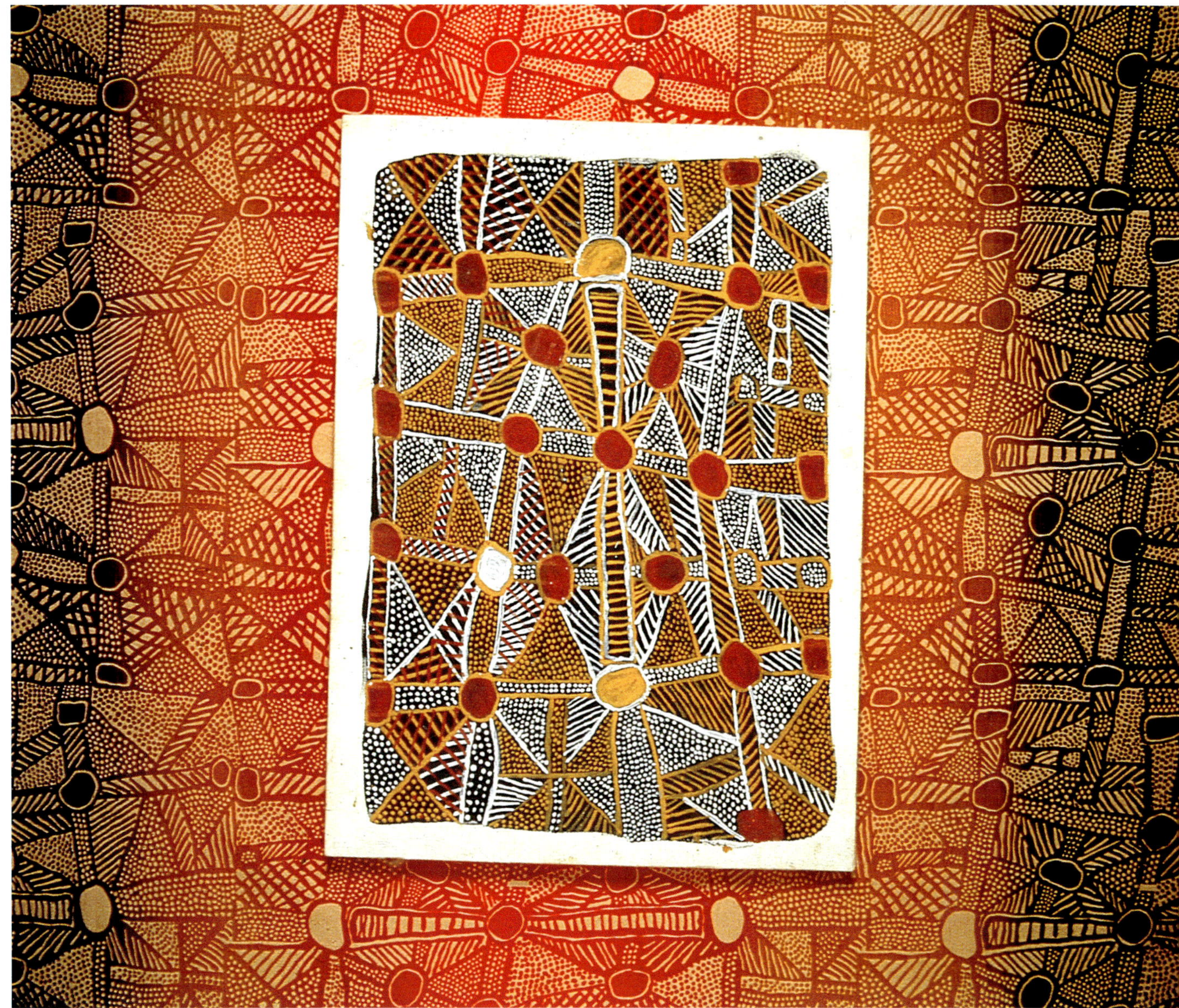

program. The employment of a male coordinator in 1989 led to the involvement of local male artists in what originally had been a women's screenprinting and dressmaking project. The smaller more intimate community meant that screenprinting was never separated from the other arts and crafts, but was literally under the same roof. Bark paintings were stored beneath the fabric print table, while carvings shared the corner of the studio shed with silk-screens. This led to an interaction between younger screenprinters and painters with older traditional artists, which produced fruitful results that might not have

occurred in a community fractured by accelerating acculturation and alcohol-related problems. Such interchange was particularly important when many of the traditional occasions for passing on skills, such as during preparation for ceremonies, had largely vanished. The involvement of several generations of Tiwi artists in the production of fabric designs at Milikapiti meant the emergence of several distinct styles of fabric in the early 1990s. This is clearly exemplified when comparing the work of Nancy Henry Ripijingimpi (deceased), an older woman artist, with younger artists such as Raelene Kerinauia or Ray Bush who were

Jilamara (Design) painting by Nancy Henry Ripijingimpi, 1991, ochres on canvas, placed on textile length (behind) with design based on painting, 1995, screenprinted cotton (photo Penelope Clay, collection Powerhouse Museum, courtesy Powerhouse Museum).

working at Jilamara Arts and Crafts at this time.

Nancy Henry's designs, with their contrasting variations of lines and dots, were eminently suitable for the screenprint medium. She was among the last artists on Bathurst or Melville islands who work in a style that was clearly in touch with pre-contact ceremonial art. Her motifs were those that were once used in a variety of forms on *tuttini* funerary poles and *wangatunga* bark baskets. More importantly, they were created with a knowledge of belief stories and ritual protocol now largely lost. This imbued her designs with an authority and clear spiritual context.

The younger artists, both in their silk-screen designs and paintings, used the same distinctively Tiwi *mulpinyini amintiya pwanga,* lines and dots, more often in symmetrical combinations that contextualise contemporary depictions of ceremonial objects or bushtucker. This superimposition of a figurative image over a background pattern is nowadays considered by local artists to be a traditional Tiwi style, but more likely reflects recent contact with neighbouring Arnhem Land culture.

This increasing concern with decorative images and technical refinement is a widespread trend in the area of contemporary Aboriginal art that continues to identify itself as traditional. Perhaps it has as much to do with lifestyle changes, and a growing consciousness that perceive that element of spontaneity so essential to any performance, sacred or otherwise.

With the introduction of textile printing in Tiwi communities, the practice of using felt pens or brushes for preparatory drawings and hand-cut stencil film for developing the screen images tended to remove the dynamic elements from Tiwi art, and emphasise instead the bold decorative patterns that perhaps were more to the expectations of a public purchasing Indigenous fabric art. The conscious early decision by Jilamara Arts and Crafts screenprinters to adapt certain designs directly from local ochre paintings revealed aspects of this art hitherto unexplored, and created a source of inspiration for local painters and designers alike.

The resulting fabric image conveyed a freshness and spontaneity

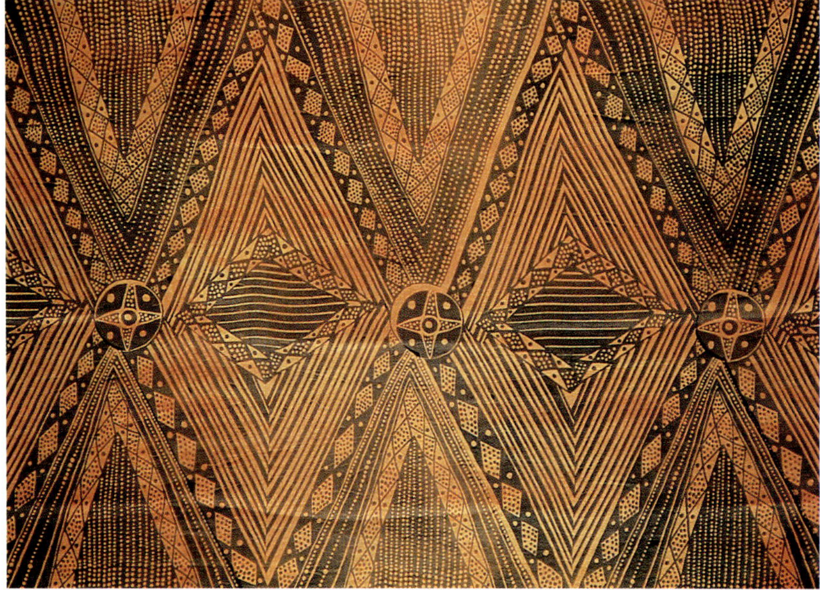

Jinani, Aileen Henry Kumarjino, Jilamara Arts and Crafts Association, 1990, screenprinted dyes on silk, 400 cm x 92 cm (collection Powerhouse Museum, courtesy Powerhouse Museum).

closer in many ways to the heart of the Tiwi artistic tradition than one initially drawn laboriously in pen or pencil on paper. Central to this is the recognition that the power of much Tiwi art rests in the personal way each artist uses and responds to an established vocabulary of symbols, lines and dots. This is heightened, furthermore, by each painter's idiosyncratic use of ochres. Any adaptation of a Tiwi design to a fabric print would suffer a loss if, in the process, sometimes seemingly arbitrary aspects of personal style were detached from the generalised traditional image. By the mid-1990s at Milikapiti, as on many other communities, there had commenced a general trend away from screenprinting towards the production of one-off artworks that could attract higher prices than a length of printed fabric. Yet the introduction of textile printing at Milikapiti had provided a crucial training resource for the younger generation of Tiwi, and subsequently became the fundamental impetus for an artistic revival there. These locally printed fabrics had been the only immediate daily contact point with an articulated style of Tiwi art and, for many beginner artists, profoundly influenced their perceptions of traditional aesthetics.

Whatever boundaries might have been crossed at Jilamara Arts and

Crafts Association between painters and screenprinters had nothing to do with the whitefella concepts of artist and craftsperson. If anything, it is about the traditional divisions in Tiwi society between the hierarchies of age and sex, kinship obligation and avoidance. Perhaps this will be ultimately the most rewarding and difficult lesson for white Australian artists to learn from Indigenous traditions: that like so much else— hunting or fishing, attending funerals or playing cards under the mangoes, playing football or just gossiping and relaxing together—art and craft is just something one does.

Based on an article by the same author first published in 1992 in *Artlink,* volume 1, number 12, pages 59–60.

my soul likes to work

making a living from fabric

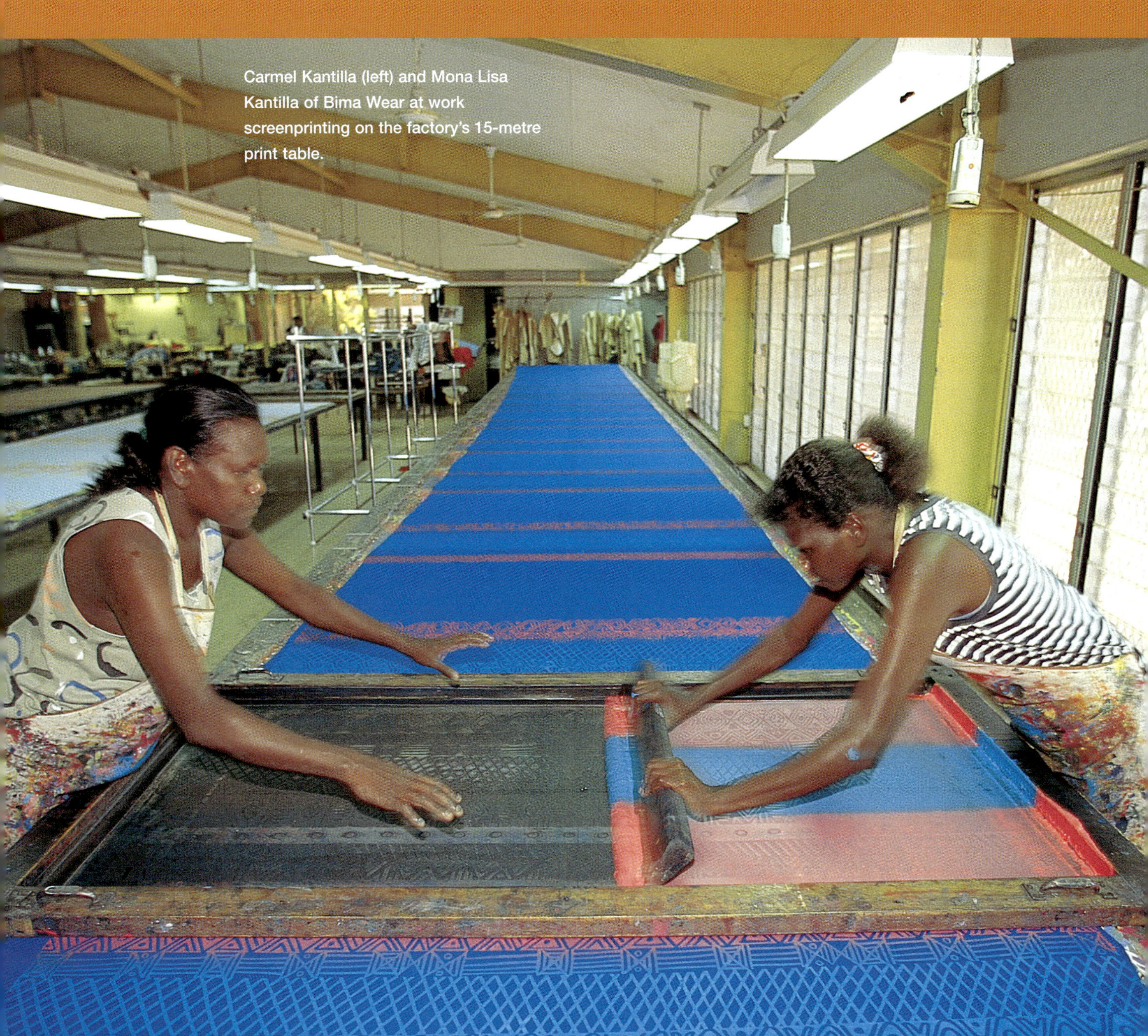

Carmel Kantilla (left) and Mona Lisa Kantilla of Bima Wear at work screenprinting on the factory's 15-metre print table.

My spirit likes to paint

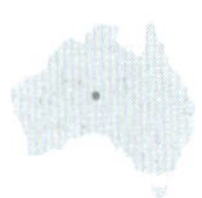

Matjangka (Nyukana) Norris,
Kaltjiti Arts and Crafts

*Ngayulu warkarinyi, palu waaka
nyangatja ngayulu puṯu wantinyi, panya
waaka nyangatja paluru wiṟu, T-shirt
palyantjaku, material palyantjaku, ka
nganaṉa puṯu waaka wiya nyinanyi,
munu mukurunganyi, raiki tjuṯa
palyantjikitja, panya waaka wiṟu*

*nguwanpa wantikatinytjaku wiya,
nganaṉa puṯu wantikatinyi. Ka nganaṉa
tjuṯa palyantjikitja mukuringanyi, panya
kutjupa tjuṯa nganaṉa katinyi Muṯitjulula
kutu munu sellamilani nyara palula.
Rawangku nganaṉa alatji palyaningi,
munu pitjala piṟuku palaṟa katinyi . . .*

*Nyangatja wiṟu mulapa, waaka wiṟu.
Tjinguṟu ngayulu nyanga palula
nintiringama munu ngayulu nyanga
palunya rawalta waakarinyi panya
waaka wiṟu nguwanpa nyangatja panya
puṯu wantikatingu waaka nyanga
palunya.*

I've been working here, it's the kind of
work I couldn't give up because it's so
good to make things like T-shirts and
lengths of cloth. We love it, and we
can't sit down and do nothing, we
couldn't give it up. We like to make a
lot of batik, and we have been doing it
for a long time. We take our craft to
Muṯitjulu and sell it there and then we
come back and make more . . .

This is fantastic work. I want to
gain a high level of skill and stay here
for a long time. I couldn't leave such
good work.

Translated from Pitjantjatjara by Suzy Bryce.

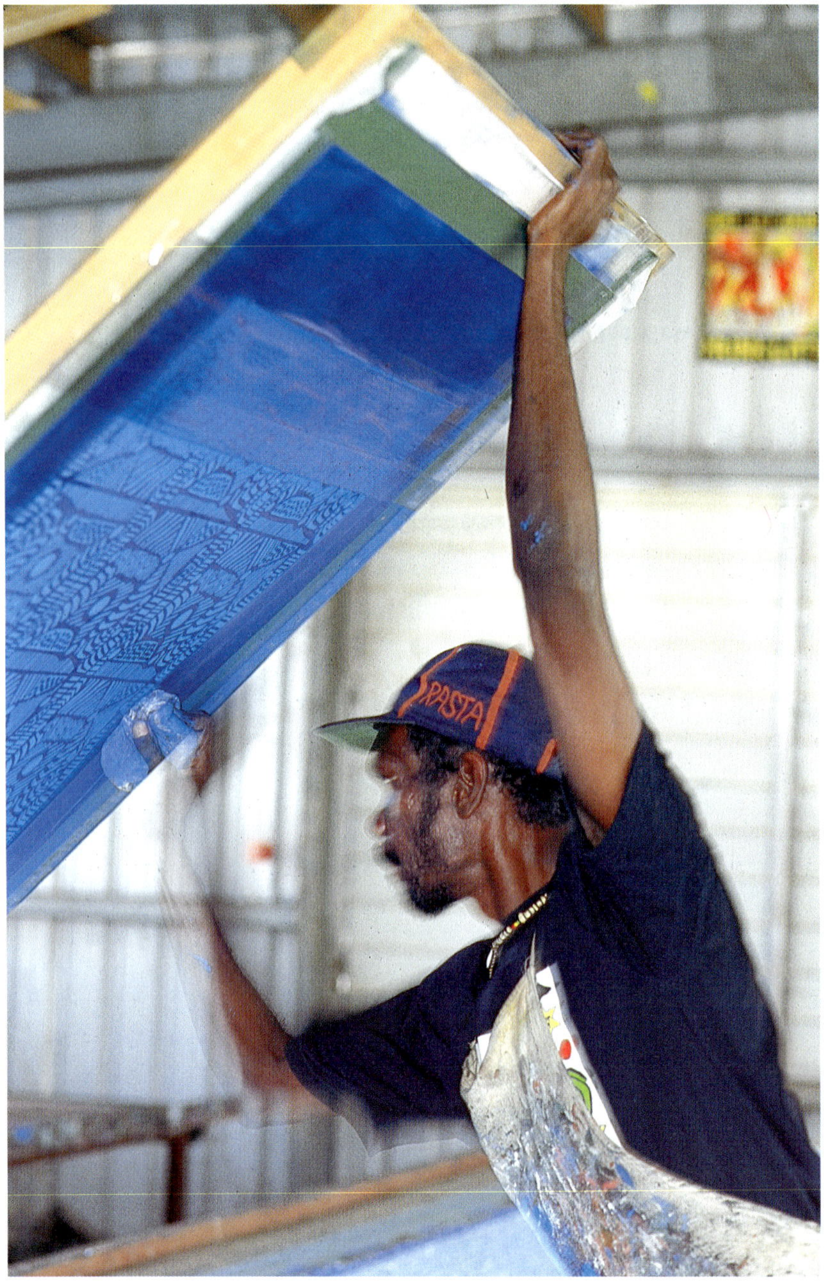

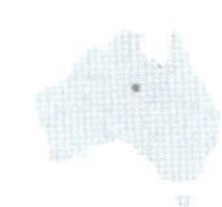

Gloria Apetyarr, Urapuntja Artists

*Inkwerelhek ingkwernetyek. Utneng
ilkelhek ingkwernetyek batik warrk-
irretyek. Akwetant anem ingkwernenh
ingkwernenh, utneng atyenh, you know,
I like work. Utneng atyenhan ilkelhetyel
warrkekarl. Pwarrkarl irrerlanem war
anerlanemel. War anerlanem pwarrkarl
irrem.*

*Atherram anwantherr
ingkwernetyel: batik, canvas.
Anwantherr atherrek warrkirretyel,
batik, painting. Atherrek. Akweteth.
Canvas and silk, batik, silk rantey batik
anyent ra. Well, atherrek anwantherr
warrk-irrem. Arrularl start-irrek, batik
anwenantherr ipmetyakenhel
ingkwerneynetyel. Atherr-antey, arrularl
start-irrek batik-angwel angwel. Well,
we can't leavem. Some people want to
buy batik or painting, atherr.*

I like to paint. My spirit likes to paint
and work at batik. I always paint and
paint and paint, and my spirit, you
know, I like to work. My soul likes
work. You get tired if you just sit down
and do nothing. Sitting down doing
nothing makes you tired.

We paint both: batik and canvas.
We work for both batik and painting.

Tiwi Design printer Osmond Kantilla
prepares a silk-screen for printing.

Always. Canvas and silk—silk that is batik. Well, we work for both. That batik that we started a long time ago, we haven't given it up, and we keep batiking. We started that dear old batik a long time ago. Well, we can't leave it. Some people want to buy batik or painting, both of them.

Translated from Anmatyerr by Jenny Green.

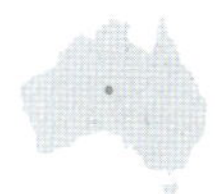

ALISON (MILYIKA) CARROLL, ERNABELLA ARTS
Ngayulu mukuringanyi rawa waakarintjikitja, waaka wiru mulapa. Minyma ini ngananya, Atipalkunya, paluru rawatu waakarinyi, kuula wiyaringkula paluru tjartaringu, munu kuwari waakarinyi. Pulkara waakaripai paluru, tjuta palyalpai scarfa tjuta, raiki wara, pulka mulapa paluru palyalpai, mapalku wiyalpai paluru.

Nyukananya panya iriti waakarinyi, palumpa year tjuta mulapa, nyangangka waakaripai tjinguru kungkawaranguru paluru waakaringu, ngananala wanala wiyalku, nganana tjitji tjuta nyinanytja nyanga paluru waakarinyi, munu paluru kuwari waakarinyi, pamparingkula waakarinyi alatjitu, munu wiru tjuta palumpa, batik paluru wiru mulapa palyani, walka wiru.

I want to work here for a long time because it is really enjoyable work. There are women here like Atipalku Intjalki who have worked here for so long. When she left school she started

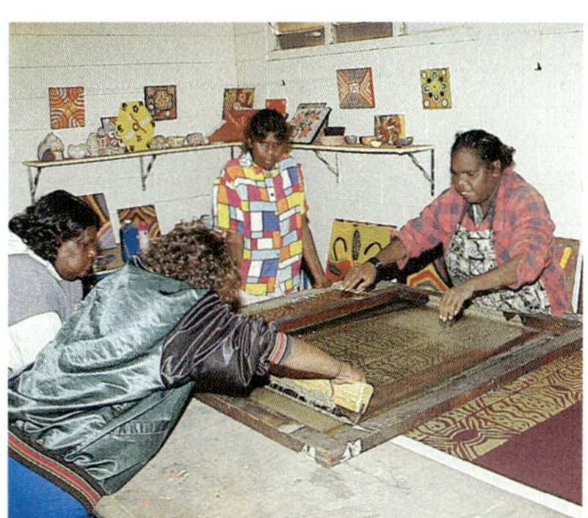

Screenprinting a cotton length at the Pink Palace, the Julalikari Arts and Crafts work area.

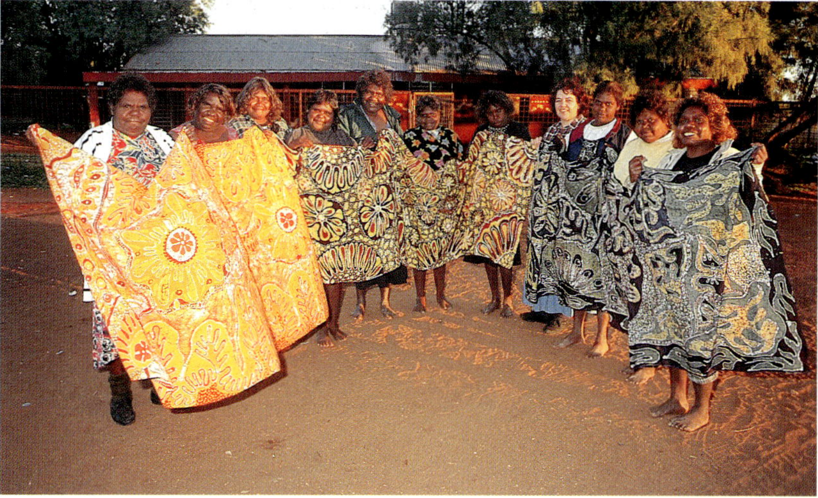

The artists of Kaltjiti Arts and Crafts display their distinctive silk batiks.

here and she is still working. She works very efficiently and makes a lot of scarves and lengths. She really makes a lot of things and finishes them quickly.

Nyukana Baker came to work here a long time ago and she has continued for many years, starting probably when she was a teenager. We are following her example until we finish, and we were just kids when she started. Now she is turning into an older woman, still a batik artist making wonderful designs.

Translated from Pitjantjatjara by Suzy Bryce.

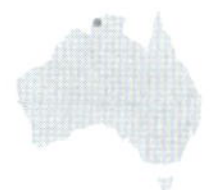

LOLA TYSON, DUNNILLI ARTS
I came to Dunnilli Arts, and I shall still be here when I get a wheelchair.

Working in a fabric workshop at an Aboriginal art centre

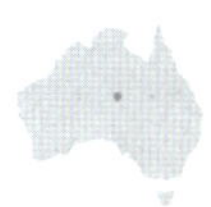

KATHLEEN WALLACE, KERINGKE ARTS
Each coordinator has brought something new to Keringke Arts. They are all so different. Some are artists and some aren't, but they've all been great. It's going really well here now. I'm really happy about that.

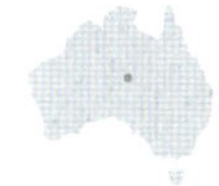

LINDA HERANGI, TITJIKALA WOMEN'S CENTRE
The main thing I do here at Titjikala is to coordinate the women and the programs they are doing. Our main funding comes from Aged Care through the council, so I spend half my time keeping the Aged Care going, and then I divide up the rest of my time between the creche, women's centre business, and other CDEP projects. Each group that I support has an Aboriginal supervisor but it still takes up a lot of time.

I bring women out here occasionally to do workshops when there is funding available. I don't have time to sit with the women and do artwork, even though I would really like to.

The women are waiting for their new arts and crafts centre. The planning is all set and the design is approved and the money is in the bank. We have been talking about a co-op for the women and setting up a home page for art and craft. We need to find funding for a coordinator, even a part-time one.

I enjoy taking the women to the markets in Alice Springs where we sell their work. Being amongst it is really satisfying. We sell artefacts and beads, silks, batiks and canvas.

The CDEP employees use the art room in the mornings, and in the afternoons women come in and do their own thing. We supply everything and when it is sold, we split the money in half, but we hope to have a better system when the new arts centre opens. We have a gallery included in the plans for the new building. Tourists come through on their way to Chambers Pillar.

Desart has been out a few times and they help us by phone. They understand a lot of legal and other things that I'm not really sure about. They plan to set up a portfolio of the artists' work. We go to the AGMs and it's good because I get to meet everyone else.

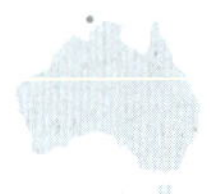

OSMOND KANTILLA, TIWI DESIGN

I started at Tiwi Design in 1983 as a trainee. At first I wondered if I could do it, I felt a bit unsure and nervous. I made a few mistakes, too. Since then I have seen a lot of changes, new ways of printing have come in and we have tried to keep up with different changes. I really enjoyed the three months I did in 1986 at Redback Graphics in Sydney with Ray Young [a trainer at Tiwi Design]. It was a chance to learn more techniques and talk with other printers. One of the designs that we are printing today, I did while I was in Sydney; it's called Pandanus. I love printing fabric, cards, tea-towels, towels, T-shirts. We print two- or three-colour designs all based on Tiwi culture. Artists come in and do new designs which we put onto screens in a darkroom. We get some strange requests at times, especially when people want their clothes printed at the last minute for ceremony.

I'm the main printer now and am teaching some of the younger boys to do it. We have six students coming over from the school every morning. It takes a bit of time for them to get used to it. We should be training more young people to work here, especially linking in with the school or attracting people who are on the dole. Some young people only play on the pool table, or drink too much beer; instead they could be having a future fabric printing. If I get sick, our organisation is in trouble, so we really need to train new printers urgently.

The big problem for us is that we can't stop to train new people, because we have to keep working to make money. A few times before, we have tried to train people, but then urgent orders have come in and the young people get tired of waiting around. Learning to print properly takes a long time.

To sell our fabric we have to promote it outside. Sometimes we are so busy keeping up with the everyday, we can't even stop to promote our fabric. We have our special shops that know us, but we need to get more known, possibly overseas.

Because our fabric is hand done, we can never make any one thing exactly the same as another. Buyers want perfection, but they must realise that it is hand done and that is different, plus it is Tiwi art and that is what makes it special. It's not some modern mass-produced thing.

Sometimes we have problems printing. You have to wait a long time for the ink to dry during the wet season. It gets very hot here then as well. In the

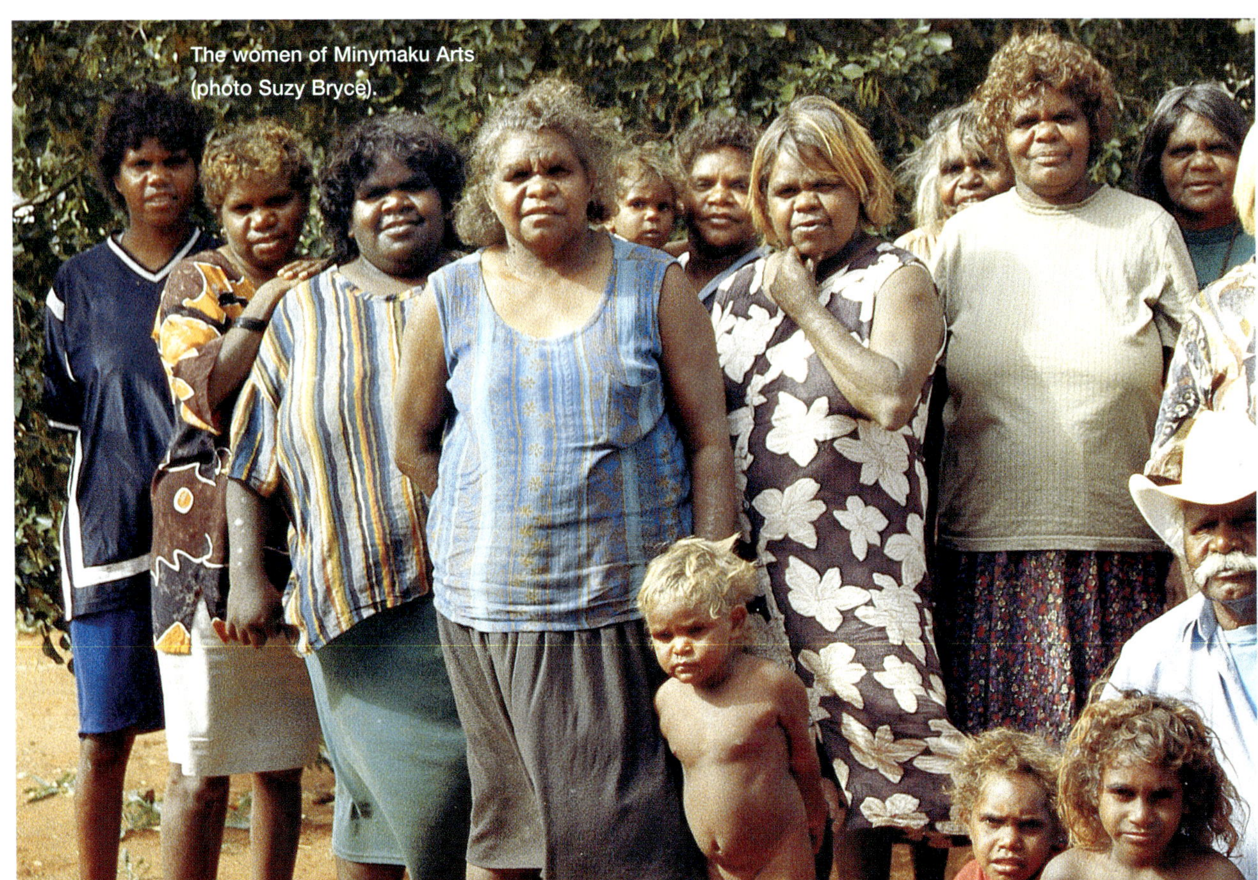
The women of Minymaku Arts (photo Suzy Bryce).

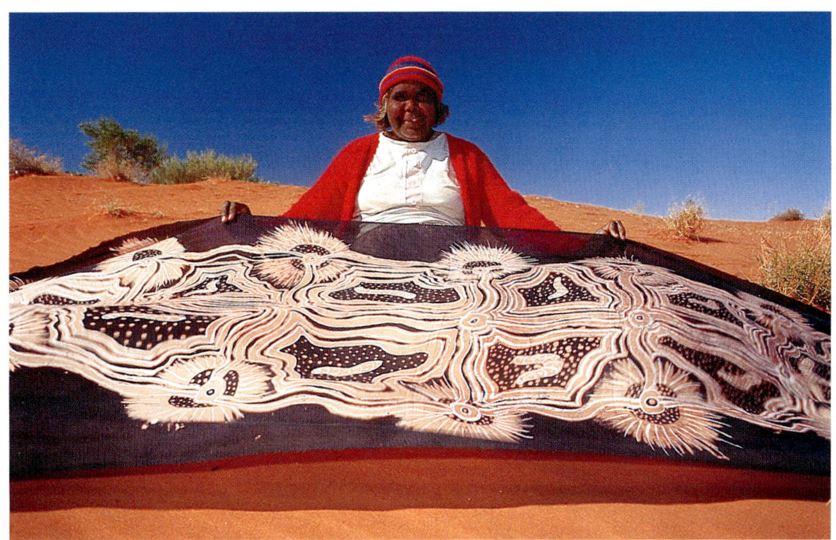

Doris Thomas of Titjikala Women's Centre spreads a silk batik to dry in the desert sun.

dry season it dries too quickly, the ink on the screen dries too. I want it to keep going though, it's a good place and good for our community.

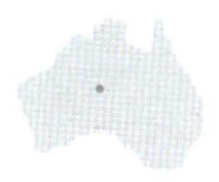

MONA MITAKIKI, MINYMAKU ARTS
Ngayulu mukuringanyi waaka craft room-ngka munu nganana pulkara waakarinyi panya nganana machine-ngku palyantja wiya waaka ngaa panya marangku palyani batiki, nyaa batik panya canting mantjini, munu piruku oil panya munu piruku brush-ngka walkatjunanyi nganana marangku palyani. Waaka pulka nyara paluru. Tjuta ngaranyi. Nganana mukuringanyi waaka paluru, rawa nganampa alatjitu ngarantjaku.

Nganana apamilanyi, nganana kutjupa kutjupa tjuta wiya, ngaltutjara. Waaka pulka palyani palu nganampa wiya. Ka nganana mukuringkupai ngananya apamilantjaku nganampa wiyaringanyi, silk material wiyaringanyi, munu cotton material wiyaringanyi, brush, uwankara wiyaringanyi, ka nganana payamilantjaku putu kulilpai. Nganana waaka wiru mulapa.

I really like working in the craft room and we work really hard. We don't have machines to print our fabrics, we do it all by hand. We do batik, do oil paint with brushes, we do it all by hand. It is a lot of work. There are a lot of us who work here. We really like this work. We want to keep doing this work of ours.

We need people to help us. We do not have all the skills to run a craft room, particularly the administration. We work very hard but don't know everything. We need help when materials get low, someone to order silk, cotton, brushes, wax—everything. We don't understand the systems to purchase these things. We do very good work.

Translated from Pitjantjatjara by Suzy Bryce.

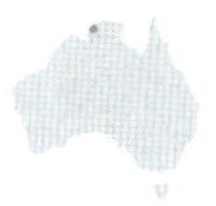

MALINDA FLYNN, DUNNILLI ARTS
It has always been a dream of mine to open my own business, and now that I have teaching and textile arts skills, I feel I have made a step in the right direction.

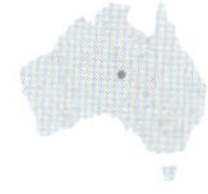

DORIS THOMAS, TITJIKALA WOMEN'S CENTRE
We might do more printing when they put the new building up—women's centre—then we can work. And the tourists can come around and get things. Some tourists said that they heard about us in Alice Springs and they saw our work and they liked it. They came down to see us and find out how we make our things. They were watching us doing our work. *Paluru tjana wangkangu nyura wirura palyanu, nganana nyangu*—they said that they liked watching us to see how we did it. Some were from America and Switzerland and also Germany.

This batik here, *ngayulu tjunu piranpa tjuta nyakuntjaku, ngayulu tjunu maku munu nyangatja tjanpi*—I did this batik for white people to look at. I put in witchetty grubs and spinifex.

My job is supervisor—lots of things to do. I make batik and T-shirt and big sheet and bags. *Ngayulu mayatja nyinanyi, paluru tjana palyani tjunguringkula, ngayulu palunya tjananya learn-milanu, palyantjaku*—I'm the Aboriginal boss here. The women sit down together and make things and I have shown them how to make things.

Translated from Pitjantjatjara by Suzy Bryce.

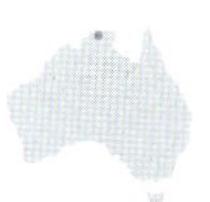

ISIAH NAGURRGURRBA,
INJALAK ARTS AND CRAFTS ASSOCIATION
Wendy Kennedy was the one that was asking people here who was interested in screenprinting. So, we had two groups: Wendy used to work with the ladies, and Ray Young used to work with us, the blokes. We used to do two-metre fabrics. The ladies used to do shoulder bags.

Wendy asked for funding to work with the screenprinting, from Adult Education, and we said, 'Kamak—good, we will do screenprinting.' So, we got more skills, because we didn't do it before in this community. We started doing screenprinting. Wendy knew Ray Young was working at Bathurst Island, and she made a phone call from here to Bathurst, and he said, 'I'll come there and teach those boys

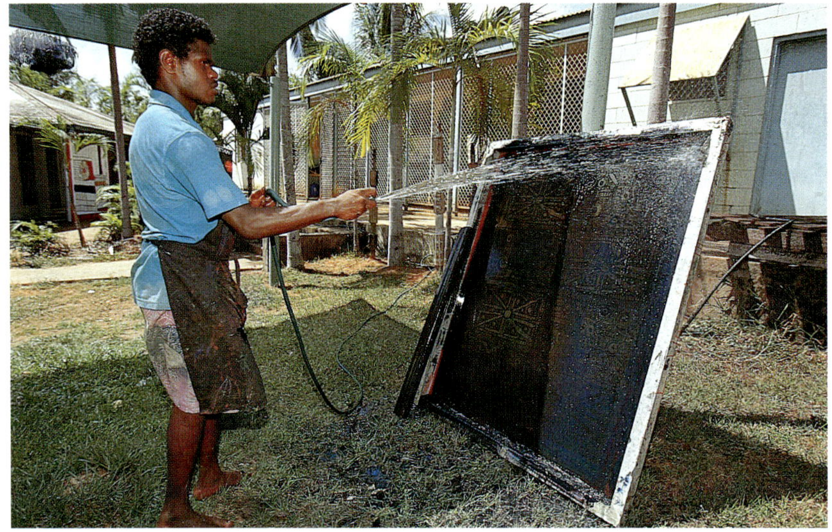

Leon Puruntatameri Jnr washes down a silk-screen at Jilamara Arts and Crafts Association on Melville Island.

skills.' He came with his wife and kids.

I started in 1985, screenprinting with Ray Young. I started working with Gabriel [Maralngurra], Neville, Michael, my brother Patrick, Barry, Kennedy, Ted and Harold. We took all those boys and we first started working in that old shed down near the council office. We didn't have any building—it was really small. We used to do fabrics—not big ones—tablecloths, T-shirts. We asked the resource centre for equipment. They gave us tables and chairs and stuff. We used to make our own screens. Ray used to help us. We had glass and we used to expose the screens from the sun. Not like now.

Wendy was asking traditional owners if we could put up a building for Bining [Aboriginal] people to work in. She asked the traditional owners and they said, 'Kamak'. We asked ATSIC and they gave us $100,000 to build this building. We designed this building. The builders worked here from Darwin—came here to decide which way this building was going to be facing. Wendy and Ray and the traditional owners said this building was going to be facing Injalak escarpment. When tourists come, we'll do screenprinting and T-shirts and

show them it's named after this hill, because there's a lot of rock art there. We are really interested in getting rock art paintings and using the designs for T-shirts.

We got that woman design— Yingana, creation mother—from up there. We took photos and brought it here, and Ray Young made that creation image. (Yingana was travelling, put those kids everywhere.) Ray brought a lot of equipment from his place—from Redback Graphics— and brought it all here. We were going really good. We didn't have any manager, used to only have Ray Young, he was the only one. And Wendy was busy working with those daluk [women]. She used to make bags for us.

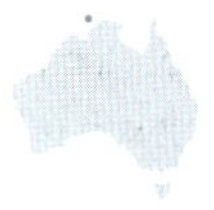

Tara Munkanome, Bima Wear

I started working here in 1980. Marie McMahon came over and taught us screenprinting onto fabric. We did batik for a little while, but I prefer the fabric printing.

We have four tables here. One seven metres, one seven-and-a-half metres, one nine metres and one—the biggest—fourteen metres. We all do the printing, two ladies at a time, across the table. It's a two-person job. We put our designs onto the screens

using rubylith film [see glossary on page 87], cut to follow the design. Then we expose them. We've fixed up one of the rooms to be the darkroom. Our designs are all done here: one's of cemetery poles, bushtucker, mango fruit. My cousin came here, too, and she did one based on Tiwi dancing. We print one screen over the top of a dyed background; we put four different inks at a time along the bottom of the screen to get a rainbow effect. They're very bright.

We also do sewing here using an overlocker. We make clothes for all the special occasions here, like for a funeral or for a concert. The community buys them.

Sometimes young girls come in for training, but not much, we're waiting for them to come.

We had a big exhibition in 1987 in Adelaide that I went to. We made fabric for that, and some T-shirts and painting. We still do this work. We sell most of it at the Darwin airport.

We have a president and a vice-president and a committee, and we meet every little while to make decisions about this place. The men mostly work at Tiwi Design, but we have some women that work there, too. There are only women working here, that's the proper way for us.

The Ernabella Arts Trading Company: Reflections on potential lost and found

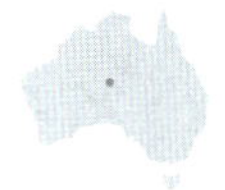

Louise Partos

Since 1988 Ernabella Arts has been producing screenprinted fabric lengths of high quality. In 1993 the artists completed a number of commissions for furnishing fabrics; clients included the Alukura Birthing Centre in Alice Springs, Uluru National Park Offices, The Underground Motel at Coober Pedy, and Community Aid Abroad. That year, Marie Warren, assisted by

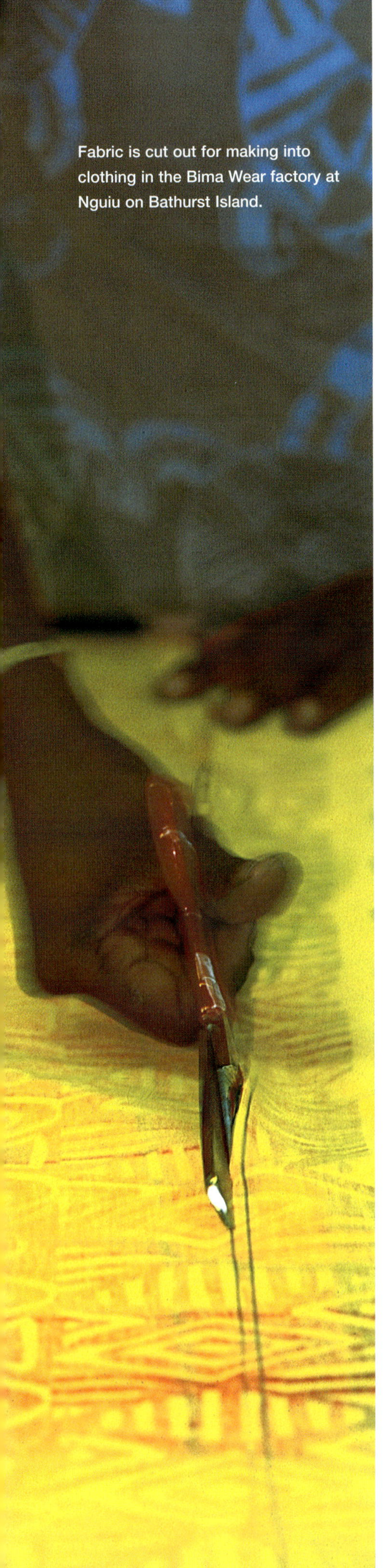

Fabric is cut out for making into clothing in the Bima Wear factory at Nguiu on Bathurst Island.

Vera Williams and Freda Shannon, printed over 2500 metres of fabric.

Following this success, investigations were made into the feasibility of the large-scale manufacture of Ernabella designs. In August 1996 the Ernabella Arts Trading Company was launched at the Fifth International Federation of Women Entrepreneurs Conference and Trade Event in Adelaide. Despite great hopes for its success, the Trading Company closed on 18 June 1997.

There were many reasons for this, and the Ernabella Arts Trading story highlights valuable lessons which must be learnt before proceeding with an affiliated screenprint-manufacturing company located at a distance. There is a definite market for Aboriginal-designed fabrics, but communication, planning, research and funding are essential ingredients for a prosperous business.

Communication is essential as goals must be common and well understood. All people involved must be working towards the benefit of the organisation. As with any business, personal issues must either be resolved or a change of personnel is required. Communication needs to be reciprocal rather than hierarchical. The Ernabella Arts Trading Company was broken into three constituencies: the decision-making side of the company was based in Ernabella; the printing happened in Sydney; and the accounting took place in Adelaide. The fractured communication resulting from such disparate locations was the single largest cause of internal conflict, and certainly contributed to the closure of the company.

Production issues and marketing strategies were never resolved. Any organisation needs to plan its strategic direction so that it can measure its performance against defined goals, and compare itself objectively with similar businesses. The decision to manufacture an Ernabella Arts Trading Company fashion range deviated from the original strength of the company: screenprinted lengths of fabric. At the

time of the launch in Adelaide, Ernabella Arts' fashion range was still in an embryonic form. Due to dwindling funds, only small runs of each item were manufactured. Prices were high and from the beginning the clothing range was not competitive.

We found that it was not wise to produce a wide range of items in the first year. Instead it seemed better to concentrate on a few bread and butter pieces, such as small items of clothing and domestic objects, and then gradually introduce new items into the range. We found that visually stimulating packaging is required and products must be well targeted and promoted.

Ernabella Arts decided not to print offshore but to concentrate on promoting and marketing an all-Australian-made product. However, prices were high and could have been cut considerably if the decision had been made to print overseas. Australian-produced screenprinted clothing is always in direct competition with cheaper imports.

One issue which haunted the Trading Company was the perception that Ernabella's designs were not recognisably 'Aboriginal'. The market demand is for Aboriginal designs but our product was perceived as being outside its boundaries. This highlights a need in the wider community for information on, and exposure to, Aboriginal art which is not dot paintings. A greater number of Aboriginal screenprinted designs in the marketplace and intelligent marketing and promotion would have greatly assisted the product.

Manufacturing away from a community base is a realistic alternative for Aboriginal communities in which large-scale screenprinting is not viable. There are successful larger businesses, such as Tiwi Design; however, unless staffing and skill levels are assured, it is a risky venture. There must be a guarantee that orders can be regularly processed and the product supplied to clients. Yet there are many

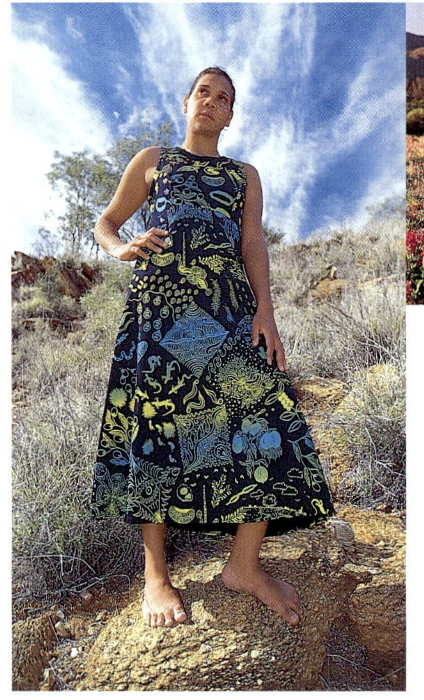

Left: Ernabella Trading Company cotton dress modelled by Amelia Forrester.
Below: Ernabella Trading Company deckchairs: (left to right) *Nguratjara (Visions of Home)*, designed by Ernabella artists, printed by Marie Warren; *Kililpi Tjuta (Many Stars)*, designed by Nyuwara Tapaya, printed by Marie Warren; *Maku (Witchetty Grubs)*, designed by Vera Mbitjana Williams, printed by Marie Warren.

cultural factors that can hamper productivity. Businesses must be both flexible enough to accommodate cultural requirements, and able to compete in a marketplace which may not be tolerant of cultural proprieties.

The ceaseless desire for 'authenticity' governs much of Aboriginal art production. Off-site manufacture, for example, means that a product cannot be advertised as totally Aboriginal made. Another drawback of printing away from communities is a loss of control. Artists may feel removed from the decision-making process, and the results. It is essential that artists have an input into business operations and, to that end, small business training recently occurred at Ernabella.

A well-planned creative business venture can, through exhibitions and sales, aid in elevating the status of Aboriginal people, assist in raising self-esteem and pride in a community, and alleviate financial dependency on systems that are inflexible and unsuitable. Financial and cultural independence are aims of any Aboriginal organisation. An off-site manufacturing company is perhaps one way to realise this.

Hot Wax: The Utopia–Yogyakarta Project

MARY-LOU NUGENT

For two weeks in March 1999 in Alice Springs two artists from Java and eight artists from Utopia, 250 km north-east of Alice Springs, worked together on a collaboration of ten large pieces of cloth. They were making batik lengths to exhibit at the Third Asia–Pacific Triennial of Contemporary Art at the Queensland Art Gallery in September 1999.

The artists had a longstanding relationship. Five years earlier, in 1994, a project was organised involving Java batik artists Nia Fliam and Agus Ismoyo, and Utopia artists Lena Apwerl, Ada Nora Apetyarr, Hilda Apwerl, Myrtle Apetyarr, Violet Apetyarr, Glory Angal, Joy Apetyarr, Rosemary Apetyarr and Barbara Weir. With anthropologist Jeannie Devitt, linguist and artist Jenny Green, and batik artist James Bennett, the group had travelled to the Brahma Tirta Sari Studio in Indonesia for two weeks'

study of batik *cap* and to review their dyeing technique. Back in Darwin, on viewing the cloths created during this workshop, the Museum and Art Gallery of the Northern Territory immediately expressed interest in buying a large number of them. This evolved into a travelling exhibition, Hot Wax, which included the works of the Utopia women, Agus Ismoyo, Nia Fliam, James Bennett and Jenny Green. The exhibition travelled throughout the Asia–Pacific region from 1995–96.

In 1999 Nia and Ismoyo were invited to exhibit in the Third Asia–Pacific Triennial of Contemporary Art. Based on the success of Hot Wax, they proposed a collaborative project with Utopia. As Nia and Ismoyo said: 'For us, this was a new development in our connection to these women. We saw it as an experiment, because at Brahma Tirta Sari Studio we have been working collaboratively for over fifteen years; but we had never extended this creative approach to include artists from outside our studio.'

In 1999 the artists from Utopia travelled to Alice Springs to work side by side, once again, with the Javanese artists. At the start Ismoyo talked of his ideas for the project—a little in English but mainly in Indonesian, with Nia translating to English. He spoke of how he and Nia work together on shared cloth, and how Aboriginal artists work in the same way, sharing canvas. He said that when they were invited to exhibit at the Asia–Pacific Triennial, they knew they would like to do an exhibition of shared works with the artists from Utopia. This was then translated into Anmatyerr by Jenny Green and Barbara Weir. The theme was taken up by the women from Utopia, and ideas flowed back and forth through the different languages. Violet Apetyarr talked about the way she and other artists from Utopia worked:

Law-akert anem anyenterrek anwenantherr, mpwarem, anyenterremel. Rather angetyek ayerrer-they angwenh, anyenterrem. Law-akert-

*rnem antey anyenterremel mpwarem.
Ingkerrek. Law-akert akin
anwekantherrenh. An ikwerareyenh
same one akin anem, Law-akert akin.
Merenp anem ikwerareyenh, merenp
akin anem, anwekantherrenh merenp
akin anem. Law-ek ingkerrek
anyenterremel. Law-ek ingkerrek
apetyemel. Anyenterremel ingkerrek mer
arrpanenh-they. Same one rernem-
apeny akin anyenterrem batik
mpwarerretyek.*

We've still got our Law, and all of us
with the Law got together to make
batik. Those two [Nia and Ismoyo]
brought their things from the north so
that we could get together. Our things
have Law and theirs are the same; they
have Law as well. Theirs comes from
the land, and ours comes from the land
as well. Everybody comes and gathers
together for ceremony. People come
from all over the place. In the same way,
we are getting together to make batik.

The Utopia artists talked about the
imagery they used in their batik. This
ranged from plants and fruits to
symbols denoting places in the
country, including intricate designs
usually painted on the body for
dancing. Well before they had travelled
to Alice Springs, the women of Utopia
had produced new designs as part of
their preparations for the workshop.

Metal *caps* of the artists of Utopia;
central design *Arlewatyerr (Goanna)*,
Hilda Apwerl.

The designs were drawn at the
outstations and faxed to Java where
they were made into *caps,* or metal
stamps. These were subsequently
brought to Australia by Nia and
Ismoyo. Some designs were
sophisticated, others very simple. As
Hilda Apwerl said of this aspect of the
project:

*Ratherr apetyek, anwenantherr apetyek,
anwenekantherrenh, nhenh-arey-
akertarl. Mpwaretyek. Alakenh tyap
anyemayt artekerrel anem, ntang,
atnyem, tyepety, atnem, tyepety
anepanemel. Urtnarl tnem nhenh, mer
anwenekantherrenh. Tyepety apmer ra.
Nhenh apek arnam arlatyey-artek
anteyarl, an nhenhel-arey arlkwetyekarl
urntem, nhenh leaf arlkwetyek.*

Those two came, and we all came, with
these things [our *caps*]. This is where
the witchetty grub is lying in the root,
these are seeds, the witchetty bush,
and the *tyepety* stories [women's stories
drawn on the ground]. Here is the
coolamon and the digging stick. This is
the place called Urtnarletnem. That is
our country, the place called Tyepety.
Here is a plant that is similar to the
pencil yam, and these ones [itchy grubs]
are crawling towards it to eat it, to eat
the leaves.

Nia and Ismoyo also talked about their
textiles: some use traditional figures
from the *wayan kuli,* the puppet
theatre; others use symbolic designs of
water, the spiral nature of life and the
potency of plants.

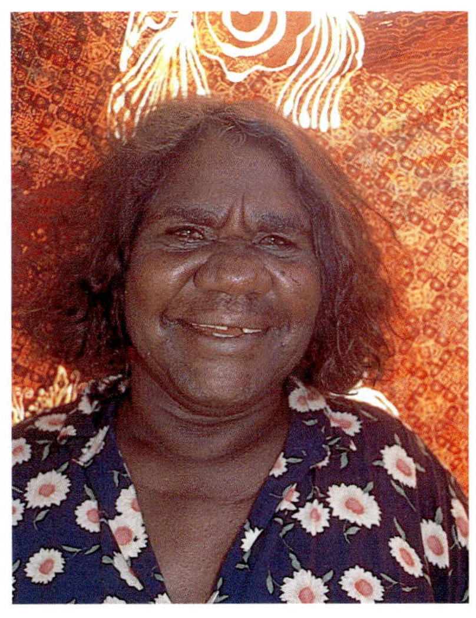

Glory Angal, Urapuntja Artists
(photo Jenny Green).

Then the batik work began. Nia
and Ismoyo had previously worked on
four pieces in Yogyakarta. These were
laid out and discussed, then given to
the women to work on. The women
began their work on four new cloths,
and in time they were handed back for
Nia and Ismoyo to continue with. The
artists discussed their work together
and planned the patterning of *caps*
and handwork to be layered in. Glory
Angal talked about the collaborative
work being done:

*Anwantherr anyenterrek apurt anem
anwantherr warrkerretyel. Mwerrarl
alanh. Arrwekelenyarl anyenterretyart-
apeny. Mwerr way. Anwantherr
ingkwernetyel anyent-antey anem.
Apurtel anem. Ikweratherr then. Cap kel
ikweratherrenh Law-akert. Same one*

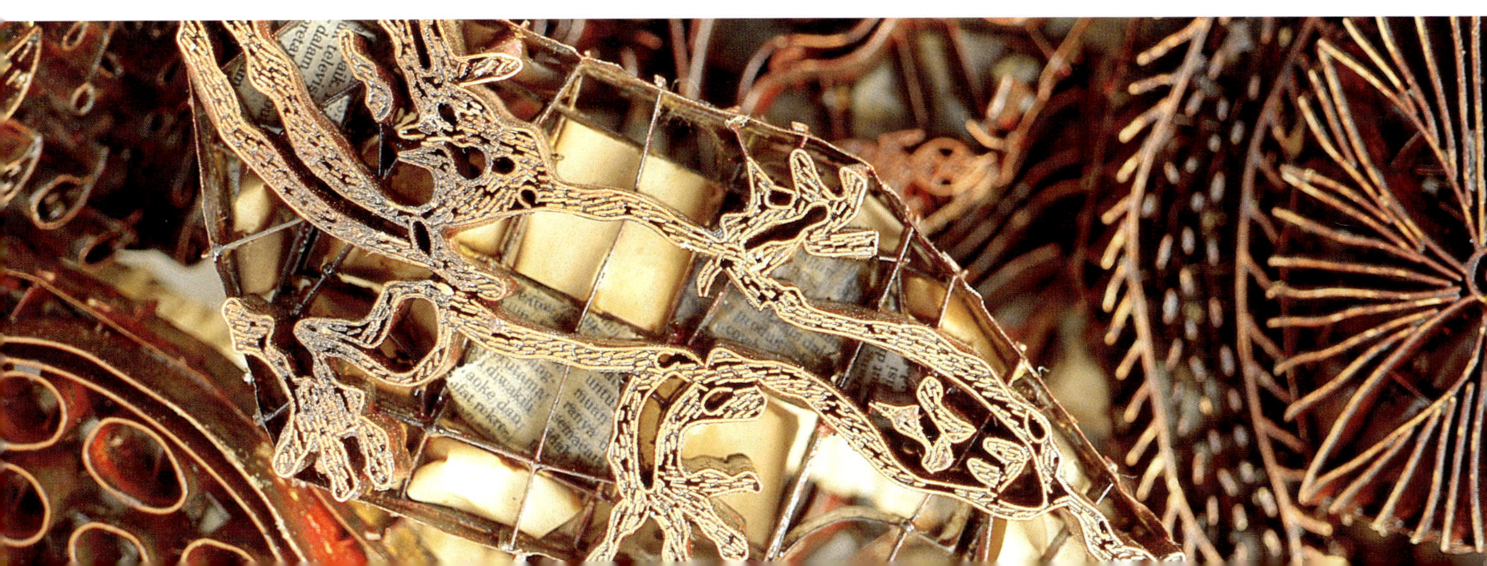

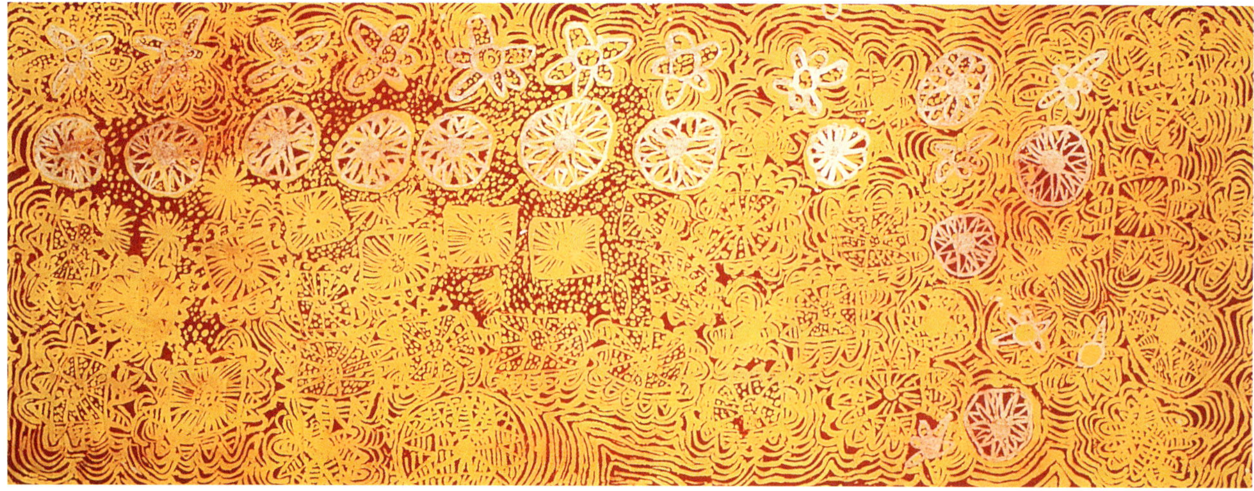

Untitled, Mavis Akemarr, Utopia, silk batik, 3 m length.

akin irrpwerl-rnem apeny arrpem rarey anetyel. Ingkerr-antey. Cap ikwerareyenh mwerr-rnem. Law-akert ikwerarey, arelhekareyenh irrpwerlekareyenh Law-akert akin.

We have all met together to work. It's good, just like the olden-time people used to get together. The proper way. Now we are all doing batik together as one, with those two [Nia and Ismoyo]. Their *caps* have Law in the same way that Aboriginal people have Law. Their *caps* are really good. They have their Law, and Aboriginal people have their own Law as well.

Of the artists working together, Nia Fliam said: 'It forces us to give and take and to gain more than the strengths of one person. We have felt drawn to explore this space of creativity with the women of Utopia. As artists from varied traditional cultural roots, we have sought to come together for a moment in time, as clouds in the sky that are layered for a moment, and then move in their separate directions.'

It is the growth of the relationships between these two groups of artists that has produced a body of work significant in its position of cultural and social exchange. This trading of ideas and technical skills has created a momentum which promises more creative output in the future. The finished works were exhibited at Queensland Art Gallery's 1999 Asia–Pacific Triennial of Contemporary Art and plans are under way to tour the exhibits worldwide.

Based on excerpts from 'The Utopia–Yogya Project Report' written by Suzy Bryce, and a catalogue entry by Nia Fliam and Agus Ismoyo for their exhibition Songs of Peace, Songs of the Ancestors: Batik from the Land. Texts in Anmatyerr collected and translated by Jenny Green.

Selling the fabric

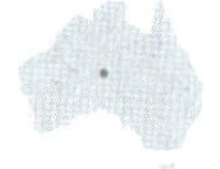

Katey Curley, Kaltjiti Arts and Crafts
Ngayuku raiki wiṟu tjuṯa, walka wiṟu tjuṯatjara palyalpaiṉa. Ka paluṟu tjana ngayuku waaka wiṟu tjuṯa iyalpai ngura kutjupa kutu, Perthalakutu, Adelaidealakutu, Sydneylakutu—wiṟu tjuṯa. Walka tjutju tjuku, kura kura tjuṯa, wantipai. Wiṟu mulapa iyalpai.

I make all kinds of lovely batik with different designs. They send my work to Perth, Adelaide and Sydney—all the good ones, and leave behind any with weak colours or patterns.

Translated from Pitjantjatjara by Suzy Bryce

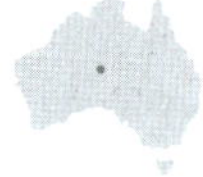

Inawinytji Williamson, Kaltjiti Arts and Crafts
I've got a large batik hanging at Murdoch University in Perth. It is a butterfly story design. Some time ago I went all the way over there and I explained the batik work to a lot of interested people. We've got pieces at The Araluen Centre in Alice Springs and others in Canberra. A while ago we went to Canberra for an exhibition of our work, batik and other things. In Adelaide we have had work in the Newland Gallery. We went down there for the opening of our exhibition. Women from Ernabella went, and we went from Fregon. Others also went from Tjurma Homelands, Mimili and Indulkana. Visitors come to Fregon and our work is on display so that they can buy it. Not long ago we were very busy with a lot of people coming and buying. People come in from Marla Bore, and the police stop in, and then the children from Victor Harbour came to the school. They like to buy the small artefacts.

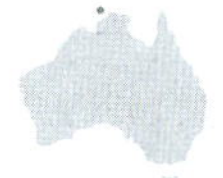

Bernadette Puruntatameri, Munupi Arts and Crafts Centre
We sell our work here on the community. People come in buy fabric and take it to the sewing centre to

have it made up into clothes. During ceremonies people come across from Jilamara Arts and Crafts Association, about an hour and a half away, to buy our work from the store. We do the same when we visit their community.

We sell our material in our little shop at Munupi Arts and Crafts, for our local people so that they can wear our Tiwi design. Then in 1995 Lyn Helms came to work here. She is a good helper, she has helped us organise our work here and have exhibitions interstate. Early this year we went to Sydney to have an exhibition at Datners Gallery in Glebe for our first solo show. We are also travelling to Switzerland with Lyn later this year to have an exhibition in Geneva.

It's very important that people from here have fabric with *jilamara* designs [Tiwi designs] on them, so when ceremony is coming up people can buy them and put colourful material around the burial poles.

Marketing Aboriginal textiles

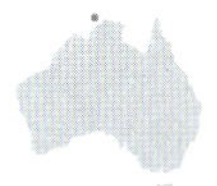

FLICK WRIGHT

Producing and promoting textiles raises a unique set of issues for Aboriginal art centres and their staff. Textiles could be described as the Cinderella of art centres, fighting for recognition as fine art, appealing to a far smaller section of the market than paintings and commanding comparatively tiny prices, yet frequently requiring a higher degree of skill to create than conventional 'fine arts'. It is an irony not lost on the staff who work with textile artists in art centres, watching the act of creation and then attempting to market the finished product.

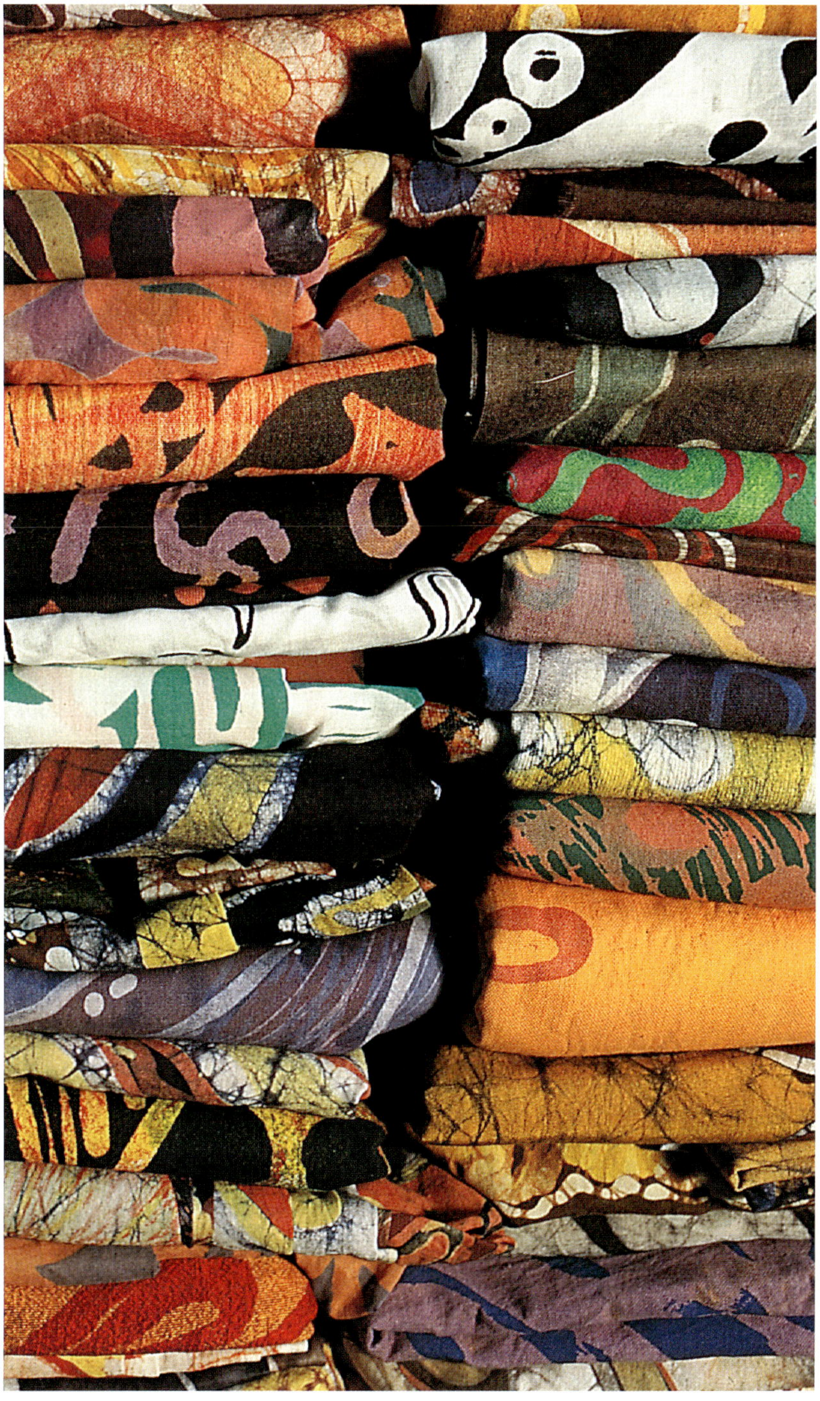

Bold batiks and screenprinted fabrics of Kaltjiti Arts and Crafts, ready for sale.

Talking about 'craft' in relation to Aboriginal art and craft usually refers to the smaller items that do not command sufficient status to be identified as 'art'; they are often produced in significant quantities and frequently presented for sale without the producer being identified. It is a schism that occurs in non-Aboriginal art and craft equally. What is lost is the understanding that the term 'crafts

person' was traditionally, and still is, used to describe an artisan who has achieved a level of proficiency in their craft.

Unlike painting, executing good textile work requires skill that cannot be 'lucked' upon. It is not enough to pick up a brush and dab some wax on a length of fabric to create a batik. Composition is only half the story. Knowledge of dyes and the different effects achieved by varying the shades and intensity of dyes, and how to make beautiful colour combinations by over-dyeing, is at least as important as composition, and gaining competence can take months and years. Important, also, is an understanding of cotton and silk and the way each reacts differently to wax, handling and dyes. At Ernabella, the fine *canting* lines and tiny drops of wax create delicate items of beauty, the linework enhanced by three, four or five separate dyeings. Handpainted silks require extraordinary skill. Anyone who has watched beginners painting on silk for the first time will have a better understanding of how difficult it is to create, for example, the fabulous lengths that emerge from Keringke Arts.

Aboriginal art centre textiles generally fall into two categories: small and cheap or big and expensive. The first group is made up of small, usually wearable, items such as scarves and T-shirts, and the second of 'pieces', the fine-art lengths and commissioned works. Whilst there is a large market for small and cheap products, among art centres it is usually licensed product, rather than handmade, so that it can compete in price with the

manufacturers of mass-produced Aboriginal-inspired, or plagiarised, designs. Fine-art pieces face stiff competition from paintings and sculptures. Ironically, the further a textile moves away from having a function, the more it is perceived to be valuable.

Over a number of years, Keringke Arts developed increasingly intricate handpainted silk scarves for a small number of retailers. The women had begun painting on T-shirts, shoes and miscellaneous prefabricated textile products and graduated to silk. The scarves were beautiful and were able to be priced relatively cheaply because of a government subsidy to artists. Demand for the items became huge and there were a constant number of back orders from retailers. Nowadays, however, the production of such articles has become rarer as the women realise that for the same amount of effort and skill they can paint in other media, and make more money.

Anne Phelan, who owns Framed Art Gallery in Darwin, has been selling textiles alongside Aboriginal and non-Aboriginal artworks and craft for years and is a long-time collector of textiles. 'There is a definite market for textiles,' says Anne. 'People are drawn to fabric textiles.' But she notes a contrast between the sales of fabrics by the

metre and lengths of silk. 'The fragility of silk lengths can scare people. I did a show of batik silk lengths last year and the art centre coordinator said, "Don't hang it near the window, it might fade. Don't hang it near the bricks, it might catch on them." In reality, who really hangs silk textiles in their own homes?' As a textile fiend who has two wonderful large fabric screenprints from Ngukurr, silk batiks form Tiwi Design and a number of Yuendumu batiks from the mid-1980s in a box under my bed, I can readily sympathise. Further, she noted that connoisseurs and collectors will buy such lengths, but 'it's hard to educate people to pay $1000 for a piece of fabric'. Framed Gallery carries hand-screenprinted fabrics on the roll from the Tiwi Islands and other Top End centres such as Injalak Arts and Crafts Association. 'The northern communities understand the importance of a wholesale to retail price structure for a retail outlet so that I can buy the fabrics at a price that can stand doubling. We had some dupion silk from Injalak last year and were buying at $40 and retailing for $80 per metre. The public loved it—didn't bat an eyelid. As long as the quality of printing and fabric is there.' Anne was disappointed that some small silk scarves she bought from a Central Australian art centre did not cope with the retail mark-up and none had sold in a year.

Very few Australian galleries and shops provide the opportunity for art centre textiles to be displayed and sold in a fine-art environment, and there are very few places where they are displayed in the same space as paintings. I have worked in an art centre—Injalak Arts and Crafts Association—that produced both textiles and artworks, and it was interesting to note the entirely different way the two types of product needed to be marketed. Galleries exhibiting Injalak's paintings were usually offered the opportunity to include textiles with the show. Most galleries were horrified

The Kaltjiti Arts and Crafts display and sales area at Fregon.

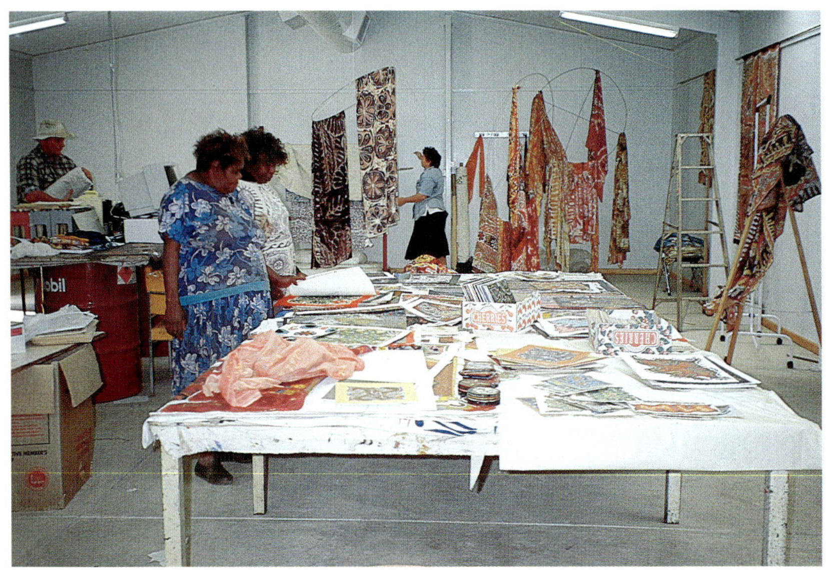

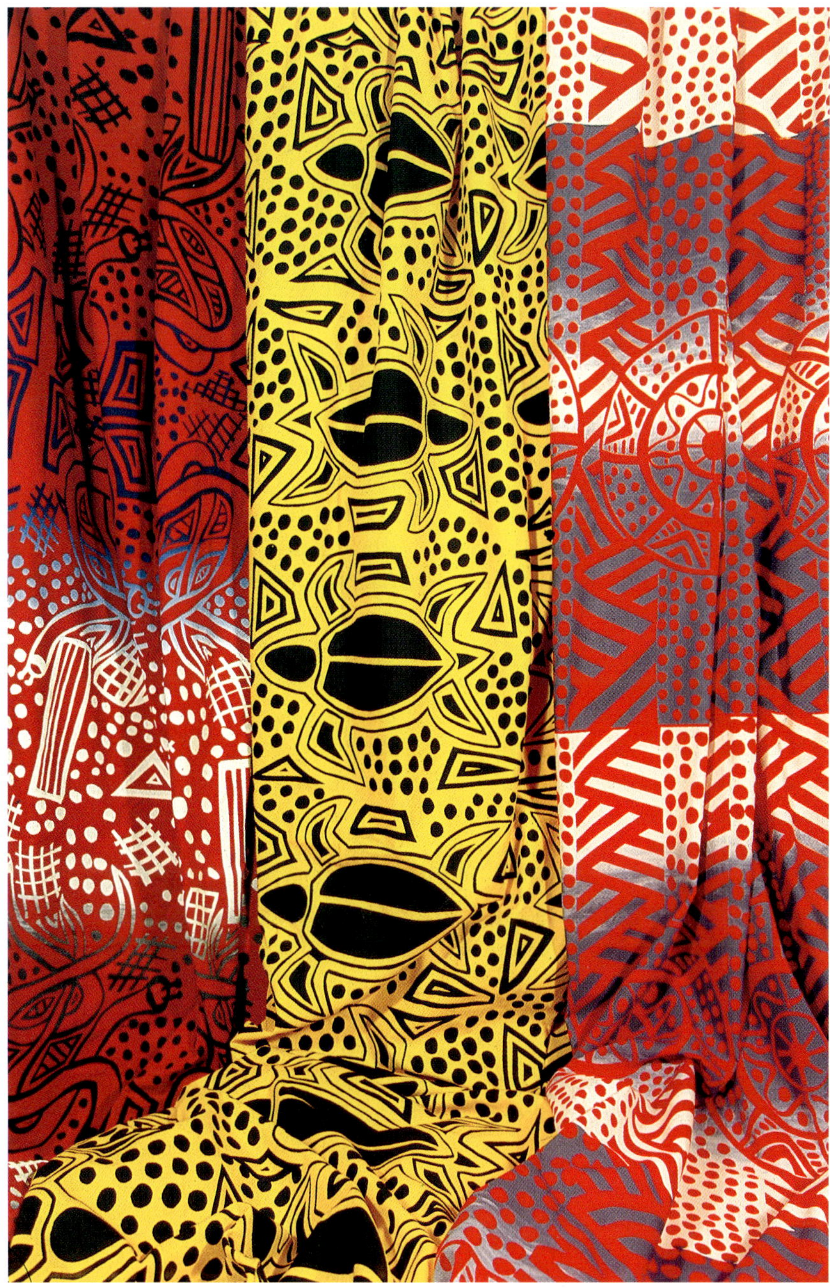

Munupi Arts and Crafts Centre screenprinted cotton fabrics: (left to right) *Yuli Worm* by Thecla Puruntatameri; *Turtle* by Reppie Orsto; and *Kulama* by Thecla Puruntatameri.

academics have been known to be staunch advocates of textiles and fibre crafts. Not all textile buyers are collectors, many people can picture a use for that length of hand-screenprinted fabric or have the perfect spot to hang a dillybag—their approach is more utilitarian.

It is difficult for art centres producing textiles to be economically viable. The cost of production of textiles is high and the potential sale price is generally low. Art centres selling handmade batik T-shirts are all aware of a ceiling of about $75 per item, no matter how beautiful the colours or design, or hours of work spent creating it. Further, such a price can only be achieved if sold directly to a customer, which is a relatively infrequent occurrence in a remote community. Art centres can wholesale the T-shirts for only approximately half that amount. Consumers baulk at paying high prices for wearable products and, yet, when the material and labour costs are added up—wax, brushes, *cantings*, dyes, T-shirts, electricity—very little is left for art centre running costs or investing in new initiatives. The lower the value of each item being sold, the more items have to be sold, packaged, invoiced and catalogued to achieve a reasonable turnover. When each product is handmade it can be a challenge to market.

Art centre staff labouring over textile sales may well look wistfully at art centres selling paintings that absorbed less than $100 in material costs, yet can sell for more than $1000. Producing textiles is more akin to manufacturing: it is important to be aware of costings so that the return for the product is not less than the cost of production. Some centres can and do

at the thought of including any sort of textiles in the show and emphatically declined. A small number were happy to take a little bit of everything and some weren't too proud to have T-shirts. Conversely, when the art centre presented a major show of textiles (featuring lengths of rather expensive dupion shot-silk) at the former Meat Market Craft Gallery in Melbourne in 1994, the exhibition organisers were also offered paintings on bark or Arches paper. In the end they decided upon small barks

because their audience was perceived to be interested in high-quality crafts but not fine art. Most gallery sales books tell the story that buyers will buy paintings or textiles, but rarely both.

The textile collector is usually a devotee. Unlike their fine-art collecting counterparts you rarely hear them discussing the investment value of their collection. Usually female, and with a passion for either fibre crafts, fabric textiles or both, they are relatively rare creatures. Craft councils are generally textile-friendly places and make deliberate decisions to subsidise the production of textiles because artists enjoy diversity and like to alternate batiking a T-shirt or length of silk with painting. However, it is important that the art centre staff and governing bodies are aware of how much this is costing the centre and have a strategy for generating enough income to pay for the subsidy. Art centres specialising in textiles do not necessarily have this luxury.

After years of training and support from successive textiles trainers and

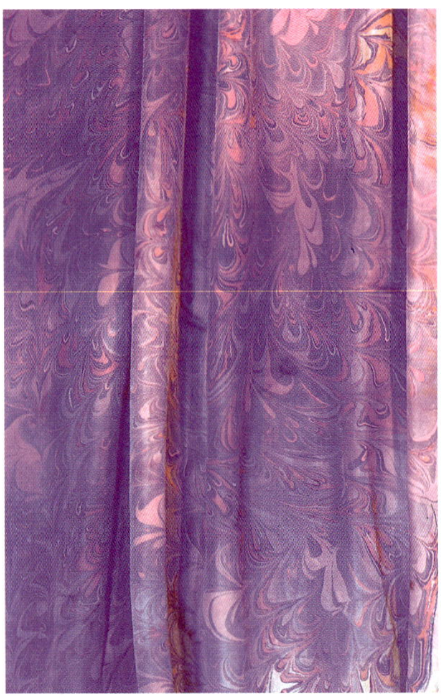

Untitled, Hermy Munnich, Dunnilli Arts, marbled silk produced by taking a 'print' from fabric paints floated on a corraghen gum bath, 300 cm x 112 cm.

specialists since the mid-1970s, the artists of Utopia in Central Australia have an international reputation for fine batik silk lengths. The Holmes à Court collection of Utopia batiks and the related catalogue have contributed significantly to the status of Utopia artists; there is a strong niche market for their work, with collectors and institutions paying more than one or two thousand dollars a piece. Utopia has more recently become famous for its painters, many of whom were batik artists throughout the 1980s and early

1990s. The most outstanding examples are Emily Kngwarray (deceased) and Gloria Apetyarr. The beautiful multilayered and textual way these artists have approached painting on canvas has been strongly influenced by their years working with batik. Somewhat ironically, because of the highly technical nature of the medium, batik making at Utopia has been largely dependent on the presence of an arts administrator or coordinator to organise materials and the facilities where the craft could be undertaken. In recent years, batik production at Utopia has slowed. It is far easier for artists without an on-site coordinator to work with less demanding and fragile media such as paint and canvas. In addition, the significantly higher returns offered by painting are very attractive.

Art centres are becoming renowned for producing 'fine art'. Textiles are still rare and only Utopia and Ernabella had achieved major national profiles by the end of the 1990s. The majority of art centres producing textiles are working hard to produce hand-screenprinted cotton and silk by the metre and the returns are much lower.

The distinguishing feature of textiles and fibre crafts is their relevance to the artists and craftspeople; they are not just a commodity produced for sale to external buyers. While not many Aboriginal artists have an interest in buying a painting to hang in their home, there is often a strong local demand for community produced T-shirts or clothes. Art centres such as Bima Wear sell most of their output locally. At Gunbalanya (Oenpelli) it was a source of pride and satisfaction to see artists, their family members, non-Indigenous staff and visitors to the community all wearing T-shirts and clothing screenprinted at Injalak Arts and Crafts Centre. Through its clothing and textiles the art centre had a visible presence throughout the community and a number of its products were

accessible to everyone. The other community-friendly aspect of making textiles such as batik is the manner of production. Women sit together around an electric frying pan of hot wax, leaning in to scoop up more wax in their *canting* or dabbing the brush, careful not to scorch the bristles on the bottom of the hot pan. Conversations ebb and flow.

As we can see, art centres and Indigenous artists producing and marketing textiles face a number of issues and constraints. In many ways they are the same as those faced by textile artists and craftspeople of any ethnic background. The making of textiles could not be described as a lucrative activity. Nevertheless, for a variety of reasons many artists and craftspeople want to work with fabrics and there is a keen, albeit small, audience for their labours. It is possible that through a commitment to continuing skills development and quality, savvy marketing and strategic partnerships with sympathetic galleries, art centres and their artists can reach new markets for their fine-art textiles and improve returns, commensurate with the work and skill of the artisans. In addition, or alternatively, art centres can choose to subsidise textile production through the sale of other products or can enter into licensing agreements to maunfacture the more labour-intensive products such as T-shirts and fabric lengths. These options have been chosen by a number of art centres in recent years with success. Marketing textiles is the challenge of getting Cinderella to the ball.

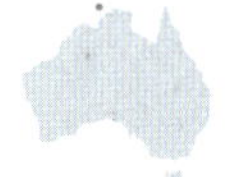

ANDREA MCNAMARA WITH GILLIAN DALLWITZ, TIWI DESIGN

It is a very long road for a product to travel: from an Aboriginal arts centre in a remote community to a city retail outlet and commercial reality. Despite the fact that this is largely uncharted territory, the idea of giving it a go seems irresistible. It's partly the lure of the dollar, mixed with inspiration from successful Australian firms like Mambo, but also an acknowledgement of the inevitability of funding subsidies being withdrawn from Aboriginal art centres. Too soon, art centres like Tiwi Design are expected to be self-sufficient. But are they ready?

Tiwi Design, on Bathurst Island, has a significant investment in the production of handprinted textiles, both historically and financially. Textile production has been happening there since the late sixties. The decorative style of Tiwi art, which has its origins in body painting, leans naturally towards repetitive pattern which has made it easily adapted to fabric. The fabrics found a ready market in the 1970s and 1980s, both on and off the island. The novelty of Indigenous designs on fabric and the fact that printed fabrics in general were popular made things look rosy for Tiwi Design. Handprinting is labour intensive, but the community was time-rich and enthusiastic, so there seemed to be no problems. It kept people busy and it brought income into the community.

The 1990s and beyond, however, have not been so good. The number of outlets for Tiwi Design fabric has decreased, there have been no new designs for a long time, the printing facilities need upgrading and there is more interest in painting, carving and pottery than fabric. The question the organisation faces is whether to stop producing fabric or to give it one last shot and set out on the road to Daimaru.*

To find a solution, this dilemma needs to be put into the wider context of what is happening in the Australian textile industry. Tiwi Design might be in a quandary, but so are many small handprinted textiles businesses in Australia. Over the last few years, several small production studios have either closed down or looked for other ways of doing things. Handprinting is just not worth it, physically or

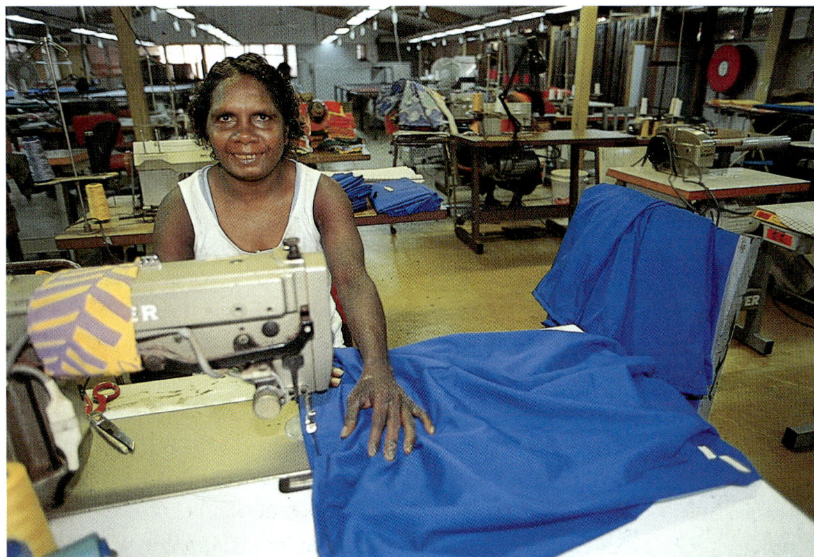

Bima Wear seamstress Antoinette Tipiloura sews a ceremonial garment.

commercially. In other words, apart from the climate and remote location, it is significant how many of the problems faced by Tiwi Design are shared by other small textile businesses.

For a start, handprinted fabric by the metre is seriously hard to sell. There are no specialty shops that sell limited edition fabrics. Retail outlets don't know how to display fabric to show it to advantage, and fabric takes up a lot of room. Lengths of fabric are not usually greeted with enthusiasm by galleries, who are more accustomed to showing paintings or three-dimensional items. The other problem is that pigment-printed fabric produced by hand has limited commercial application. It will not meet the required standards of, for example, a Martindale rub test.[†] It won't meet the required Australian standard for wash and colour fastness, which is essential if the product is to go into department stores. The big fashion manufacturers are not interested in the fabrics if they don't fit in with the colour and style predictions of what will sell. What this all means is that the audience for handprinted fabrics is a small niche market.

If fabric by the metre is hard to sell, making things might seem to be the solution. However, the problems relating to product development and manufacture are definitely

compounded by isolation. There is no solid manufacturing base close to Tiwi Design on Bathurst Island and transport costs add up. Plain fabric has to go to the island to be printed, then to the manufacturer, then back to the island and eventually distributed to the consumer. Distance makes quality control at the manufacturing end difficult. The choice of plain cloths to print on is limited; it is hard to source good fabrics from the one salesman who makes the trek to the Top End, and Darwin is hardly a textile Mecca.

Any increase in demand for handprinted textiles can be a problem

* Daimaru is a Japanese-owned department store located in Melbourne's CBD. It stocks a product mix which appeals to locals and tourists alike, which makes it an ideal outlet for Aboriginal products.

[†] The Martindale rub test is the industry standard by which manufacturers know the longevity of the fabric they are using. A fabric is categorised for usage according to the number of 'rubs' it will withstand. The higher the number of rubs (e.g. 50,000) the better for use in commercial furnishing contracts.

because production is limited by the manufacturing process. While handprinting offers a quick turnaround time and low minimum quantities, it's only good until you get either successful or tired.

So, once demand increases, the logical thing would be to outsource the fabric printing. This would free time for other things, like that popular notion that emerged in the 1990s of working on the business, rather than in it. But, in the last fifteen years, the Australian textile industry has shrunk and many fabric converters have closed, unable to compete with off-shore prices. Current trends indicate that textiles of the future will have minimal decoration. The spotlight has moved to constructed fabrics. New high-performance yarns and computerised production methods are all the go. Jacquard woven fabrics outlast printed furnishing fabrics and are more cost effective. Placement prints on garments have been usurped by embroidery which is now very economical using computerised systems. Demand for printed fabrics has dropped and the factories close.

Bima Wear dresses await shipment from the factory at Nguiu on Bathurst Island.

Why not go off-shore for printing? The price per metre is definitely cheaper but the minimum quantities are higher, and a substantial sum has to be paid up front. There is also the issue of whether 'Australian made' is a significant aspect of the product's saleability.

After all attempts to outsource printing and manufacturing have failed, the answer might be to build another print table, employ more printers, instigate more efficient procedures and develop new markets; but that's a short-term solution. There is no point in printing more fabric or developing new designs if it is still not clear who and what it is for.

It's easy to say that the answer lies in new designs for a market prepared to pay a bit more. However, this raises issues of quality. Is a market with money interested in Indigenous textiles, let alone those which are pigment printed on ordinary fabrics, and which are usually a little bit faulty in that handprinted kind of way? It is a vicious circle, because the tropical climate and the existing print facilities make it almost impossible for Tiwi Design to produce the flawless fabric a discerning consumer is likely to demand. Such a market is not in Darwin, but probably somewhere like Daimaru, in Melbourne.

An answer could be to license the designs. That way, all manufacturing problems belong to the licensee. More and more art centres are negotiating good reproduction deals for artists. Why not talk to the surf and swimwear companies in Queensland to see about the possibilities for licensed design? This is a potentially huge market, but licensing designs still doesn't solve what happens to the print facility at Tiwi Design on Bathurst Island.

One successful move that Tiwi Design has made is to invite textile artists and designers to work at their facility. The resulting fabrics can be seen as true limited edition pieces and, therefore, are taken more seriously by galleries. This is one way to produce covetable (and more expensive) fabrics and means that Tiwi Design no longer works in isolation. The next step is to form strategic alliances with people in urban Australia, with manufacturers, fabric suppliers, potential licensees and customers.

Before packing the bags for the journey south to Daimaru, some strategic planning needs to take place. For a start, is Daimaru the ultimate destination? The answer lies in serious market research and analysis to define who Tiwi Design's customers are and what they want to buy. Some of the findings of such research may be

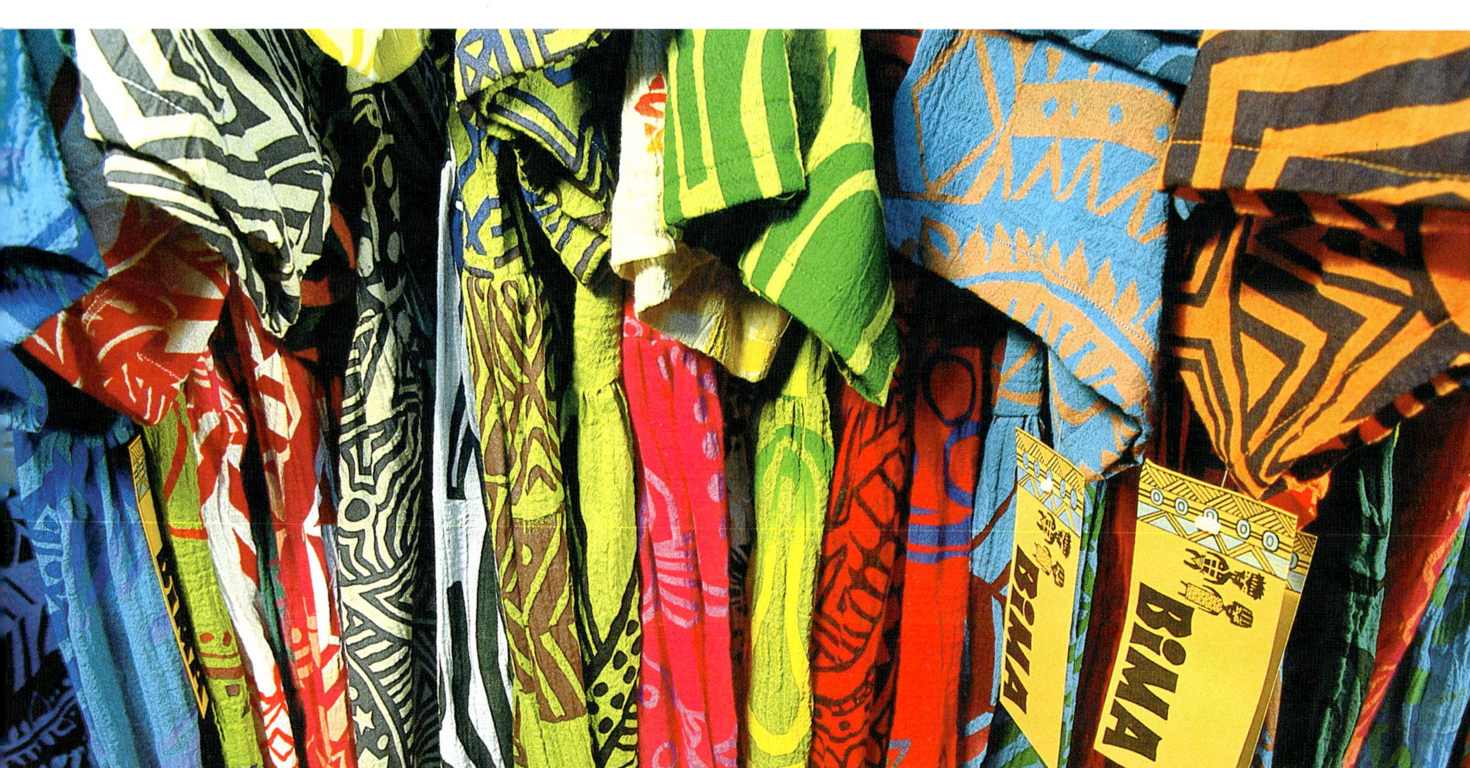

unwelcome, but too much has happened for too long on an *ad hoc* basis. Tiwi Design needs to establish where it wants to be, plan the appropriate route to get there and seek advice along the way. It is a long way south, but Tiwi Design has to start some time, and the beginning of a new century is as good a time as any to let the journey begin.

Textile collections: Dealing with documentation

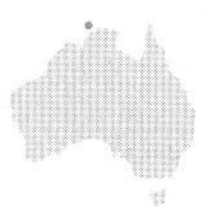

GRACE COCHRANE, POWERHOUSE MUSEUM

The Powerhouse Museum in Sydney is a museum of applied arts and sciences, and within its huge collection of about 300,000 objects it has strong holdings of contemporary textiles made by Aboriginal artists in Central and Northern Australia. What does it mean to have these works included in this kind of collection, and what are the issues in relation to collecting and displaying them that may be useful to others?

Textiles in context

The only one of its kind in Australia, the Powerhouse Museum collects and exhibits objects in the broad fields of decorative arts and design, science and technology and social history. The museum aims to include Aboriginal and Torres Strait Islander material culture in all relevant collection areas. Most of the textiles from Central and Northern Australia have been acquired by the decorative arts and design curatorial department, where they are located (as are ceramics and woodwork by Aboriginal artists) into the wider Australian collections of contemporary crafts and design. Here they form part of the broad story of Australian textiles development and of the long histories of batik, printed fabrics and basket-making from many other parts of the world. The

Powerhouse Museum acknowledges the connections between decorative arts and design, and 'art' and, therefore, appreciates the links between these contemporary textiles and the paintings and prints also made by many of the artists. However, unlike many other gallery collections, 'art' is not the primary means of validation for the textiles. This is mainly because we believe textiles to have their own significant histories and traditions that can include connections with art, but also because, in New South Wales, paintings are the province of the Art Gallery of New South Wales. Similarly, historical material is collected by the Australian Museum in Sydney. We aim not to duplicate their responsibilities, so, while occasionally acquiring works overlapping their fields of interest, we are more likely to borrow their objects for exhibition.

Within the Powerhouse Museum, two Indigenous curators specialising in Koori history and culture, and an Indigenous education and visitor services officer work as part of teams that develop a range of exhibition programs. Along with other objects acquired as decorative arts and design, the textiles made by Indigenous artists are, at times, of interest to curators in other areas. Curators of social history, for example, are interested in the stories of a wide range of Australian cultural 'communities' and their expressions of identity. Their focus is on New South Wales groups in particular, like the Koori community at La Perouse and, in the context of textiles, the Yurundiali screenprinting workshop at Moree. In the area of engineering and design, those researching product design are interested in screenprinted furnishing fabrics from Tiwi Design and Ernabella Arts, and those dealing with manufacturing technologies will consider Arnhem Land basketry used for fishing. A chemistry exhibition in the sciences area includes a basket from Maningrida because of the dyes that were used, and the curator of

health and medicine is interested in batiks from Utopia that show plants used as bush medicine.

Textiles in focus

A good deal of effort at the Powerhouse Museum is put into the documentation of objects, as they are acquired in the belief that it is better to get it right now rather than have someone invent a story in a hundred years' time! Thus, notes are made about the artist, the context in which the artist works (like clan affiliations or the development of an art centre in a community), the process of production, issues of protocol regarding naming the artist and the ownership of the work and, as far as we can be sure, the aspects of the work that might contribute to its meaning, as well as what we believe to be the significance of the work to our collection. Because we are some distance from Central and Northern Australia and are not able to travel frequently, it was decided when writing the museum's collection development policy for decorative arts and design in the late 1980s, to focus—to start with, anyway—on a few centres where we could develop a continuing relationship and build knowledge over time. Ten years later, we believe we have a good collection, some long-term relationships with art coordinators and agents which we value enormously and, especially, some memorable and rewarding experiences of meeting and working with artists. And we have learned a great deal.

Textile tensions

A number of issues crop up from time to time that affect our ability to do our job well and which may be of interest to art centres as well as other collecting institutions.

A continuing issue is that of distance. The role of reliable, informed and ethical agents remains central to our task of collecting information and maintaining awareness of the development of artists' work. In many cases this role is carried out by community art coordinators, and theirs is not always an easy job as they work between artists, suppliers and the market. The viability of the centres in which they work is, in my view, essential to our good links with the artists themselves. We have also enjoyed strong relationships with some key dealers, who provide the same ethical service from a different perspective or distance. However, as with any artist working anywhere, a clear communication path between artist and agent must be established so that all the appropriate copyright or licensing permissions, documentation and payments remain correct and coherent, for the artist primarily—but also for those collecting their work.

In the places where artists employ,

Makoto Tomana, curator from the Hokkaido Museum of Modern Art, Sapporo, Japan, looks at Alison (Milyika) Carroll's batik with Nyuwara Tapaya and Daisy (Nyukana) Baker during a visit by Ernabella artists to the Powerhouse Museum in 1995. Batiks from Ernabella and Utopia were included in the exhibition Contemporary Australian Craft organised by the Hokkaido Museum of Modern Art and the Powerhouse Museum, which toured Japan in 1999 (courtesy Powerhouse Museum).

through their council, a coordinator to manage such business, the process is usually fairly streamlined. However, where a number of agents compete for an artist's work, the records of that work are inconsistent and dispersed and opportunities for continuing professional and legal contact become very confused. This is not an issue for Indigenous artists alone: all artists involved in the art marketplace have to decide who will represent them and what that representation entails. However, it is more difficult where there are great distances to cover in order to contact artists, where social conventions and language can create barriers to explanation and understanding, and where artists are not in a position to keep their own records. Furthermore, the unscrupulous can exploit an artist who does not have first-hand experience of an art world that has—often quite contrary to Indigenous conventions—particular notions and expectations of ownership, authorship and rights, and practices that include 'selling-on' at a profit.

We are very well aware, for example, that practically the whole of the contemporary Western art world rests on the concept of the author as an expressive individual. Yet, Indigenous authorship is linked to a wider notion of custodianship and may be multiple or collective, as well as

individual. If someone asks 'whose is this?' without realising the potential for ambiguity between 'making', 'owning' or 'being responsible for', the answer can clearly vary. There can be a difference, for instance, between who might physically make a batik and whose motifs the maker may include along with his or her own. There will also be times when an aspect of the process is assigned to others; cooperative assistance on a textile work is often carried out in the same way as for many paintings. Yet, this practice has caused concern in the art marketplace, especially where it has been exploited by dealers aware of the value of a 'name'. One is reminded of the similar anxiety amongst glass collectors when American glass artist Dale Chihuly, blinded in one eye through a car accident, employed teams of glass-blowers to make his pieces (in the best Venetian traditions), which he then signed as the artist. With textiles, the introduction of new techniques, like the use of batik stamps of personal totems that can be shared within a family group, can stimulate creativity through new patterning possibilities while at the same time adding to the complexities of authorship for collecting institutions. For distant museums, it can be difficult without expert and consistent advice at the point of acquisition to determine whom to properly acknowledge.

There have been a number of outstanding projects where Indigenous artists have reproduced their works in forms or materials made elsewhere: drawing on etching plates to be printed in a workshop, painting on ceramic plates that are fired elsewhere or designing screens for semi-commercial textile production in the city. Here the artists remain in control of the meaning of their work, although it is transferred to another form.

However, somewhat problematic, in my view, are the instances where, from time to time, artists working within Western conventions and experiences want to make

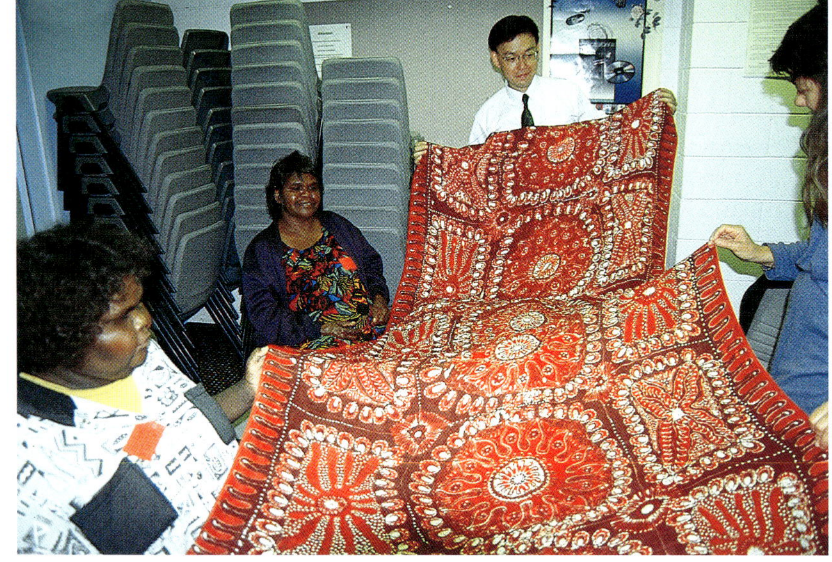

'collaborative' works with people outside their own cultural group. They see working with artists whose cultural practice is very directly related to traditions, like tribal Indigenous artists, as an opportunity to enrich their own experience and perhaps that of the artists with whom they might work, through a 'meeting of ideas'. Unless the experience is of artists simply working alongside one another so that the contributions remain distinct even if on the same work, or where there is a very genuine commitment to a long-term shared experience and understanding, I am, so far, not altogether convinced that the eventual 'shared' meaning, and especially the authorship of these works, is always quite agreed or understood. 'Collaboration', 'contracting' and 'co-operation' in this context are terms and practices that need a good deal of consideration.

A further serious issue for museum records is the development, since the mid-1980s, of spelling systems for Aboriginal languages. Earlier efforts to transcribe Aboriginal names and place names often failed to cater for sounds unique to, for example, Arandic languages. Reviews of written names have refined inconsistencies in the spelling of artists' names, but in doing so have also added to the confusion for curators whose task it is, in the interests of the documentation of artists' work, to seek consistency within and across collections. In my experience over a twelve-year period, the spelling of names and kinship names (by which many artists are known) has changed several times (e.g. Pula/Pwerle/Apwerl and Pitjara/Petyarre/Apetyarr), making even the most informed curator's job difficult. The confusion can be further exacerbated if the artists themselves sign their names on their work using an earlier spelling, perhaps one used in often inconsistent and unreliable local clinic records or passport documentation. Furthermore, much Aboriginal work is also held in

overseas art museums, where contact with centres of change is even more difficult, resulting in what must now be wildly inconsistent records both within and between collections, worldwide.

Clearly these anomalies will be clarified over time, but until the informal arrangements between galleries, museums, curators and dealers of Aboriginal artworks on the one hand, and regional language centres and dictionary projects on the other hand, are formalised, these problems will continue. The onus is

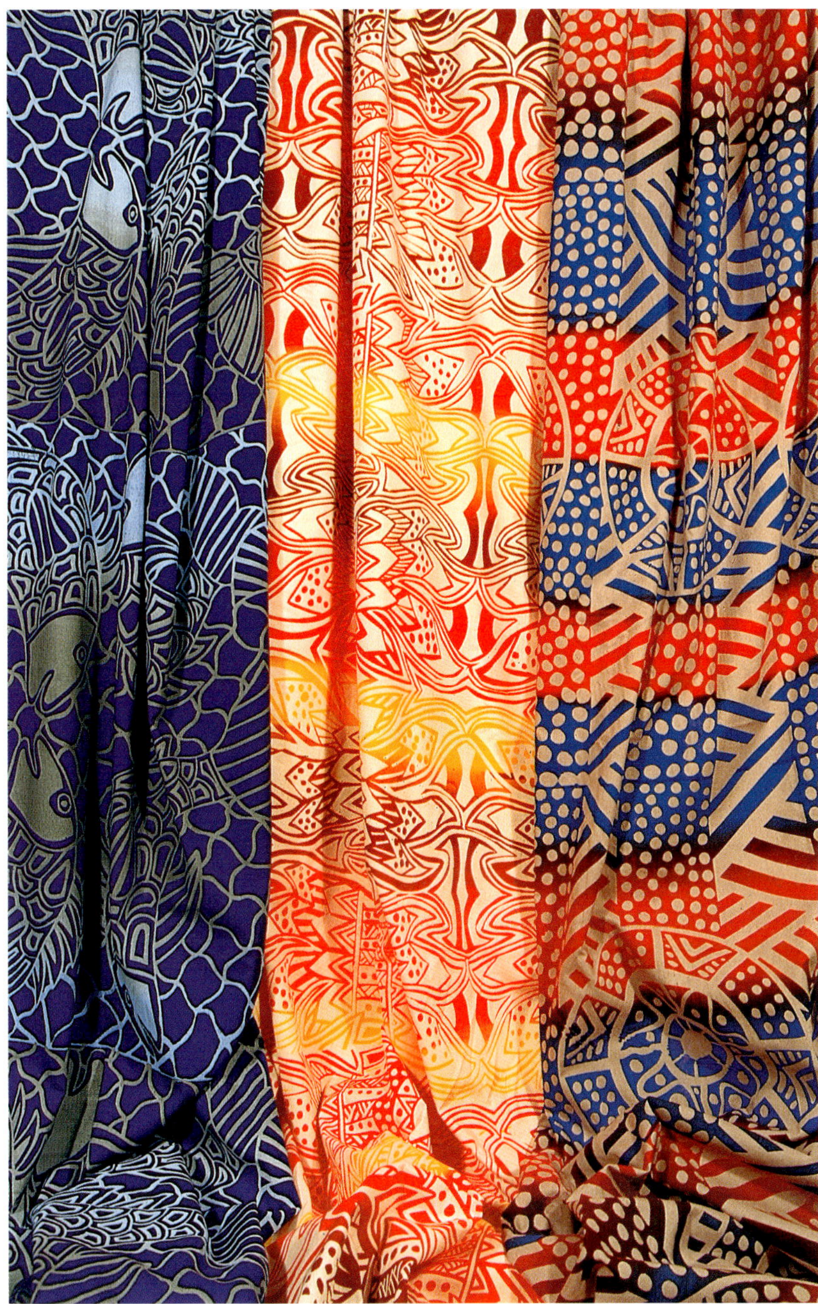

Munupi Arts and Crafts Centre screenprinted cotton lengths: (left to right) *Fish* by Fatima Kantilla, *Bushfire* by Thecla Puruntatameri and *Kulama* by Thecla Puruntatameri.

currently on the informed curator to liaise with language centres in order to ensure that records reflect current usage. However, I would argue that this is not a one-way responsibility, and the implications for the permanent record of an artist's work and career must also be a consideration for language centres, even if the solution is simply to try to disseminate their decisions to all those who are involved in responsible documentation.

Again, we accept that the current time limits set by copyright law cannot apply where Indigenous ownership or responsibility is collective or passed on through generations, but I am not sure at what point, or how, a museum can obtain new information about changes to the custodianship of certain works. We have to be careful to allow ambiguities and variations to be understood or allowed for when applying our museum-cataloguing conventions. Clearly, it is essential for institutions like ours to receive very informed and accurate data at the outset; it is very hard to retrieve or add more information later.

A final comment concerns what is actually made. In all instances, other than basket- and bag-making, textile designing and making is a non-traditional activity, a 'new' form of expression, although the designs usually come directly from continuing traditional cultural practice. Many of the processes of working in new media are also connected to traditional culture, such as the practice of working in a group and sharing work within a family. Perhaps, because the textiles themselves are not linked to functional, material, cultural practice, most objects made are not used by the artists or the people around them (except, for example, for basketry and for clothing by Bima Wear and Jilamara Arts and Crafts Association). By and large, what is made is an expression that is certainly coming from cultural traditions but which is not part of ceremony; it is made for pleasure, for expression and education and, above all, for income. It is not surprising, then, that the attraction of art forms that bring a greater monetary return, combined with declining financial support for art centres, is forcing a shift from textile making to painting and prints that can find a more viable

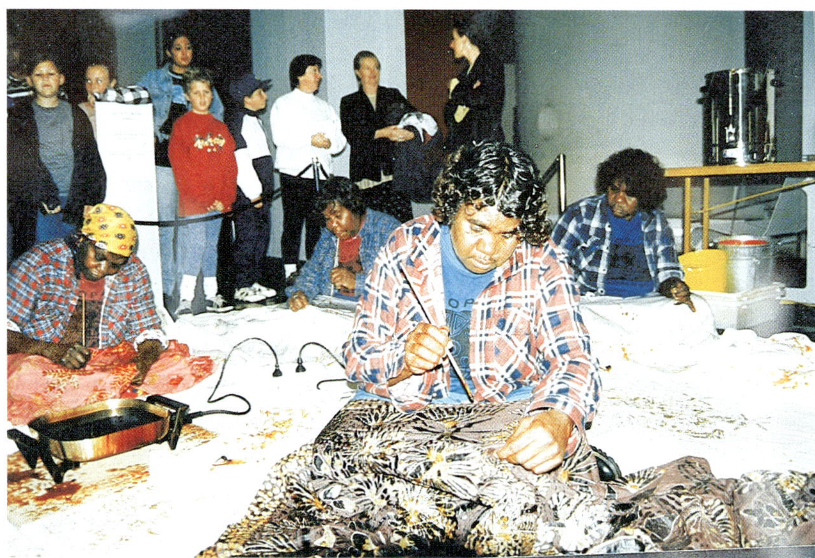

Gladdy Akemarr, Nora Akemarr and Glory Angal from Utopia in Central Australia make batik at the Powerhouse Museum as part of the 1997 Festival of the Dreaming (photo Grace Cochrane, courtesy Powerhouse Museum).

place in the hierarchies of the established art market.

What is the solution? Silk batik lengths are generally offered as artworks to be hung on a wall. They are very labour intensive to make and require considerable skilled assistance in the provision of materials and maintenance of skills. They cost much less than a painting to buy, but comparatively few private collectors of paintings will also collect a batik hanging. They, therefore, have little market outside the collecting institutions who are interested in them as cultural artefacts; the art world, with its established hierarchies, does not place a high investment value on them. Screenprinted-textile workshops do design for production, but must address the changing tastes of fashion and furnishing markets. Others make or contract out production clothing, like T-shirts and scarves, but few of these, other than commercially successful textile companies like Desert Designs and Balarinji, can attract an income comparable to that possible for good artists through the art market.

It may be that artists will choose to continue making textiles because it suits them, because they enjoy the process and because it means something to them. And it may be that centres will be funded to maintain this

important activity. But it may also be that in order to continue at all there may have to be some review of what is actually being made and what else might be possible. Public taste in furnishings and fashion is as fickle as the views of the art world.

I hope this work continues, because in whatever direction it moves in the new century, the development of textile production in Central and Northern Australia remains a most significant cultural phenomenon.

appendices

Appendix 1: Techniques

Batik

Batik is the process of creating designs on fabric using a wax resist. The wax is applied to the cloth by means of a brush or *canting*. A *canting* is a traditional Indonesian tool with a hollow metal vessel at one end. The *canting* holds the wax and allows the artist to 'draw' with the wax onto the cloth. At Utopia a *cap* is sometimes used: a custom-made stamping tool (usually made of copper or bronze) based on the artist's design. The *cap* is dipped into hot wax and stamped onto fabric. Ernabella Arts and Kaltjiti Arts and Crafts at Fregon use a brush to apply the wax.

The wax is applied successively between dyebaths of different colours. Each waxing masks out a bit more fabric, the dipping in dye ensures that each waxed section will result in a different colour. This continues until the artist is satisfied with the colour and design. Dyes need to be light-fast cold-water dyes as hot dyeing melts the wax from the fabric. Naphthol dyes, which are fibre-reactive, are most commonly used.

After a final rinse in water, the fabric is hung in the shade to dry. Sunlight causes the dyes to fade or become 'fugitive', so all dyeing must be performed in the shade for best results. The wax is finally removed from the fabric, usually by boiling in water with a little caustic soda and soda ash added. For extra finishing some fabrics are dry-cleaned.

Based on The Utopia Batik Training Program written by Jan Ross Manley

Lino-block printing on fabric

Block printing is the process of carving a block to form a raised surface onto which ink or dye is applied. The block is then printed, or pressed, onto the surface of the fabric.

Squares of linoleum are usually used for fabric printing. A design is drawn onto the block and then lino-carving tools or knives are used to remove the background. Ink or dye are then applied to the raised area or 'positive image' using rollers dipped in colour. This block is then printed onto the surface of the fabric in a repeat or sometimes random manner.

A fabric ink or dye can be used. Ink is fixed onto the fabric by heat. Dye must first be thickened with a thickening agent, such as Manutex, to allow the ink to adhere to the block. The fabric is then steamed to fix the colour into the fabric and the Manutex is washed out in water.

Screenprinting

Screenprinting is the technique of transferring images onto fabric with a silk-screen (a fine mesh—usually synthetic fibre, not silk—stretched across a frame) and a squeegee. Ink or dye is forced through the screen, which has been masked or covered in certain areas to form the image or design.

There are many different ways to mask a screen. Tiwi Design and Ernabella Arts use photo emulsion to develop images permanently onto the screen surface. A negative image is placed on the surface of a screen which has been coated with light-sensitive emulsion. The screen is exposed to light (either outdoors in sunlight or with a lamp in a darkroom) causing the image to develop on the surface of the screen. The unexposed emulsion is washed out leaving the 'positive' image exposed to the screen.

Rubylith film can also be used to mask the screen. The film is cut into a design which is then adhered to the silk-screen; the film blocks ink from passing through the screen's mesh.

The image can be printed in repeat on specially designed tables, as a random print, or one-off T-shirts can be printed using a carousel.

Handpainting with fibre-reactive dyes

At some art centres, artists work with handpainted silks using fibre-reactive dyes. This process, developed relatively recently, involves using a gutta resist to define the design. Gutta is a thick honey-like substance which prevents the dyes from bleeding, so confining the colours to selected areas. It is applied usually from a bottle with a fine nozzle allowing the designs to be rendered in great detail.

Dyes are then painted into the spaces enclosed by the gutta. The dyes are called fibre reactive because they react with the fibres in the cloth immediately transforming the fibres' chemical make-up. After the dye painting process has been completed, the cloth is steamed to fix the dye and the gutta is washed out. Some guttas are coloured and this colour remains in the cloth. This process is best suited to silk fabrics. Sometimes the silks are stretched across a frame to make painting easier and more precise.

Appendix 2:
Art centre directory

Central Australia

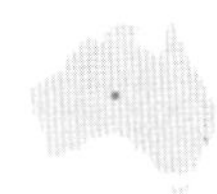

Ernabella Arts Inc., Ernabella

Ernabella Arts at Ernabella began operation in 1948 and is believed to be the oldest continuously operating Aboriginal art centre in Australia. Ernabella is situated 440 km south-west of Alice Springs, just over the Northern Territory border in South Australia on the Anangu Pitjantjatjara Lands. In its early days the centre produced handspun yarn and woven woollen goods from the wool of Ernabella sheep. Today it has an international reputation for its fine art work. Batik, one of the high-profile products of Ernabella Arts, was first introduced in 1971. In addition to batik, paintings on canvas, handpainted seed jewellery, prints on paper, wood carvings and handpainted ceramics are all made at Ernabella. Fabrics using Ernabella designs are manufactured under licence off-site.

Artworks from Ernabella are included in the collections of all of the major public galleries of Australia and in significant international collections. Ernabella artists have won many prestigious art awards and have exhibited in major exhibitions in Indonesia, Japan, Malaysia, the Americas, Western Europe and the United Kingdom. The artists have travelled to Asia, Africa and around Australia demonstrating their craft and participating in workshops.

Julalikari Arts and Crafts, Tennant Creek

The women's art and craft program, run through the Julalikari Council in Tennant Creek, 500 km north of Alice Springs, had humble beginnings. It was set up in 1994 in a tin shed with few resources and under difficult physical conditions. In early 1995, the program moved to a disused house in Mulga Camp (one of ten urban Aboriginal living areas in the town).

The Pink Palace, as it is known locally, was originally a hostel for Aboriginal stockmen coming into town from out bush. The building had many uses before being renovated and decorated to become an art and craft centre. It is now a meeting place and workplace for women from the area, a thriving vibrant facility for a group of artists serious about their work.

A variety of artwork is created by women at the Pink Palace: paintings, prints, ceramics and sewn garments. The women have gained a strong reputation for their handpainted and handprinted textiles. The fabrics produced have bright clear-cut designs, colours are vigorous and bold, and they are distinctive amongst Central Australian textiles.

Julalikari Arts and Crafts is a relatively young art centre but artists have been involved in exhibitions in Tennant Creek, at the Araluen Centre in Alice Springs, and in Canberra. The program has an annual end-of-year exhibition in Tennant Creek which has a dedicated following amongst the locals of the town.

Kaltjiti Arts and Crafts, Fregon

The Fregon community is set on sweeping sandy plains cut by winding creeks and punctuated by rocky outcrops at the foot of the Musgrave Ranges, 500 km south-west of Alice Springs. It was established in 1961 as an outstation of Ernabella, 65 km to the south. Strong geographical, cultural and family connections exist between the two centres, and because art and craft activities have been popular at Ernabella since the 1940s, the artistic influence from that centre has been very strong. In 1973 the art centre at Fregon opened as Aparawatatja Arts and Crafts, eventually to become Kaltjiti Arts and Crafts.

In the early 1970s, artists at Kaltjiti Arts and Crafts sewed and produced tie-dyed fabric. Batik was introduced in the mid-1970s and has become the most successful and popular technique practised at Fregon. The centre's range of textiles, however, is broad and includes handpainted scarves, screenprinted lengths that are sometimes made into bags, and batik T-shirts.

The Ernabella influence was initially strong in Kaltjiti batik work; however, as the years have passed, Fregon artists have developed their own individual style. The immediate natural environment around Fregon provides the single most important influence on artists, and Kaltjiti designs have a strong organic feel.

In 1997 the centre obtained funding from ATSIC to screenprint fabric using designs generated as a result of a workshop with Johanna Weiss. Five designs were transferred onto hemp/cotton, cheesecloth and cotton and have been used to make curtains, bags and clothing. Designs from the workshop were also used on T-shirts and other items. The centre has continued to use designs on a number of products and has also branched out into licensing sarongs and T-shirts.

Kaltjiti Arts and Crafts has participated in many exhibitions including the Indigenart Gallery Exhibition in Singapore, Italy and France; in the 1996 Adelaide Fringe Festival; in the annual Central Australian Aboriginal Art Exhibition at the Araluen Centre in Alice Springs; and at the Winkiku Centre at Uluru.

Based on personal communication with Bev Peacock, Kaltjiti coordinator.

Keringke Arts, Ltyentye Apurte

Ltyentye Apurte, or Santa Teresa, lies 80 km east of Alice Springs and is home to approximately 500 Eastern Arrernte people. The community lies at the foot of a range of tabletop hills overlooking a sweeping plain.

The art centre at Santa Teresa, Keringke Arts, was established in 1987. Local artists initially adopted a style similar to the Hermannsburg watercolour school of painting. Since then, however, the imagery in their work has grown more symbolic with the connection to their Indigenous heritage gradually growing stronger. The majority of Keringke artworks are not accompanied by specific stories, yet artists do draw on a strong traditional narrative for inspiration, structured around age-old motifs, landscape forms, the elements, daily life, food gathering, and the flora and fauna of the local countryside.

To the present day, all artists at Keringke Arts have been women, who produce a wide range of textile items, including silk scarves and lengths, as well as handpainted furniture, works on paper and canvas, and ceramics. Keringke Arts' international reputation has been built on their luminous and highly decorative silk painting. They have further strengthened their profile through the production of decorative homewares: the surfaces of tables, chairs, boxes, mirror frames and ceramic pots have been adorned with their signature style.

In 1988 Keringke artists were the first Aboriginal people to exhibit in the annual National Australian Craft Show, held in Sydney. Their work is held in the collections of many Australian and international museums and art galleries around the world. Keringke artists have also executed numerous commissioned projects including rug and calendar designs.

Minymaku Arts, Amata

Minymaku Arts was formed by the artists and craftspeople of Amata community and Tjurma Homelands. Amata sits in the picturesque Musgrave Ranges in the far north of South Australia on the Anangu Pitjantjatjara Lands, approximately 150 km south of Uluṟu and approximately 500 km south-west of Alice Springs. Minymaku Arts operates from the Amata Arts Centre and the Tjurma Homelands craft room situated side by side and located centrally within Amata. Minymaku means 'belonging to women'.

Batik became popular among Pitjantjatjara women during the 1970s. It was introduced to Amata in 1975 by trainer Vivienne McKlintock and quickly became as popular as it was in Ernabella, 150 km to the east. The Tjurma Homelands artists, as Minymaku Batik, developed a reputation during the 1980s for beautiful work. Today, their intricate batik pieces combine many layers of bold warm colours and abstract representations of their landscape.

The artists of Minymaku have exhibited in most capital cities, and their work is held in the collections of the Museum of Victoria and the Araluen Centre in Alice Springs.

Based on information from the Minymaku Arts website.

Titjikala Women's Centre, Titjikala

Just off the old South Road that follows the original Ghan railway track, about 100 km south of Alice Springs, lies the small community of Titjikala, originally set up as a stockcamp for nearby Maryvale Station. About 180 people, from predominantly Luritja and Pitjantjatjara language groups, live here.

The Women's Centre at Titjikala has been in operation since the early 1990s. It is establishing itself as a working studio for artists to practise their craft and train in new areas. Titjikala textile artists work in screenprinting and silk painting, and are particularly interested in lino-block printing.

The Titjikala Women's Centre has been in several local exhibitions in Alice Springs, and regularly sell their work at markets and art fairs.

Urapuntja Artists

Urapuntja Artists is located at Utopia on the Angarapa Land Trust in the south-eastern region of the Northern Territory and to the north of Alice Springs.

Batik has been synonymous with Utopia since the technique was introduced to the community in a training program run by the Institute for Aboriginal Development in the late 1970s. Pitjantjatjara artists skilled in the Ernabella method of batik-making shared the technique with the Utopia women, who quickly became adept in the craft.

Over the years these batiks have evolved into works of art on fabric, characterised by a spontaneous fresh style. Strong ties to land and to *awely,* or women's ceremony, provide a rich spiritual and creative reserve for artists. The silks are a mosaic storyboard of camp life, of the gathering of bushtucker and of nurturing and maintaining clan and country.

Artists combine various methods of wax application in the batiks. Wax can be painted directly on the fabric or worked with a *canting* tool or *cap* printing block, a technique acquired during a cultural exchange to Indonesia in 1994.

Utopia artists' work is held in collections around the world and they have given many workshops in their craft, both locally to other Aboriginal communities and internationally.

Top End

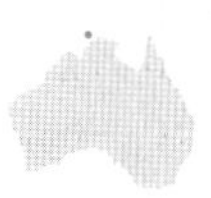

Bima Wear, Bathurst Island

Bima Wear began as a sewing enterprise at Nguiu on Bathurst Island in the early 1970s when visiting nuns started teaching sewing to local women. The name Bima is the name of the wife of the legendary figure of Purrukapali and is also an acronym of the Bathurst Island Mothers Association and the Bathurst Island Mission Auxiliary.

In 1975 the fledgling business moved to new premises. By then, women at Bima Wear were making garments from fabric printed at nearby Tiwi Design. By 1976 fourteen women were employed as seamstresses and as clerical workers, and about 300 garments were made every week. Most were sold at the Nguiu Ullintjini Store and a small number were sent to Darwin; uniforms were also made for local schools.

Bima Wear was incorporated in 1978 and expanded over the following years till it was producing 17,000 articles per year. Much of this was sold outside the island, but until the early 1990s, Bathurst Island residents were the main consumers of Bima Wear product.

Screenprinting—mainly motifs and placement printing—began in 1982. Some designs were sold to Bima Wear by other artists from the community. Around this time the art centre began selling finished garments directly to the public from their showroom. In 1989, after a workshop run by Marie McMahon, Bima Wear artists began screenprinting repeat images on lengths of fabric.

By the end of the 1980s Bima Wear was a successful business. In 1990 they exhibited handpainted silks and prints on paper at the Powerhouse Museum in Sydney. Their work also travelled from 1989–90 in the touring exhibition Australian Fashion: The Contemporary Art of Dress.

Based on an extract from *Kiripapurajuwi Skills of Our Hands: God Craftsmen and Tiwi Art* by Kathy Barnes.

Dunnilli Arts, Nungalinya College, Darwin

Dunnilli Arts is a textile training and resource centre in Darwin. It draws clients from the Top End, in particular artists from Darwin, western and eastern Arnhem Land, Central Australia and the Kimberley.

During the mid-1980s, Darwin Aboriginal textile artists were having difficulty in pursuing their craft. Many were clients of the Northern Territory Government Housing Commission; its policies forbid operating a business from home. Some lacked knowledge of copyright, taxation, licensing and other issues associated with running a small business. Dunnilli Arts was established at Darwin's Nungalinya College to address these community needs. The Larrakia people of Darwin gave the name for the art centre, Dunnilli, meaning 'to make something special'.

The centre operates on two levels: as an art practice workshop and as a training centre. Government funding and monies from sales fund its operation. The work produced consists mainly of fabrics for day and evening wear, and for homewares such as tablecloths, aprons and placemats. These are sold locally through the art centre and at the Northern Territory Parliament House shop in Darwin. At least twelve exhibitions are booked annually in southern states.

Based on personal communication with Jillian Thompson.

Injalak Arts and Crafts Association, Gunbalanya

The rugged sandstone plateau of the Arnhem Land escarpment, an area of deep plunging gorges, huge boulders and wide overhanging rock platforms, rises to the east of Gunbalanya (Oenpelli) home of the Injalak Arts and Crafts Association. Gunbalanya billabong at the centre's rear is surrounded by open flood plains and overshadowed by Injalak hill, a place rich in rock-art paintings and a source of inspiration for local artists.

Gunbalanya is a small Aboriginal township close to the East Alligator River in western Arnhem Land, approximately 300 km east of Darwin. In 1925 the Church Missionary Society took responsibility for the community but the mission now has only a minimal influence. Gunbalanya has an Aboriginal population of approximately 1000 people who are predominantly Kunwinjku speakers with English as a second language.

A screenprinting course in 1986 led, eventually, to the funding of the Injalak Arts and Crafts Association. At first, artists worked in a small shed, but then a purpose-built centre was officially opened in late November 1989. The centre is long and flanked on either side by covered verandahs where the artists work. Injalak Arts and Crafts Association produces a diverse range of art and craft, including screenprinted fabric lengths, tablecloths, tea-towels, T-shirts and cushions. The imagery is often based on the abundant rock art that can be found in the area.

Jilamara Arts and Crafts Association, Melville Island

Milikapiti on Melville Island, just to the north of Darwin in the Arafura Sea, is home to Jilamara Arts and Crafts Association. The community was introduced to textile design in 1986 when Ian Foster and Heather Read conducted a six-month community employment program to train six women in basic screenprinting and sewing techniques. In 1989 the organisation was incorporated and James Bennett began working as the art centre coordinator. He introduced

fibre-reactive dyes screenprinted onto silk lengths and scarves. A printing studio was built with two ten-metre tables, and textiles became a major source of revenue for the centre.

All Jilamara artists have unique and individual styles. Some adhere very closely to Tiwi traditions by employing a wooden comb to apply dots to their canvas or sculpture, others use coconut sticks, and some use contemporary Western brushes to make their individual marks.

The centre currently produces screenprinted silk lengths using fibre-reactive dyes, and cotton lengths printed with inks. T-shirts are sold within the community, with multicoloured designs particularly popular in recent years.

Jilamara Arts and Crafts Association is starting to license some of its designs to manufacturers and designers within the fashion industry. Negotiations to print very high-quality silk scarves in Italy is currently under way. The scarves, slickly packaged and marketed to the higher end of the fashion market, may prove lucrative for Jilamara artists as significant royalty payments have been negotiated.

Information provided by Felicity Green, former coordinator at Jilamara.

Munupi Arts and Crafts Centre, Melville Island

The Munupi Arts and Crafts Centre is in the community of Pularumpi on Melville Island, just north of Darwin in the Arafura Sea. Pularumpi has a population of approximately 370 people, although this figure fluctuates as people move from one community to another to visit family or country. *Munupi* means 'country' or 'land'.

What started as a centre primarily for the women of Pularumpi to take sewing classes, has grown steadily over the last decade to became an incorporated artists' association with a dedicated art and craft centre employing a full-time coordinator. Munupi Arts and Crafts currently produces painting, pottery, wood carving, printed fabric, lino-block prints and etching.

Munupi artists' fresh and uncomplicated approach has led to a unique style using rich vibrant colours.

Tiwi culture and the Tiwi Islands inspire Munupi artists. Ideas come from designs traditionally used to decorate ceremonial poles, spears and bark baskets, as well as the diverse elaborate markings painted on the face and body during ceremonies.

Tiwi Design, Bathurst Island

Tiwi Design (formerly Tiwi Designs) is one of the oldest and the best known Aboriginal-run printing workshop of its kind in Australia. It was established in 1969 at Nguiu on Bathurst Island, just north of Darwin in the Arafura Sea, both to promote Tiwi culture and to create employment.

Tiwi Design's initial output was block prints on paper and fabric domestic items, such as linen placemats and wall hangings. After some early success, a print table was installed in 1976 and the product expanded to include fashion items and soft furnishings. Tiwi Design T-shirts also became very popular during the 1980s.

Imagery has evolved from the earlier isolated figurative motifs to the more recent distinctive, multicoloured-striped effect achieved by mixing ink directly on the screen.

Tiwi Design has, over the years, enjoyed considerable commercial success, with a number of its designs, such as the well known burial pole design, being continually in print for a number of years. The printery has always been run and staffed by men who strive to maintain a handmade product.

With the recent downturn in the domestic textiles market, Tiwi Design is currently investigating new directions.

Information provided by Margie West.

Appendix 3:
List of contributors

Mary Akemarr is an artist with Urapuntja Artists.

Glory Angal is an artist with Urapuntja Artists at Atneltyey.

Gloria Apetyarr is an artist with Urapuntja Artists at Atneltyey.

Kathleen Apetyarr is an artist with Urapuntja Artists at Iylenty (Mosquito Bore).

Myrtle Apetyarr is an artist with Urapuntja Artists at Iylenty (Mosquito Bore).

Violet Apetyarr is an artist with Urapuntja Artists at Atneltyey.

Hilda Apwerl is an artist with Urapuntja Artists at Stirling Station.

Lena Apwerl is an artist with Urapuntja Artists at Iylenty (Mosquito Bore).

Daisy (Nyukana) Baker is an artist with Ernabella Arts at Ernabella.

James Bennett is the curator of Oceanic Art at the Museum and Art Gallery of the Northern Territory.

Marlene Boko is an artist with Titjikala Women's Centre.

Ron Brien is the executive officer of Desart in Alice Springs.

Kelli Bruce is an artist with Dunnilli Arts at Nungalinya College in Darwin.

Suzy Bryce is a freelance language consultant based in Alice Springs.

Alison (Milyika) Carroll is an artist with Ernabella Arts at Ernabella.

Grace Cochrane is curator of Australian decorative arts and design at the Powerhouse Museum in Sydney.

Katey Curley is an artist with Kaltjiti Arts and Crafts at Fregon.

Margaret Dagg is an artist and translator at Ernabella.

Gillian Dallwitz is the former coordinator of Tiwi Design at Nguiu on Bathurst Island. She now works in Melbourne.

Malinda Flynn is an artist with Dunnilli Arts at Nungalinya College in Darwin.

Djankawu Garrawurra is an artist with Dunnilli Arts at Nungalinya College in Darwin.

Jenny Green is an artist, and was formerly an arts and crafts teacher at Utopia. She is now a linguist at the Institute for Aboriginal Development in Alice Springs.

Linda Herangi is the coordinator of the Titjikala Women's Centre at Titjikala.

Winifred M. Hilliard was the first coordinator of Ernabella Arts at Ernabella where she lived for twenty years. She now lives on the Central Coast of New South Wales.

Peggy Napangardi Jones is an artist with Julalikari Arts and Crafts at Tennant Creek.

Nyurpaya Kaika is an artist with Minymaku Arts at Amata.

Osmond Kantilla is a printer with Tiwi Design at Nguiu on Bathurst Island.

Rosie Kunoth Kngwarray is an artist with Urapuntja Artists at Arlparra.

Andrea McNamara is a trainer with Tiwi Design at Nguiu on Bathurst Island.

Mona Mitakiki is an artist with Minymaku Arts at Amata.

Tara Munkanome is an artist with Bima Wear on Bathurst Island.

Angelo Munkara is a printer with Tiwi Design at Nguiu on Bathurst Island.

Janice Murray is an artist with Jilamara Arts and Crafts Association on Melville Island.

Isiah Nagurrgurrba is a printer with Injalak Arts and Crafts Association at Gunbalanya in Arnhem Land.

Matjangka (Nyukana) Norris is an artist with Kaltjiti Arts and Crafts at Fregon.

Mary-Lou Nugent is a former project officer at Desart. She now works at Old Parliament House in Canberra.

Louise Partos is the former coordinator of Ernabella Arts at Ernabella. She now works with the Museum of Victoria in Melbourne.

Bernadette Puruntatameri is an artist with Munupi Arts and Crafts Centre at Pularumpi on Melville Island.

Tim Rollason is the former coordinator of Keringke Arts at Ltyentye Apurte. He now works with Desart in Alice Springs.

Doris Thomas is an artist with Titjikala Women's Centre.

Lola Tyson is an artist with Dunnilli Arts at Nungalinya College in Darwin.

Kathleen Wallace is an artist with Keringke Arts at Ltyentye Apurte.

Penny Watson is an art lecturer with the Batchelor Institute of Indigenous Tertiary Education in Alice Springs.

Margie West is curator of Aboriginal art at Museum and Art Gallery of the Northern Territory in Darwin.

Inawinytji Williamson is an artist with Kaltjiti Arts and Crafts at Fregon.

Flick Wright is a freelance arts consultant specialising in Indigenous art centres. She is based in Wangary in South Australia.

glossary

Anangu	a Pitjanjtatjara word meaning 'people'; may be used in a general way to mean 'Aboriginal person' or, more usually, to denote a person from the Western Desert region
art coordinator	the manager or administrator of an arts centre, usually employed from outside the local community and answerable to an Aboriginal committee of artists
ATSIC	Aboriginal and Torres Strait Islander Commission
awely	an Alyawarr and Anmatyerr word meaning women's ceremony; Anmatyerr is spoken by many of the artists from the Utopia area
batik	see techniques on page 81
canting	a traditional Indonesian tool with a hollow metal vessel at one end; the *canting* holds hot wax and allows the artist to 'draw' with the wax onto the cloth as part of the batik technique
cap	a traditional Indonesian custom-made stamping tool (usually made of copper or bronze) used for applying wax to cloth as part of the batik technique
kwertengerl	an Anmatyerr word meaning the manager of ceremony; Anmatyerr is spoken by many of the artists from the Utopia area
outstation	small Aboriginal communities established away from larger communities and usually located in, or close to, traditional country
photo emulsion	a light-sensitive fluid used for making photographic screens for screenprinting (see techniques on page 81)
rubylith	a film used in silk-screenprinting (see techniques on page 81)
silk-screenprint	see techniques on page 81
Tjukurpa	the 'Tjukurpa', or 'Dreamtime' or 'Dreaming' as it is sometimes loosely translated into English, is fundamental to Central Australian Aboriginal life. It defines traditional Aboriginal law and religion and encompasses the land and its creation and all that exists. Different language groups of the Centre have different words and spellings for the same concept, sometimes capitalised and sometimes not. Some of these are: Tjukurpa (Pitjantjatjara language), Altyerre (Arrernte), Jukurrpa (Warlpiri) and Tjukurrpa (Pintupi–Luritja).
tyepty	an Anmatyerr word meaning a storytelling game of drawing in the ground; Anmatyerr is spoken by many of the artists from the Utopia area

bibliography

Barnes, K. 1999, *Kiripapurajuwi Skills of Our Hands: God Craftsmen and Tiwi Art,* ATSIC, Darwin.

Caruana, W. 1993, *Aboriginal Art,* Thames & Hudson, United Kingdom.

Eickelkamp, U. 1999, *Don't Ask for Stories: The Women From Ernabella and Their Art,* Aboriginal Studies Press, Canberra.

Green, J. 1998, 'Singing the Silk', in *Raiki Wara,* ed. J. Ryan, National Gallery of Victoria, Melbourne.

Kleinert, S. & Neale, M. (eds) 2000, *The Oxford Companion to Aboriginal Art and Culture,* Oxford University Press.

Maynard, M. 2000, 'Indigenous Dress' in *The Oxford Companion to Aboriginal Art and Culture,* (eds) S. Kleinert & M. Neale, Oxford University Press.

Morphy, H. 1999, *Aboriginal Art,* Phaidon Press, United Kingdom.

Ngaanyatjarra, Pitjantjatjara & Yankunytjatjara Women's Council 1999, *Nganana Rawangku Altji Wararipai (We Have Been Doing This Work for a Long Time),* Ngaanyatjarra, Pitjantjatjara & Yankunytjatjara Women's Council, Alice Springs.

Nugent, M. 1998, *Desert Art,* Jukurrpa Books, Alice Springs.

Partos, L. 1998, *Warku Irititja Munu Kuwari Kutu* (Work From the Past and the Present), catalogue of an exhibition by Ernabella Arts, Ernabella Arts.

Ryan, J. 1998, *Raiki Wara,* National Gallery of Victoria, Melbourne.

West, M. 1988, Art for money's sake: The art and craft enterprises on Bathurst Island, unpublished MA thesis, Australian National University, Canberra.

West, M. 1989, Yirrkala art enterprises, unpublished report prepared by the Museum and Art Gallery of the Northern Territory for the Department of Aboriginal Affairs Review Committee on the Aboriginal Arts and Crafts Industry.

Wright, F. 1999, *The Art and Craft Centre Story: A Survey of Thirty-Nine Aboriginal Community Art Centres in Remote Australia,* undertaken by Desart Inc., vol. 1, report, Aboriginal and Torres Strait Islander Commission, Canberra.

Wright, F. & Morphy, F. 2000, *The Art and Craft Centre Story: A Survey of Thirty-Nine Aboriginal Community Art Centres in Remote Australia,* undertaken by Desart Inc. vol. 2, summary and recommendations, Aboriginal and Torres Strait Islander Commission, Canberra.

Wright, F. 2000, *The Art and Craft Centre Story: Good Stories From Out Bush,* undertaken by Desart Inc. vol. 3, examples of best practice from Aboriginal community art centres in remote Australia, Aboriginal and Torres Strait Islander Commission, Canberra.